Globalisation and Peri-Urban Transformation

A comparative analysis of the governance characteristics of the three Indian cities

Globalisation and Peri-Urban Transformation

A comparative analysis of the governance
characteristics of the three Indian cities

Tathagata Chatterji

COPAL PUBLISHING GROUP

Inspiring for a better future through publishing

Published by Copal Publishing Group
E-143, Lajpat Nagar, Sahibabad,
Distt. Ghaziabad, UP – 201005, India

www.copalpublishing.com

First Published 2017

ISBN: 978-93-83419-45-6 (hard back)
ISBN: 978-93-83419-46-3 (e-book)

Typeset by Bhumi Graphics, New Delhi
Printed and bound by Bhavish Graphics, Chennai

Contents

Preface

Over the past two-and-a-half decades—ever since the beginning of the economic reforms in the early 1990s—Indian cities have been undergoing massive changes. The changes are most vividly visible at the fringe areas of the big cities – which have become the location of choice for the globalised Information Technology (IT) sector. As an architect–urban planner, I had the opportunity to closely observe the changing peri-urban dynamics, due to the process of globalisation. I was soon confounded by the complexities of the issues involved and developed a keen interest to delve deeper. The generous scholarship from the University of Queensland enabled this to happen—by allowing me to do a PhD on the subject. This book is an outcome of that research and for that I shall always remain indebted to The University of Queensland.

I was truly fortunate to have two outstanding and sympathetic advisors for my research: Associate Professor John Minnery and Associate Professor Glen Searle. My sincerest gratitude goes to them for their support, guidance, encouragement and constructive criticism for the entire length of my study. My research also substantially benefitted from advice, comments and suggestions from Prof. Swapna Banerjee-Guha, Prof. Bibek Debroy, Partha Sarathi Banerjee, Dr. Loraine Kennedy, Prof. Kevin O'Conner, Dr. N. Sridharan and Dr. Elisabeth Storm. I would like to thank them all.

I received cooperation, help and information from a large number of people during my fieldworks in Bangalore, Delhi and Kolkata. While it would not be possible to name them individually, I would like to thank the following in particular for arranging a large number of interviews: Dr. S.K. Biswas, Kathayani Chamaraja, Col. M. S. Dahiya, Sunil Kaul, Subinder Khurana, Dr. A. Ravindra and Debashish Sen.

Opportunities for lecturing and tutoring in courses like Asian Metropolis, Urban Governance and Management and Development Planning in Developing Countries at the University of Queensland, broadened my horizon and allowed me to see the ongoing changes in India in the larger context. For providing these opportunities, I would like to thank Dr. Derlie Mateo Babiano, Dr. Iraphne Childs and Dr. Thomas Sigler. A special 'thank you' is due to Isabel Buitrago-Franco, my fellow traveller in the PhD process, for regular stimulating discussions, thoughtful comments and consistent encouragements. I would like to thank Judith Millington for her very diligent proof-checking the manuscript. I would like to extend my appreciation and thanks to Rishi Seth and the staff of Copal Publishing, for publishing the book. In this context, I would also like to acknowledge my thanks to Lambert Academic Publishing Saarbrücken, Germany, for allowing me to bring this book as an updated edition of my earlier published book titled "Local Mediation of Global Forces in Transformation of the Urban Fringe: The Story of India's Regional IT Clusters (ISBN: 978-3-659-52416-5)". The earlier edition was published by Lambert Academic Publishing Saarbrücken, Germany.

Finally, I would like to thank and express my gratitude to my family members. This book would not have been possible without their support and understanding. My father Dr. Biswapati Chatterji and mother Ms. Mridula Chatterji encouraged me to fulfil my goal and provided necessary courage. My wife Sushmita left her job in Delhi to be with me as a pillar of strength throughout the arduous process of research, fieldwork and writing. She not only transcribed several interviews and went through my writings repeatedly, but provided huge emotional support through her patience and daily prayers.

List of abbreviations

ABIDe – Agency for Bengaluru Infrastructure Development

BATF – Bangalore Agenda Task Force

BDA – Bangalore Development Authority

BJP – Bharatiya Janata Party

BMRG – Bangalore Metropolitan Regional Governance

BRICS – Brazil, Russia, India, China and South Africa

CCWS – Cyber City Welfare Society

CDP – Comprehensive Development Plan

CIVIC – Citizen's Voluntary Initiatives for the City

CPI(M) – Communist Party of India (Marxist)

DDA – Delhi Development Authority

DCP – Directorate of Town and Country Planning

EGL – Embassy Golf Links business park

FDI – Foreign Direct Investment

JAFRA – Joint Action Forum for Resident Associations

GDP – Gross Domestic Product

GFC – Global Financial Crisis

HAL – Hindustan Aeronautics Limited

HIDCO – Housing Infrastructure Development Corporation

HUDA – Haryana Urban Development Authority

IIMB – Indian Institute of Management Bangalore

IT – Information Technology

ITES – Information Technology Enabled Services

ITPL – Information Technology Parks Limited

KSIDC – Karnataka State Industrial Development Corporation

KBITS – Karnataka Biotechnology and Information Technology Services

KEONICS – Karnataka Electronics Corporation

KGA – Karnataka Golf Association

KMDA – Kolkata Metropolitan Development Authority

MCG – Municipal Corporation of Gurgaon

MNC – Multinational Corporation

NASSCOM – National Association of Software and Service Companies

NCRPB – National Capital Region Planning Board

NGO – Non-governmental Organisation

R&D – Research and development

SEZ – Special Economic Zone

STPI – Software Technology Parks of India

TMC – Trinamool Congress

TCS –Tata Consultancy Services

WTO – World Trade Organization

WBEIDC – West Bengal Electronic Industries Development Corporation

1
Introduction

1.1   Research rationale

This book explores how variations in sub-national and local political cultures impact urban development patterns by mediating forces emerging out of global economic demand and a uniform national regulatory regime. The increasing importance of urban regions following globalisation[1] has, in recent times, sharpened the focus on the role of the local governance institutions in promoting economic growth and generating employment. Beset with problems of deindustrialisation, flight of capital and shrinking revenue base, cities in the Global North have increasingly turned 'entrepreneurial' to attract capital to their respective cities (Harvey 1989). Entrepreneurialism in urban governance has also emerged on the opposite side of the global spectrum in transitional economies like China (Chien 2008) and India (Kennedy 2007; Shaw & Satish 2007).

Recent research exploring the changing role of urban governments in promoting economic development has progressed along two divergent pathways—'structural' and 'agential'. Structuralist theorists argue that contemporary urban changes are part of a wider political economic process like globalisation and reconfiguration of scalar relationships across the multiple levels of governance (Brenner 2004; Jessop, Brenner & Jones 2008; MacLeod & Goodwin 1999a). The roles and responsibilities of the local agents are marginal in this conceptualisation, as global and national forces almost predetermine local policies. The variations that occur between the cities are mainly due to institutional path dependencies (Brenner & Theodore 2002a). On the other hand, 'growth machine theory' (Logan & Molotch 1987) and 'regime theory' (Stone 1993) traversing the agential track suggest that powerful informal coalitions between political and business interests take the lead in shaping the direction of local economies to suit their own agenda.

---

[1] The term 'globalisation' in this book primarily means economic globalisation in the contemporary sense, unless specifically clarified otherwise.

However, given the dynamic interrelationship between the larger structural context and the political choices of the local actors in the real world, examples of absolutist theoretical positions are hard to come by. DiGaetano and Strom (2003) synthesised the structural and agential strands and suggested adaptation of an integrated framework to compare the governance characteristics of the cities in the Global North. In the framework suggested by them, structural factors like globalisation or state rescaling provide the overarching environment, but the local political agents, informed by a place-specific cultural milieu, also play important roles in guiding local growth processes – at least in federal political systems. Thus local socio-political dynamics, actor relationships and embedded social settings are contextualised within the broader processes of state restructuring induced by global forces.

There is, however, a dearth of theoretically grounded research about comparative urban governance of the fast-changing cities in transitional economies of the Global South (Keivani & Mattingly 2007; Shatkin 2011). Keivani and Mattingly (2007) also emphasised the need for greater research about the impact of globalisation in the peripheral areas of the cities. Unlike the cities in the Global North, where major economic momentum informed by compact-city debates is being concentrated in the central city areas, much of the impact of the economic changes in developing countries, particularly in fast growing Asian economies, can be seen in the peripheral areas of the big cities (Keivani & Mattingly 2007; Webster 2011). Urbanisation is increasingly happening over an extended metropolitan region, far beyond the formal administrative boundaries of the core cities. As the peripheral areas of the big cities have turned into dynamic urban spaces, Keivani and Mattingly (2007) stressed that research should be focused in these areas:

> In particular, views are needed that encourage debate on the following: The impact of globalisation on urban governance in developing cities, including changing power relations, administrative restructuring, internal conflicts and competition; The impact of globalisation on the local economy in peripheral and informal neighbourhoods; Globalisation and contested claims on urban space, particularly in respect of peripheral land in developing countries; The effect of this competition on the livelihoods of the low-income people. (Keivani & Mattingly 2007, p.470.)

However, the bulk of the scholarly research on urban economic transformation in developing countries has focused on China and Southeast Asian cities. Comparatively, there is very little research on Indian cities. This is understandable, as economic reforms in these regions preceded those in India by several years, even decades. Taking note of this, Shatkin (2011), while delivering a lecture at Harvard University, called for enhanced research focus on contemporary Indian cities and specifically pointed out the need to analyse the roles of the local agencies in Indian cities, as they attempt to mediate global economic forces in managing urban transition. This book attempts to partially bridge this gap through a comparative analysis of the development of the IT clusters in three metropolitan regions of India to show how local planning cultures mediate global economic forces in shaping transformation of the urban fringe.

India is a good example to explore the local–global interface in urban transformation, as it is a major transitional economy and India's urban centres have been undergoing dynamic changes since the beginning of economic reforms in the early 1990s. The changing nature of urban India and the rise in middle-class consumerism have drawn much global attention in recent years. Despite these changes, India, however, continues to grapple with a high degree of poverty in the rural areas, where 70 percent of the people live. It is widely recognised that globalisation has increased regional unevenness and urban–rural disparities (Ghosh 2010). These developmental dichotomies are sharply etched in the Indian political systems and play out most vividly in the context of land use change in the fringe areas of the big cities to accommodate the spatial demands of the IT outsourcing industry.

The IT services[2] sector provides a useful lens to explore the changing peri-urban dynamics of Indian cities. Much of the economic growth in Indian cities has come about due to outsourcing of Information Technology (IT)-enabled back-office services from the Global North. The Indian IT sector, which predominantly consists of software development, call-centres and other knowledge intensive services (rather than electronic hardware manufacturing), was export oriented from its

---

[2] The term IT services in this book has been used in the broad sense to include software development; other IT enabled services (ITES) and routine Business Process Outsourcing (BPO). But unless specifically mentioned, hardware manufacturing is not included. Chapter 5 provides a full sectoral break-up.

very inception and is seen as a prime exemplar of the 'new economy' in the Indian context. However, at the same time it also remains an 'enclave' economy (D'Costa 2011; Upadhyan & Carol 2007). The employment generated by the IT sector is miniscule compared to India's total workforce, and on the whole, the contemporary IT-driven Indian economy exemplifies the exclusionary 'jobless growth' syndrome (Ghosh 2010; Kundu 2011).

Production spaces for this 'enclave' economy are coming up in the form of gated 'enclaves'—business parks and IT-centric Special Economic Zones (SEZ)—which are located at the fringe of big cities, within the catchment area of a large, educated labour supply. The emergence of high-tech, high-security production spaces and associated consumption spaces like luxury condominiums and shopping malls lined with designer showrooms, at the outer periphery of Indian cities, beside the old rural habitats, has created a fragmented landscape marked by sharp discontinuities between formal and informal spaces. It is also a landscape filled with everyday tensions and contradictions at multiple scales between people of contrasting lifestyle – the new urban middle class tied to the global information economy and the existing rural population tied to the local bazaar economies. (Banerjee-Guha 2008; Dupont 2007)

This book attempts to increase understanding about the actors, interactions and outcomes of this interplay of local and global forces, by comparing and contrasting the planning regimes of Bangalore, Kolkata and the National Capital Region of Delhi, three competing sub-national urban regions, located in three corners of India (see Figure 1.1), having contrasting socio-economic and political cultures, under the overarching environment of the post liberalisation Indian state. DiGaetano and Strom's (2003) integrated framework developed to compare economic governance of the cities in the Global North is tested in this research as the analytic lens to compare the governing regimes of the Indian cities as they attempt to manage transformation of the urban fringe.

The following section provides a background about the development of the regional IT clusters of India. Section 1.3 then defines the research problem and research questions. Section 1.4 highlights the significance of the research. Section 1.5 provides a brief outline about the research approach. Section 1.6 sets out the structure of the rest of the book.

Figure 1.1 Major IT clusters of India [*Source:* Modified by author over map retrieved from http://www.mapsofworld.com (Accessed 9 January 2013)]

1.2   Research background

The availability of a large technical labour pool, which provides a 60–70 percent cost advantage over developed countries, has allowed India to become the leading player in the global back-office outsourcing market, accounting for a 58 percent market share (NASSCOM 2012). Over the years, IT services have become the major stimulant behind

India's economic growth. In 2011, the IT sector contributed 7.5 percent of India's GDP, 25 percent of the export earnings and generated (directly and indirectly) about 11.7 million jobs (NASSCOM 2012).

The nature of the IT outsourcing industry, which is overwhelmingly oriented towards English-speaking countries (USA alone accounts for 65 percent of the export revenue), has led to clustering of the IT firms around the biggest cities of India, where there are high concentrations of people with technical and English communication skills (NASSCOM 2011; Parthasarathy 2004). Seven big urban agglomerations (Bangalore, Hyderabad, Chennai, Mumbai, Pune, Kolkata and the National Capital Region (NCR) centring around Delhi) together account for 92 percent of the export trade volume (NASSCOM & A.T. Kearney 2009). As may be seen in Figure 1.1 five of these cities are located in the southern part of the country, while the NCR is in the north and Kolkata is in the east.

There is increasing regional competition amongst the Indian cities to attract the IT industry, due to the sector's high-profile globalised image, contributions towards economic growth and middle-class job prospects. To attract the IT sector, the local governing regimes are providing subsidised land and a host of other incentives to facilitate development of high quality production and consumption spaces matching global corporate specifications in the fringe areas of their cities. The most significant part of the state action is to facilitate conversion of agricultural land at the peri-urban belt for urban usage. In most cases, this is being done by invoking the Land Acquisition Act of 1894, which was originally enacted during the colonial period and empowered the state to acquire private property for 'public purpose' such as building of railways, roads, hospitals, etc.

However, lateral expansion of the urban footprint to accommodate such exclusionary enclaves of private accumulation through conversion of agricultural lands has generated a deeply divisive development debate in India (Banerjee-Guha 2008; Dupont 2007). In recent years large numbers of agitations and protests have erupted in the rural areas of several regions, over land acquisitions to build SEZ, tech-parks, residential townships and other infrastructure associated with the modernising economy (Banerjee-Guha 2008; Nielsen 2010). The new economic spaces are closely tied to global economic networks but their linkages with the local neighbourhoods and surrounding rural communities are ambiguous. Insertion of the IT clusters at rural peripheries of Indian cities has unleashed powerful new forces tied to the global corporate economy, generating certain new opportunities. It has, however, also increased livelihood vulnerabilities for a large rural population.

Tensions and contradictions associated with the changing space relations at the outer peripheries of Indian cities reflect these dichotomies. Understandably the local governing regime and planning systems have a crucial role in this arena – mediating the tensions and building bridges of reconciliation. To understand the political dynamics which underpin the planning decisions, it is also necessary to situate the tensions over peri-urban transformations (to meet the spatial demands of the IT-services and other knowledge driven sectors), within the larger panorama of changes going on in India with increasing globalisation and the neoliberal turn of the state. In the democratic polity of India, with 70 percent of the population still being rural, rural discontents are politically problematic. For example, the Telugu Desam Party's defeat in Andhra Pradesh in 2004 (Sainath 2005) and the Left Front's defeat in West Bengal in 2011 (Chakrabarty 2011) are commonly attributed to rural backlash over the incumbent government's rapid urbanisation and industrialisation drives.

In this scenario, the power of India's state planning institutions to aid production of globalised IT clusters by reconfiguring rural landscape at the urban fringe rests on forging a broad consensus across the political spectrum. Taking off from this broad standpoint, this book will illustrate (by comparing the planning cultures of Bangalore, NCR and Kolkata) that even amongst the largest metropolitan regions of India, operating within the same macroeconomic framework, there is substantial unevenness in engagement patterns with the global economy and in managing resultant urban spatial transformation. This will be used to provide a nuanced understanding of the processes of urban economic governance. The following section outlines the specific research problem and questions.

1.3.   Research problem and questions

Fringe areas of the big Indian cities have seen the emergence of gated technology clusters due to the regulatory conditions of the national state and competitive rescaling strategy of urban governments. While these technology clusters are articulated with the global economic networks, their linkages with local neighbourhood networks and communities are debatable. Land-use conversion in the peri-urban areas to accommodate these new economic spaces is leading to escalation of tensions but also generating new opportunities for accumulation. The roles of the various stakeholders and the local and global dynamics that play out in this context are poorly understood. This research seeks to increase understanding about the actors, interactions and outcomes of the interplay of local and global forces.

1. What are the global and national forces leading to formation of technology clusters at the fringe areas of Indian cities?

2. How do differences in local political dynamics in different socio-political contexts impact on the development of the IT clusters?

3. Who are the key actors and what are their roles in the development of India's regional IT clusters?

4. How are the planning mechanisms of the Indian cities trying to deal with the tensions between the technology clusters and the local communities?

1.4   Research significance

As already discussed in Section 1.1, there is a dearth of comparative research about the planning and governance cultures of Indian cities. Particularly, there is a lack of understanding about the roles of local political actors, about how they navigate the global forces and steer the economic direction of their cities. This research attempts to partially address this gap by comparing and contrasting the planning regimes of Bangalore, Kolkata and the National Capital Region of Delhi, three competing sub-national urban regions of India, having contrasting local political–economic cultures, under the overarching environment of the post-liberalisation Indian state.

By focusing on a comparative sub-national framework, the research highlights the differential impacts of different local governance regimes operating under the same national macroeconomic and regulatory environment, in managing land use and livelihood changes at the urban fringe. The research aims to deepen our understanding about the importance of local political institutions in charting local economic development by mediating forces emerging out of global economic demand and a national regulatory regime. The research looks at the changing dynamics of the fringe areas of the Indian cities through the prism of the IT outsourcing industry, which is amongst the most important segments of the Indian economy and has substantially contributed to India's impressive economic growth in recent decades. Restricting the focus to a common economic environment of IT services allows us to control many regulatory variables which creep into more generalised comparisons of urban governance. The research also contributes to urban governance theory by testing the applicability of an integrated urban governance framework developed in the context of the Global North, to a wider geography of the Global South and in the context of rural–urban transition.

1.5   Research approach

The research uses a multiple case-study approach directed by the comparative urban governance framework. It is based on two rounds of fieldwork at the three case study locations—Bangalore, Delhi NCR and Kolkata. The IT clusters in the Delhi-NCR are located across the administrative domain of three states: Delhi, Gurgaon (Haryana) and Noida (Uttar Pradesh), with Gurgaon being the most advanced (Maitra 2008). Therefore, the case study in this book primarily focuses on Gurgaon, but also takes into consideration that growth of the IT industry in Gurgaon has not happened in isolation, but is due to its location within the extended NCR metropolitan belt.

The research uses both qualitative and quantitative data. While quantitative data were taken from reputed secondary sources, qualitative data were obtained through detailed semi-structured interviews with planning agency officials, real estate developers, IT executives and civil society activists. Altogether seventy-five interviews were conducted, with each interview involving discussions for forty-five to ninety minutes. In several cases more than one person was present during the interview. When the local community leaders were interviewed, usually there were ten to twelve persons present, and several of them shared opinions and information. However, these have been recorded as single interviews. Information and opinion obtained through interviews was triangulated through cross-verification from multiple sources and angles.

1.6   Book structure

The remaining part of the book is organised as follows:

Chapter 2 includes a literature review about economic globalisation and its resultant transformation of urban space. After discussing contemporary literature on the impact of globalisation on the urban economy, the role of government institutions in urban transformation, and resultant social tensions, the chapter establishes that there is a gap in our understanding of the dynamics of global economic process on the transformation of Indian cities and suggests a theoretical framework to fill this gap.

Chapter 3 then sets the discussion about India's economic liberalisation and urban transformation. After providing a brief overview about the development planning process in India, this chapter discusses the literature on restructuring of urban space due to regional economic competition in India, peri-urbanisation and emerging land conflicts. The chapter concludes by establishing the gap in knowledge about the transformation of the fringe areas of Indian cities due to global forces.

Chapter 4 explains the research methodology adopted for this book. After discussing the reasons behind the adoption of a sub-national research framework, it provides justifications for the choice of particular case study locations. The chapter describes how data analysis was carried out and also highlights the constraints and limitations of the research.

Chapter 5 analyses the structural context and the prevailing socio-political milieu within which the Indian IT industry is situated. Following an overview of the Indian IT industry and various sub-segments, this chapter focuses on the major national and sub-national level IT policies. The chapter concludes by discussing trends and patterns contributing towards the formation of regional IT clusters.

Chapter 6 contains a case study of the IT clusters in Bangalore, capital of the Karnataka state and the global face of the Indian IT industry. After providing a background to the growth of Bangalore's IT cluster, the chapter discusses the state-level political–economic culture of Karnataka, which nurtured the development of the industry. It then focuses on the spatial implications of the IT services on the urban development pattern and illustrates the same through a detailed case study of one IT business park. The chapter concludes by analysing the roles of various stakeholders associated with the growth of Bangalore's

IT cluster and its urban transformation by using DiGaetano and Strom's integrated framework.

Chapter 7 contains a case study of the IT clusters in the NCR belt with a focus on Gurgaon, which has seen dynamic growth but has followed a different trajectory from that of Bangalore. The chapter begins by providing a background to the growth of the service sector economy of Delhi and its eventual spill over into Gurgaon. After that it discusses regional socio-political cultures. It then focuses on the spatial implications of the IT services on the urban development pattern of Gurgaon and illustrates the same through a detailed case study of one IT business park. The chapter concludes by analysing the roles of various stakeholders associated with the growth of Gurgaon's IT cluster and its urban transformation by using DiGaetano and Strom's integrated framework.

Chapter 8, through a case study of the IT clusters in the Kolkata (the capital of West Bengal), presents a contrasting development pattern to Bangalore and the Gurgaon (NCR). Despite strong efforts by the state government, Kolkata's IT cluster remains the smallest amongst the top seven cities in India. While the business press frequently writes about the 'huge growth potential' of the region, local educated youth continue to move out to more dynamic cities. After providing a snapshot about the growth of the IT sector in Kolkata, the chapter discusses political impediments which have prevented the sector from realising its 'full potential'. It then focuses on the spatial implications of the IT services on the urban development pattern of Kolkata and illustrates the same through a detailed case study of one IT business park. The chapter concludes by analysing the roles of various stakeholders associated with the growth of Kolkata's IT cluster and its urban transformation by using DiGaetano and Strom's integrated framework.

Chapter 9 synthesises all the above discussions about the development of IT clusters in the fringe areas of three metropolitan regions of India and addresses the research questions. After sequentially addressing the research questions, the chapter discusses the broad theoretical implications arising out of the research and contributions to knowledge and understanding of urban governance literature. It then provides pointers to further research possibilities. The chapter concludes by summarising the major findings of the research.

Globalisation and restructuring of urban space

2.1 Introduction

This chapter contains a literature review pertaining to the key areas of research, which are: globalisation; the impact of globalisation on the urban economy; the role of government institutions in urban transformation; and the resultant social tensions. The discussion is organised as follows: Section 2.2 provides a brief overview of how economic globalisation has increased the importance of select urban regions as well as the competition between the cities. Section 2.3 then deals with the resultant spatial implications—expansion of urban footprints and discontents arising out of this process—with reference to fast-growing Asian cities. Section 2.4 then takes up the issue of changing patterns of urban governance and the emergence of entrepreneurial urban governance. Section 2.5, the final section, synthesises these discussions to establish that there is a gap in our understanding of the impact of global economic process on the transformation of Asian cities and suggests a theoretical framework to fill this gap.

2.2 Globalisation and urban economic competition

While flows of trade, cultural norms, religious practices, political ideas and movements of people across international borders have been going on for thousands of years, advancement in communication technology, and reduction in regulatory control by nation states on economic matters since the late 1970s, are leading to an unprecedented increase in global interconnectedness in economic, political and social spheres. This phenomenon of progressively increasing and deepening of transnational transactions has come to be loosely termed as 'globalisation' without being explicitly defined in academic and non-academic discourses (Eriksen 2007). According to Held and McGrew (2007), globalisation is a process that brings a transformation of the spatial organisation of social relations, generating transnational flows and networks of activities, interfaces and the exertion of power relations. Giddens (1999) defined globalisation as intensification of the social relations across the globe, in such a manner that local happenings in different places are shaped by incidents happening in distant, far away, lands.

Though multidimensional in scope, globalisation is largely driven by economic and technological processes, which are being facilitated due to gradual adaptation of capitalist free-market-oriented neo-liberal state policies by the major nation states in the world (Eriksen 2007). Tariff barriers and protectionist regulatory practices of earlier periods have come down with the advent of supra-national economic regimes like the General Agreement on Trade and Tariffs (GATT) and its successor, the World Trade Organization (WTO). While most of these multilateral platforms started off with nations of the Global North, the gradual inclusion of major non-Western economies like Brazil, Russia, India, China and South Africa (BRICS) from the 1990s has vastly expanded the scope of international trade and helped the spread of the capitalist free-market-oriented trade networks to a truly global scale. The global financial crisis (GFC) of 2008 and the continued economic stagnation of the USA and the Euro-zone have further increased the clout of the BRICS countries in the world economy.

A key attribute of this contemporary economic globalisation is the concept of 'disembedding', which also has strong political and cultural connotations. With the increase in the speed of communication, intellectual ideas, investment capital and technological developments are 'disembedded' or 'lifted-out' of their original localities and are rapidly transmitted across the globe (Giddens 1999). Progressive reductions in tariff barriers and protectionist regulatory policies by the nation states are enabling many of these capital and intellectual transactions to be carried out by transnational business networks. The increasing global mobility of financial capital and the speed of communication mediated by transnational corporations are contributing towards disembedding the production processes of goods and services from their established locations to new geographies offering greater capital return (Giddens 1999).

With greater global integration, the Fordist-era production paradigm with its emphasis on mass manufacturing-oriented vertical production chains is being rewritten. Advancements in transportation and communication technology allow the firms the flexibility of sourcing individual components from a range of suppliers spread across the globe and dispersing the production process itself to distant locations to leverage labour cost differentials (Sassen 2001). Fundamental changes in the post-Fordist industrial economy are characterised by an escalation in the importance of knowledge and capital flows in the production processes. The increase in corporate productivity is more dependent on the application of knowledge and information to management, distribution and production processes rather than the old factors of production like capital, labour and natural resources (Castells 1996). Economic growth has become delinked from employment generation, as the production centres became geographically dispersed to destinations of cheaper labour (Amin & Thrift 1992; Drucker 1987).

There is a general consensus in the academic and professional literature that globalisation has increased the economic importance of cities as hubs, where knowledge, capital and information networks converge (Castells 1996). The new world economy is essentially an urban economy, with cities contributing 80 percent of the global GDP (UN Habitat 2011). However, all regions and cities are not equally impacted by globalisation, and the neoliberal market-driven economic processes are inherently disequalising. Castells (1998, p.162) observes "Globalisation proceeds selectively, including and excluding segments of economies and societies in and out of the networks of information, wealth and power that characterise the new dominant system". Thus the top 100 large urban regions of the world contribute 35 percent of the global GDP (UN Habitat 2011).

In this process of spatial or territorial articulation of capital, technological and information flows in select urban regions, globalisation has played a paradoxical double role, by being simultaneously a process of dispersion and one of convergence (Amin & Thrift 1992; Sassen 2001). Spatial dispersal of the modern industrial production process has been accomplished through globally extended corporate chains which include elaborate processes of subcontracting, joint ventures, and strategic alliances between corporate groups across nation states. However, the challenges of managing such complex and extended networks required the centralisation of control functions—corporate headquarters and linked producer services, such as insurance, finance, advertising, marketing, etc. All top tier 'global-cities' like London, New York, Sydney and Hong Kong have high concentrations of high-value producer services and knowledge-intensive creative sector jobs, while more labour-intensive processes have been dispersed to lower wage geographies (Hutton 2003; Sassen 2012).

On the opposite side of this global spectrum, new economic flows become concentrated in a select few urban clusters in the developing world, like the Pearl River Delta (China), Jabotadetabek (Indonesia), Bangkok Eastern Seaboard (Thailand) and Bangalore (India) (Hamnett & Forbes 2011). Firms tend to concentrate in those urban regions which offer greater opportunities for capital accumulation through economies of scale, specialisation of services, and access to advanced communication networks and capital markets; while skilled people move in to locations offering opportunities for professional advancement (Sassen 2012). Convergence of both capital and talent has led to the emergence of certain urban regions as the strategic sites for the new global economy.

While it is established that globalisation has enhanced the economic importance of urban regions, it has also generated competition between the cities. Technological advancements and liberalisation of economic policies have made it easier to relocate to destinations offering greater opportunities for wealth maximisation through lower input costs or higher productivity. During the 1980s and 1990s, the early phase of globalisation, the diminishing role of the nation state in commercial issues and the rise of supra-national bodies (e.g. WTO, EU, ASEAN) led to a perception that such business relocations were purely market driven. This perception gained further strength due to devolution of administrative powers in several spheres, from the nation-state to sub-national units, which ran almost in parallel to the process of economic liberalisation across the globe. All major developed and developing countries undertook substantial devolution and decentralisation during the 1990s, though there are wide variations in forms and contents of such devolution, depending upon the specific local context (Cheema & Rondinelli 2007). In this scenario, the emergence of the urban nodes was envisaged as being due to apparently horizontal and seamless flows of knowledge, power and information, with minimal state intervention (Castells 1996) in an emerging free-flowing borderless world (Ohmae 1995). Subsequent studies, however, demonstrate that such flows are in effect channelised through determined actions by the nation states to boost the productive capacity of strategic urban regions within their territorial jurisdiction, in the face of rising economic competition (Brenner 2004; Cox 1997; Pemberton & Searle 2012; Swyngedouw 1997).

During the post Second World War period of the developmental state, public agencies held crucial roles in economic matters, and often shaped locational decisions concerning major investments within their administrative domains. While in the Soviet Union and other socialist countries, bureaucratic central planning through public sector investments guided industrial locations, European welfare states also did so for private investments through the rubric of balanced regional development (Brenner 2004). Most post-colonial Afro-Asian states also followed the path of state-led industrialisation through central planning, partly as a legacy of the anti-colonial movements that associated market capitalism with imperialism, and partly due to scarcity of indigenous expertise in most spheres of the modern economy. India was a pioneer in this and adopted public-sector-led industrialisation in the 1950s to 'fast-track' modernisation, guided by Prime Minister Nehru's 'mixed-economy' model. One of the first objectives of the newly independent Indian state was to overcome the spatial distortions of the colonial era when industrial growth was heavily concentrated around the port cities of Calcutta (Kolkata), Bombay (Mumbai) and Madras (Chennai). However, such balanced regional development objectives—what Brenner (2004) termed as 'spatial-Keynesianism'—gave way substantially from the 1990s, with the rolling back of the national-state's regulatory mechanisms.

2.3   Urban spatial restructuring

While globalisation has led to concentration of economic flows in select urban centres across the world, these cities themselves are continuously being reshaped and reconfigured, socially and spatially, through the flows of these networks. The process of urban transformation is integral to the process of macroeconomic restructuring and technological advancement brought forward through globalisation (Castells 1996). However, the scale and nature of such transformations are not uniform, and are governed by the degree of the particular city's integration into the global network, as well as other place-specific factors. Patterns of spatial reconfiguration of old industrial cities of Europe, through inner-city regeneration, differ substantially from the horizontally expanding Asian mega-cities, which again, are very different from the suburban sprawl of the North American cities. For contextual relevance, discussions in this section are mostly around Asian cities.

In the Asian regional context, one of the most visible outcomes of contemporary economic growth is the emergence of mega-urban regions encompassing several cities, towns and rural areas, such as: Hong-Kong–Shenzhen–Guangdong, Jabotadetabek and the Bangkok Eastern Seaboard (Hamnett & Forbes 2011). Similar patterns of mega-urban industrial corridors have started taking shape in India as well, such as Baroda–Surat–Mumbai–Pune or the National Capital Region, centring around Delhi (Mohan & Dasgupta 2004; UN Habitat 2011).

Recent studies in urban geography suggest two crucial spatial characteristics of these globalising Asian cities. Firstly, spatial demands of the global economy have generated centripetal forces, leading to horizontal expansion of the core cities towards the outer periphery. Secondly, the fringe areas of the big cities are increasingly gaining in economic importance, vis-á-vis the core areas, as places of production for the global economy. According to Webster (2002), foreign direct investment (FDI) in Asia is overwhelmingly concentrated at the fringe areas—within a 200 km radius of the big cities—and infusion of large scale global capital has stimulated mass-scale peri-urbanisation from the 1990s.

Webster (2002) attributes rising demand for land in fringe areas to a combination of three major factors. Firstly, modern 'just-in-time' manufacturing processes require large perimeter single-storey structures, which are not feasible in the core areas due to prohibitive land costs and planning restrictions. Secondly, the government agencies have increasingly adopted a cluster approach to group production facilities in planned industrial clusters, having well-developed infrastructure facilities. Such clusters are usually managed by single intermediaries, who act as buffers between the individual firms and the local governments. Thus the investors are spared the trouble of dealing with multiple agencies. Thirdly, and most importantly, "the investors require relatively easy access to a core city that offers high level business and personal services, and access to major government decision makers", suggests Webster (2002, pp.9).

Apart from these external economic causes, peri-urbanisation is also resulting out of the internal restructuring processes of the core city areas. For example, tightening of environmental regulations is leading to relocation of the manufacturing industries to industrial clusters in the fringe areas, while demand for more affordable housing is steering the urban middle class towards the periphery (Dupont 2007). Thus demands for space in the fringe areas of the Asian cities are not happening in isolation but rather in consort with the overall spatial dynamics of the city region. The core areas in Asian cities are not getting hollowed out in the way the American cities did during the 1950s. The spaces vacated by the manufacturing industries and other lower tier activities are being filled by retail, entertainment and high value producer services (Hutton 2003). To accommodate these demands, government-planning agencies are opening up the rural hinterlands of the big cities through large scale public investments.

Rapid expansion of the footprint of the Asian cities over their rural hinterlands is resulting in a complex, patchwork quilt urban landscape marked with profound discontinuities with pockets of rural vernacular in the midst of the modern cities (Marshall et al. 2009; Narain & Nischal 2007). The fringe areas of the Asian cities are characterised by high population densities, poor slums, haphazard conversion of agricultural land to urban usage, diverse sources of income, lack of regulatory mechanisms, contested land tenure, pollution and environmental degradation, intensified resource exploitation, economic dynamism, inadequate service infrastructure and fragmented and uncoordinated administration (Allen, Davila & Hofmann 2006; Dupont 2007; Tacoli 2006; Webster 2002).

Dynamism and change are inherent in the context of the fringe spaces and thus they cannot be constructed in static terms. Competing interests of small farmers, the urban middle class, industrial entrepreneurs and informal settlements all coexist. Spatial boundaries, land use characteristics and the occupational structure of the population in the fringe areas are in a constant process of change with the gradual expansion of the city. Allen, Davila and Hofmann (2006) suggest that socially and economically the urban peripheries constitute a heterogeneous mosaic subjected to rapid changes over time. Taking note of the rapidly changing boundaries of the peri-urban areas due to expansion of the urban functions, Webster (2002) moved away from spatial specificity and defined 'peri-urbanisation' as a process in which rural areas located at the outskirts of established cities become more urban in character, in physical, economic and social terms, often in piecemeal fashion.

Globalisation has not only added additional dimensions to this complicated peri-urban dynamic, by introducing new sets of actors and capital flows, but has also substantially altered the transformation process, through a new set of ideas about city building. In this neoliberal model, the process of land development by large scale private developers and partnerships between the private sector and government agencies has become the preferred mechanism, leading to increasing commoditisation of land and intensification of disputes. It is where, "the forces of globalisation and localisation intersect" (Webster 2002, p.6). The intersection of such local and global forces is generating new claims and conflicts but has also added new opportunities.

Relationships between globalisation and local economic development are complex and multidimensional. Reviews of the existing literature on the peri-urban transformation of the Asian metropolitan regions do not indicate any clear picture. Several studies indicate that globalisation has brought new economic opportunities for the local communities. For example, the *hukou* system in China, which restricts access to educational and health services for the migrant population, has stimulated rental housing demand in the fringe areas, benefiting local land tenure holders and has thus succeeded in generating a synergy of interests between the external investors and the local population for peri-urban industrialisation (Webster 2002). In the fringe areas of Quanzhou (China) and Hanoi, entrepreneurial village cooperatives have, through their own initiatives, converted agricultural lands for middle and higher income housing estates and thus upgraded their livelihood options (Leaf 2002).

Later studies, however, have brought out increasing contestation over the fringe spaces between the local communities and the local government agencies, which promoted a neoliberal growth agenda. For example, research on Hanoi brings out increasing incidences of peri-urban land conflicts due to the market-oriented reforms under *doi-moi* (Labbé 2011). At the crux of the dispute lies the process of land-use conversion. A clutch of real-estate interests, backed by the local government, has appropriated large agricultural land holdings to facilitate high-quality master-planned projects, as against the slow and incremental developments initiated by the entrepreneurial members of the local community. Feeling threatened about their livelihood, a large section of the local community has begun to actively oppose the local government's initiatives. In Metro Manila as well, Kelly's (2006) research shows conversion of agricultural land to urban usage has increased livelihood vulnerabilities for the small and marginal farmers. But on the other hand, land conversion has hugely benefited the landed big farmers.

Across South and Southeast Asia, there is a steady decline in the percentage of the population depending on agriculture as the primary means of livelihood, although the rate of decline in rural agricultural dependency is much less than the proportionate increase in the national GDP for the urban-oriented industrial and service sector opportunities, contributing to increasing rural–urban disparities (Cook 2006). Nevertheless, studies on rural transformations indicate increasing occupational diversification of the rural households to non-farm activities and greater mobility. Such diversifications of livelihood options are particularly common for the households in the peri-urban areas due to the availability of greater economic opportunities with urbanisation (Tacoli 2006).

Rigg (2006) observed that globalisation has led to the emergence of an increasingly differentiated pattern of landscape in Southeast Asia, in which 'rural' has been delinked from 'agricultural'. Industrialisation due to globalisation has augmented, rather than supplanted, employment opportunities. Farming continues to be the mainstay of the village economy but its capacity to support households financially is diminishing. In the peri-urban areas of the big cities like Beijing (Liu et al. 2010), Metro Manila (Kelly 2006) and Hanoi (Labbé 2011), the dynamics of farming and non-farming activities by the rural household are gradually changing, with the younger generation opting for an urban livelihood. Yet, as Rigg (2006) suggests, there is a reluctance to give up agricultural land, which the peasants wish to retain as a form of insurance against future uncertainties. Diversification of livelihood options, often within the same households, is contributing towards blurring of the boundaries between urban and rural in the physical as well as socio-economic landscapes in the peri-urban areas.

The larger picture that emerges out of these ongoing contestations over the peri-urban space in Southeast Asia, between the local communities and the urban expansion process fuelled by the globalised new economy, is about the changing power dynamics at the local scale. It comes out implicitly through the research of Kelly and Labbé that the process of livelihood transformation, particularly when it is related to the vulnerabilities generated through conversion of agricultural land to non-agricultural usage, are deeply entwined with the political dynamics on various planes influenced by the developmental priorities of the state agencies and everyday politics at the local level (Kelly 2006; Labbé 2011). However, neither of these papers analysed the political economic characteristics of the governance regimes, nor did they attempt to distinguish between regimes at local and national scales, which are particularly relevant for large countries with more federal characteristics like India. What are the political–economic priorities? How do the priorities of the local regime differ from those of the upper tiers of governance? How are the global processes translated to the local scale? How does increasing competition between the cities for global investments contribute to these processes? These questions are explored in the next sections.

2.4   Entrepreneurial governance and urban regimes

The increasing importance of urban regions following globalisation has in recent times sharpened the focus on the role of the local governance institutions in promoting economic growth and generating employment. Beset with problems of deindustrialisation, flight of capital and a shrinking revenue base, urban governance regimes of the countries in the Global North have increasingly turned 'entrepreneurial' to attract capital to their respective cities (Harvey 1989). Departing from their old, restricted municipal roles, urban governments have expanded their ambit to promote local economic development by aligning with the business sectors and local communities. Entrepreneurialism in local governance is also becoming evident in the emerging economies of China (Chien 2008; Shen 2004) and India (Kennedy 2007; Shaw & Satish 2007).

Recent literature, exploring the relationship between urban governance and local economic development, has developed along two broad strands: the structural context of urban transformation, and its agential aspects. According to Hay (2002), the structural approach explains political events and outcomes in terms of larger and contextual factors, while the role of the local actors is relatively less significant. Globalisation itself is seen as an irreversible process of structural transformation of the international political economy. The larger political economic context almost predetermines the course of local economic direction for large globalising urban regions.

On the other hand, the agential approach emphasises the role of actors and local coalition groups (e.g. political parties, business chambers, civil society organisations) in shaping the course of political events and outcomes (Hay 2002). In this approach, which has also been termed as 'intentionalist', local political actors exert considerable control in steering local economic directions towards pro- or anti-growth, according to their political choice. Actors sharing similar economic viewpoints come together to forge coalitions. The character of the local governance regimes is shaped through processes of collaboration and contestation between the rival coalition groups (Leftwich 1995; Logan & Molotch 1987; Stone 1993). Thus in the intentionalist approach, local actors are responsible for the emerging course of economic direction—at least in a liberal democratic environment.

However, given the dynamic interrelationship between the larger structural context and political choices of the local actors in the real world scenario, examples of absolutist theoretical positions are hard to come by. As the writings of DiGaetano and Strom (2003), Gissendanner (2004), Minnery (2007) and Ataöv and Eraydin (2011) suggest there are moves towards a synthesis of the two strands. DiGaetano and Strom argue that actor relationships need to be understood by situating the discourse within the overarching structural context and also the embedded socio-political culture. They proposed adoption of an integrated framework, informed by structural, agential and cultural parameters.

Urban governance theorists, like Goodwin and Painter (1996), Macleod and Goodwin (1999b) and Brenner (2004), following structuralist logic, have claimed that the emergence of this entrepreneurial form of urban governance is a corollary to the wider process of state restructuring with the gradual spread of neoliberal ideology, resulting in alteration of scalar arrangements of power between multiple levels of governance. Devolution of power from the national state has flowed down the spatial scale to strengthen the role of the city governments. Brenner (2004) identified a strategic rationale behind this empowering of urban governance, where national governments sought to derive advantage in the competitive global economy by strengthening governance capacities of their major urban centres, so as to provide better and quicker responses to global economic challenges. Brenner (2004, p.295) termed this whole process "Rescaled Competition State Regime".

Rescaling of urban governance through political–economic empowerment has enabled several cities to enhance their competitive edge through comprehensive urban transformation. For example, in Europe, several globally connected high-tech industrial enclaves have developed around airports or transit routes like the Schiphol airport zone of Amsterdam and the ICT clusters of Ørested in Copenhagen due to initiatives of entrepreneurial planning agencies to strategically position their cities in the emerging knowledge economy (Brenner 2004). To develop the production spaces for the new economy, the parastatal agencies have often teamed up with private capital. New modes of governance have emerged through the formation of private–public partnerships and greater engagement between state and non-state actors in policy formulations and administration. Urban economic governance is no longer restricted to the domains of the formal institutions of the state, but rather expanded to include civil society organisations, NGOs, trade bodies and a range of non-state actors. Thus, the bigger political context of state restructuring due to economic globalisation has almost set the course of the local economic direction for large globalising urban regions.

However, developmental pathways of the territorially competing regions, even under broadly similar market-driven economic environments, do not follow any set pattern. Reflecting on the diverse trajectories of post-globalisation transformation of the cities of the old industrial economies of the West, Brenner and Theodore (2002b, p.344) attribute this diversity to institutional path dependencies, as they observed, "the effects of neoliberalism must necessarily be understood in contextually specific ways: they hinge upon the path dependent interaction of neoliberal programs, with inherited institutional and social landscapes". However, this emphasis on institutional path dependencies is unable to account for differences among sub-national regions under broadly similar institutional environments (Ataöv & Eraydin 2011; DiGaetano & Strom 2003).

Secondly, institutional structures within the same territorial authority often undergo changes in economic conditions, state spatial strategies and local political alliances. Drawing examples from changes in London's economic governance over the past three decades including the London Development Agency, the Greater London Authority and the Pan-London Local Enterprises Partnership, Pemberton and Goodwin (2011) claimed that such changes were more to suit the shifting electoral compulsions of the governing political parties over time, rather than due to changes in the external economic environment. Research about changing governance characteristics in Birmingham and Brisbane also indicate that although in the contemporary situation urban planning tools may be driven by national and state governments to achieve broadly similar objectives of economic growth through spatial regeneration, similarity in outcomes is not assured, due to the influence of the local socio-political factors, which may resist or embrace the changes, guided by the strategic logic at the local scale (Pemberton & Searle 2012).

Reshuffling of institutional structures and economic policies to suit partisan needs of the governing regimes is more frequently undertaken in the countries of the Global South than in the industrialised countries with stronger institutional structures. This is largely due to the fact that most developing countries are also new to the norms and standards of democratic functioning. Even in more established democracies, such as India, the balance of power is more heavily tilted towards the executive arm (compared to the legislative and judicial arms)—due to the lingering influence of the colonial state. Thus the governing regimes of the developing countries are relatively less constrained by institutional norms and practices, compared to the matured industrial democracies of the Global North (Leftwich 2010).

In such a context, the institutional framework by itself is inadequate as a basis for assessing directions, as developmental outcomes frequently depend on the political will of the actors to *implement* the policy, rather than the policy itself (Leftwich 2010). Drawing on examples from the industrialising countries of Asia where historically the state has played a more direct role in steering growth than in the liberal market economies of the West, Leftwich (1995) underscored the importance of place-specific political factors in influencing developmental trajectories. According to Leftwich (1995), following are the defining characteristics of these economically successful 'developmental states': the existence of a determined and powerful local 'developmental' elite; close ties between private capital and state bureaucracy; a powerful and relatively autonomous economic bureaucracy; and a pliant civil society. The developmental elites are not static or monolithic entities, but rather a shifting coalition of diverse interests. Political leadership has the crucial role in forging such developmental coalitions by negotiating the processes of contestation and collaboration in the local political terrain. While the structural configuration of the developmental coalitions range from institutionalised and formal to tacit and informal, they all tend to share a broad consensus on political goals and economic strategies. Politically motivated developmental strategies, crafted by these coalitions of state and non-state elites, are central to understanding variations in economic development, rather than just the formal institutional rules of the game. In this conceptualisation, members of the elite coalitions are rational actors, whose shared economic agendas are essentially shaped by the political calculus. Motivated self-interest is the glue which binds the coalition together. Although the notions of 'partnership' and 'network' between the state and non-state actors dominate the contemporary literature on governance, these relations are complex with several possibilities of tensions and conflicts due to the multiplicity of interests involved at various scales (Minnery 2007). The nature and scope for collaboration or conflict between the state and non-state actors are thus contextual.

At the urban scale, coalitions between local politicians and business interests have for a long time been a feature of the city politics in the USA and have been studied under the rubrics of the 'growth machine' (Logan & Molotch 1987) or 'regime' theory (Stone 1993). Regime theory seeks to explain close synergies that exist between municipal (city hall) level politicians and local business interests (e.g. real estate, construction, retail, entertainment) and circumstances which almost inevitably necessitate their working in tandem (Stone 1993, 2004). They work closely through formal and informal channels to perpetuate governance arrangements in such a way as to prevent taxes, legislation or any other hindrances from coming in the way of business profitability, in spite of 'official' political change. Irrespective of the party in power, the 'growth machine' of the local economy rolls on through the nexus between political and business interests that gives short shrift to environmental and social concerns.

However, the rootedness of these theories in the American urban political context, centring on traditions of official contributions from local business towards electoral campaign financing, and the ideological similarity of the two major political parties, which leads to formation of such coalitions or patronage networks, makes it difficult to apply the theories to other countries (Davies 2003; Pierre 2005). Nevertheless partnerships and coalitions between political and business interests in a broader sense have become the dominant paradigm in contemporary economic development strategies under neoliberalism, though manifestations of such elite coalitions, degree of collaboration or contestation are contextual. Rational choices of the individual actors in the partnerships and thereby the nature of their collective relationship are shaped by place-specific factors including degree of local autonomy, modes of raising revenues, the nature of public participation in governance and differences in power relationships between the constituents of the coalition (Davies 2003; Kantor, Savitch & Haddock 1997).

Earlier studies on globalising Asian cities noted the important roles played by local actors in the urban transformation. Drawing reference from Hong Kong, Shen (2004) argued that there are close synergies between a city's economic competitiveness and characteristics of its governing regime. In recent years, cities in China have seen increasing economic competition sparked by ambitious local government officials, keen on demonstrating their entrepreneurial prowess to the higher leadership (Shen 2007). Similarly, in the extended metropolitan region of Bangkok, the local political leadership plays an important role in translating national growth objectives at the ground level. Powerful businessmen–politicians have emerged as local chieftains, who are becoming intermediaries for economic growth through global flows, but who also enrich their own political and commercial interests in the process (Shatkin 2004). Observing the influence of these local elites in shaping place-specific economic agendas, Shatkin (2004, 2007) called for an actor-centred perspective while analysing urban changes, rather than merely focusing on macroeconomic factors.

However, Ramsey (1996) suggests that actions by the political actors are not purely based on rational choice but are also rooted in a socially embedded cultural milieu. Values, norms, traditions and beliefs influence the political choice of the actors. Social communities, and hereditary castes, tend to have different values and beliefs. Political actors seldom operate in isolation from these larger social processes and are also influenced by differential power relationships across the communities (Caulfield & Wanna 1995). Thus affluent and educated communities are better able to articulate their demands and exert greater weight in policy decisions. Specifically discussing planning cultures of the cities, Castells (2005) argued that globalisation and developments in communication technologies have radically altered the material basis for urbanism.

Thus, it is necessary for the planning practices in different cultural and economic settings to acknowledge these changes and reorient their priorities to meet the new challenges. Differing from this logic, Friedman (2005) claims that vast variations in the urban quality of life between cities and rootedness of urban planning in local institutional frames negate any possibilities of arriving at a homogenised planning culture, even in an increasingly globalised world.

Comparative analysis of urban governance through the prism of culture helps in explaining how embedded social and historical factors enable specific modes of governance to function in the context of structural changes. But on the other hand, cultural traditions are often inward looking and resist changes brought about by external forces. In this context, cultural analysis becomes useful to see continuities in institutional norms and policies, but also blurs the vision about ongoing changes.

2.5   Integrated framework for analysis of urban governance

Each of the analytical pathways based on structural changes in the global economy and resultant state restructuring, rational choice by the political actors in the governing regime or embedded place-specific cultural context, opens up substantial, albeit partial, windows to view contemporary urban changes. However, when it comes to comparison of sub-national governance regimes of a large and populous country like India, having huge regional cultural diversities along with entrenched caste and class interests, a more integrated approach is essential. Combining the facets of structural, agential and cultural factors, DiGaetano and Strom suggest such an integrated model.

In the integrated framework, DiGaetano and Strom (2003, p.373) define urban governance as "the process of coordinating political decision making" which they construe as "a series of intermediations across the structural, cultural and agency levels of governance". In this, they argue that more than the formal structure, the political institutions in the cities are linked by informal arrangements, which determine the modes of governance or characterise the regime type. The following three basic premises undergird this framework:

In the contemporary era, globalisation and state devolution provide the overarching structural environment within which the institutions of urban governance are inscribed. Economic globalisation proceeds unevenly. A city region's position in the national and international hierarchy is based on the proportional composition between 'new' and 'old' economy segments. Mobility of capital due to global financial integration has created an environment of competition between the cities. New institutional forms are emerging as cities embrace partnership with non-state actors.

Place-specific political culture 'mediates and filters' the impact of change in economic and political culture over the institutional milieu of urban governance. Thus in regions having strong statist traditions, the effects of globalisation are blunted and diluted. Conversely, regions having a strong private-sector-oriented culture are likely to facilitate globalisation.

Operating within the external structural context, the political actors may either become agents or resistors to institutional change, depending upon the rational choices of the constituents of the coalition and their cultural orientation. Devolution of power from upper tiers and economic changes provide opportunities for local political elites to expand their coalition by incorporating new stakeholders. But the new economy may also threaten the institutional support base, if it erodes the existing economic opportunities of powerful groups. Thus a political coalition which overtly depends upon trade unions tied to the old economy or on a statist political culture will tend to resist globalisation. Whereas, actors tied to the new economy will advocate reforms and restructuring.

DiGaetano and Strom argue that operating within the overarching structural environment, it is the interplay between the contextual factors of agency and political culture that define the local institutional milieu and, in turn, account for differences in economic development patterns between cities. There is a set of four basic criteria to understand this dynamic interplay. Firstly, there are 'governing relations' or the mode of interaction between government officials and private business interests. Secondly, there is 'governing logic' or the manner in which political decisions are made. Thirdly, there is the question of who the 'key decision makers' are—that is, the various combinations of politicians, bureaucrats, civil society activists, etc., which comprise the inner core of the governing coalition. Lastly, there is the question of what the 'political objectives' behind decision making are—these can be direct material or tangible benefits, purposive or non-selective tangible benefits, and symbolic non-tangible benefits. Based on these four criteria, they identify five major modes of governance, which are:

- *Clientelistic* – This mode of governance is shaped around politicians and favouring business interests based on particularistic exchange. The governing logic in this is often linked to direct material benefits.

- *Corporatist* – This mode of governance is formed around defined public–private partnerships. In this, the governing logic requires the elite corporate business houses and leading politicians to form a coalition through consensus. This mode of governance seeks to advance local economic development through joint and collaborative work between the corporate sector and the political set up (i.e. through specialised task forces, committees, etc.), but does not provide any direct or tangible benefit to the political leadership.

- *Managerial* – This mode of governance is based on formal bureaucratic exchange. Authoritative decisions are taken by bureaucrats and politicians, but do not entail consensus building with the business sector. Thus managerial decisions, involving the private sector, often lead to contracting out of specific civic services, but do not lead to institutionalised task forces between state and non-state actors.

- *Pluralist* – This mode is characterised by the balancing of interest amongst competing groups. Consensus building between diverse groups is the overriding governance logic in this context.

- *Populist* – In this mode of governance, a high degree of grass-root level mobilisation is involved. The governance logic is based on democratic inclusiveness. The key decision makers in this scenario are elected politicians and community activists. Business interests take a back seat in this regime.

Table 2.1 summarises the five governance modes discussed above.

DiGaetano and Strom (2003) provided a broad brush cross-country categorisation of the urban governance systems of Britain, USA, France and Germany, by analysing public–private partnerships. However, a more nuanced analysis was carried out by Ataöv and Erayidin (2011) as they analysed the economic governance responses of two Turkish metropolitan regions, in the context of globalisation and state restructuring. Restricting the external environment to the Turkish national structural context enabled the authors to investigate how embedded cultural factors and local actors had responded differently to economic opportunities.

Table 2.1 Modes of governance and their characteristics [*Source*: Adapted from (DiGaetano & Strom 2003)]

		Clientelistic	Corporatist	Managerial	Pluralist	Populist
Governing relations		Particularistic personalised exchange	Exclusionary negotiation	Formal bureaucratic or contractual	Brokering amongst competing interests	Inclusionary negotiation
Governing logic		Reciprocity	Consensus building	Authoritative decision making	Conflict management	Popular support mobilisation
Key decision makers		Politicians and clients	Politicians and powerful civic leaders	Politicians and civil servants	Politicians and organised interests	Politicians and community movement leaders
Political objective		Material	Purposive	Material	Purposive	Symbolic

However, on the whole, there is a paucity of comparative research about the governance characteristics of the cities of the Global South. Specifically reflecting on the peri-urban transformation in the globalising regions of East Asia, Webster (2011, p.635) observed, "urban regime theory would appear to have considerable relevance in explaining peri-urban dynamics, but it is an intellectual framework that has been underutilised to date by scholars of East Asian peri-urbanisation" (Webster 2011, p.635). A similar view was expressed by Shatkin (2011) while delivering a lecture on state, space and citizenship in contemporary urban India at Harvard University. In particular, Shatkin discussed the dearth of literature which links how local political processes respond to global economic forces. The next chapter discusses the available literature on globalisation and urban restructuring in India. And in doing so, it points to the serious knowledge gap which this book intends to address.

2.6   Summary

This chapter discussed the key issues pertaining to the transformation of urban regions due to economic globalisation. Market-driven global economic flows have increased the importance of select urban regions as strategic hubs and have increased competition between the cities. State restructuring and devolution of power from the upper tiers have strengthened the scope for entrepreneurialism at the urban scale to meet global economic challenges. Competitive pressures are forcing the state agencies to depart from their earlier emphasis on balanced regional development and development of backward regions, to channelising new investments into specific urban nodes, which have become strategic sites for articulation into global economy. One of the major spatial consequences of this competitive rescaling in Asia is the growing trend of large scale peri-urbanisation around the metropolitan cities, as the state agencies are opening up land at the fringe areas to meet the demands of the globalised economy. Rapid expansion of the urban footprints is in turn causing conflict over conversion of rural land for urban usage. Transformation of the fringe areas of the metropolitan cities in Asia is thus closely allied with the global economic processes.

However, economic competition and state restructuring do not necessarily spark entrepreneurialism in urban governance. There are differences in how cities respond to the external economic environment. There is however a research gap about the interface between the local and global forces in this scenario, which is particularly important in understanding how changing modes of urban economic governance impact transformation of land and livelihood of the people at the urban fringe. The existing literatures neither ask how the composition of the local governance shapes its engagement pattern with the external economy, nor do they explain what role the political objectives of the local regime play in mediating the impact of the global economic forces in particular ways.

DiGaetano and Strom (2003) developed a framework for comparative analysis of urban economic governance by combining structural, agential and cultural factors for cities in the advanced industrial economies. However, there is a dearth of use of such a comparative research framework to analyse the characteristics of the globalising urban regions of Asia in general and India in particular.

Liberalisation and urban transformation

3.1   Introduction

This chapter covers the literature review on post-economic liberalisation urban changes in India. The discussions are organised as follows: Section 3.2 provides a brief overview of the development planning process in India. Section 3.3 then focuses on the opening up of the Indian economy and globalisation. The next section, Section 3.4, then takes up the issue of changing patterns of urban governance in India and its scalar relationships. Section 3.5 then discusses restructuring of urban space due to regional economic competition, peri-urbanisation and emerging land conflicts. Section 3.6, the final section, concludes the discussion by establishing the gap in knowledge about the transformation of the fringe areas of the Indian cities due to global forces.

3.2   Development planning process

Since independence in 1947, India has faced several formidable challenges to its political and economic stability, due to the partition of the country, caste and linguistic divides, communal riots and natural calamities as well as malnourishment, food crises and illiteracy. All these issues have had their own impacts on the development-planning process. This section, however, provides a brief overview of only those salient features of the planning process which have a more immediate influence on the line of enquiry of this book, so as to situate the contemporary issues of globalisation and urban economic transformation in a larger historical perspective.

India adopted a parliamentary democratic form of political system and a socialist welfare-oriented economic system upon independence. Although largely modelled on the Westminster system, framing of the Indian constitution was also influenced by the American, Canadian and Australian constitutions. It has a federal structure with explicitly defined powers and responsibilities for the central (or national) government and the state (or provincial) governments (Rao & Singh 2005). The economic policies, under the leadership of Prime Minister Nehru (1947–64), were influenced by the Keynesian distributive ideology and the centralised planning system of the Soviet Union. Under Nehru's nation-building drive, import substitution and national capacity building were the prime objectives. And although the stated development model was 'mixed-economy', 'commanding heights' of the economy and crucial infrastructure sectors were reserved for the public sector, state-owned enterprises (Guha 2007). The role of private enterprise was relegated to less-important domains.

At the apex of the national development planning process was the Planning Commission, which was entrusted with formulating five-yearly plans for the functions that were directly handled by the central government (e.g. National highways, telecommunications, energy) and also allocated central funds to the state governments through a consultative process (Rao & Singh 2005). The five year economic plans, from the 1950s, laid emphasis on rapid modernisation, by building, through state initiative, heavy engineering and mega infrastructure projects; and creating specialised institutions of higher education in science and technology (Guha 2007). The planning policies also attempted balanced growth across the country by directly channelising public sector investments and providing incentives for the private sector to locate in backward regions.

Nehru's emphasis on higher education led to the establishment of several good tertiary academic institutions, particularly in the areas of science and engineering. Establishment of these institutions laid the foundation for India's later surge in the IT sector, but there were criticisms of perceived elitism, and neglect of primary education. Thus while India now produces the third highest number of engineering and technology graduates worldwide (Gereffi, Wadhwa & Rissing 2008), it also has the largest number of illiterates, as the literacy level had only improved from 12 percent in 1947 to 74 percent in 2011 and is below the world average (Census 2011). Emerging from the shadows of mercantile capitalism, the credo of Nehruvian planning was self-reliance in every sphere. As Guha observed, Nehruvian technocrats would make their own steel and machine tools rather than buy from outside, self-reliance became the index of development and progress. From soap to steel, cashew to cars, Indians would meet their material requirements by using Indian land, Indian labour, Indian materials and above all, Indian technology. (Guha 2007 p.209)

Power plants, dams, steel mills and other heavy engineering facilities developed by the modernising state were held as temples of secular India by Nehru. These large-scale engineering projects generated much hope in the initial years; however, these were not able to bring in a general economic improvement in the country. The annual economic growth rate hovered between 3 and 4 percent in the 1950s, 60s and 70s and was frustratingly termed the 'Hindu rate of growth' by economists (Basu & Maertens 2007; Dohrmann 2008). The major policy objectives of the post-colonial Indian state were not economic efficiency, but import substitution, employment generation and balanced regional development.

During the colonial era, industrial developments in India were heavily concentrated around the port cities of Calcutta (Kolkata), Bombay (Mumbai) and Madras (Chennai) (Ray, SC 2011). One of the foremost objectives of the national government during the 1950s was to overcome this spatial distortion and develop the hinterlands by channelising new investments. The 1960s and 70s were marked by more pronounced leftward orientation and centralisation of India's political and economic policies under Indira Gandhi's (1966–77 and 1980–84) regime (Guha 2007). Private sector industrial production also came under increasing state control. Quota restrictions and production upper limits were imposed, and more and more sectors began to be reserved for the public sector (Sinha 2005). These measures not only reduced efficiency in industrial production, but also severely increased scope for political and bureaucratic corruption, and came to be commonly termed as the 'license-permit-quota raj' (Guha 2007). The objectives of balanced regional development through public sector investments also started taking a back seat when locational decisions for the public sector units began to be guided by narrower political objectives. Projects in opposition-ruled states were delayed or stalled, while influential politicians began to lobby for units to be set up in their constituencies, to boost local employment and by extension, their own re-election prospects.

3.3   Economic restructuring and liberalisation

India's autarchic developmental regime started to be rolled back from the mid-1980s, through gradual economic liberalisation. Reductions in import restrictions, particularly for computers and high technology equipment, received a major boost during the period of Rajiv Gandhi's

Prime Ministership (1984–89), which subsequently led to the foundation of India's impressive growth in the IT sector. However, a paradigm shift in the Indian political economy began with the comprehensive structural reforms initiated in 1991, in response to a major balance of payment crisis and pressures from the IMF and the World Bank (Basu & Maertens 2007). But the economic liberalisation in India has moved at a slower pace compared to China, Brazil and Russia. Successive central governments led by various political combinations had broadly followed the policies of slowly and gradually opening up to a market economy and this has often been termed as "reforms by stealth" (Jenkins 2000, p.172). Large numbers of politicians believe the neoliberal market economy to be detrimental to the poor, while another influential section of economic nationalists try to protect domestic business interests (The Economist 2012c).

Nevertheless, since the early 1990s, the Indian economy has been on the upswing. The national GDP, which had increased from USD 36.6 billion in 1960 to USD 268 billion in 1991, climbed to USD 1.89 trillion—or the 9th largest in the world—by 2012, although in terms of per capita GDP India continues to lag behind at 125th position (World Bank 2012). India still accounts for the largest component of the poor population of the world, though the high growth rate in recent years has enabled large sections of the population to be lifted out of abject poverty, as the headcount ratio based on USD 1.25 per day declined from 59.8 percent in 1981 to 41.6 percent in 2005 (Ghosh, J 2010).

The post-reform decades had also seen worsening of rural and urban inequalities as well as increasing regional disparities, largely mirroring the trend in China and other developing countries. Between 1993–94 and 1999–2000, India's rural Gini index increased from 25.8 percent to 26.3 percent, while the urban Gini index increased from 31.9 percent to 34.8 percent (Ghosh, J 2010). There are rising concerns that economic growth is bypassing the vast and populous states of the north and central Indian heartlands (Ghosh, J 2010; Kavi-Kumar & Viswanathan 2008; Purfield 2006). However, the vertical disparities between the rich and poor and rural–urban divides are considered to be of more pressing concern compared to the spatial inequalities across states—which the scholars attribute to the federal structure of governance in India (Biau 2007; Ghosh, J 2010; Shankar & Shah 2003). Under the federal political structure of India, regional political actors exert greater pressure over the central government's allocation of resources, and thus it is politically difficult for the national government to prioritise certain states or regions of the country.

Over the years, the Indian economy had been going through a process of structural change, with the service sector becoming the most dominant component (Basu & Maertens 2007; Bosworth, Collins & Virmani 2007; Ghosh, J 2010). As shown in Figure 3.1, the contribution of the primary sector, which accounted for over 55 percent in 1951–52, has declined to just 14.6 percent and the share of the secondary sector has increased from 15.4 percent in 1950–51 to 28.5 in 2009–10 (Reserve Bank of India 2012). But most importantly, the contribution of the tertiary sector, which comprises of activities such as business services, real estate, finance, insurance, tourism and logistics, has climbed up from 29.3 percent in 1951–52 to 56.9 percent by 2009–10. The rate of expansion of the service sector picked up greater momentum following the economic liberalisation in the early 1990s with India's growing export of IT-related business services. Domination of the service sector also distinguishes the post-globalisation Indian economy from those of China and other Asian 'tiger' economies. Growth in China and the ASEAN countries is primarily driven by the export-oriented manufacturing sector, whereas the service sector contributes the bulk of India's export earnings (Prime 2009).

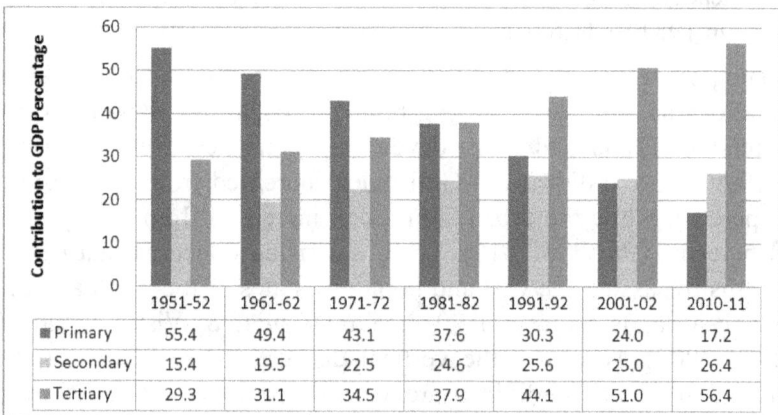

Contribution to GDP Percentage	1951-52	1961-62	1971-72	1981-82	1991-92	2001-02	2010-11
Primary	55.4	49.4	43.1	37.6	30.3	24.0	17.2
Secondary	15.4	19.5	22.5	24.6	25.6	25.0	26.4
Tertiary	29.3	31.1	34.5	37.9	44.1	51.0	56.4

Figure 3.1 Structural change in the Indian economy

Note: Primary sector includes agriculture, forestry, fishing, mining, etc.; Secondary sector includes manufacturing, construction and utilities; Tertiary sector includes business services, tourism, real estate, transportation, etc. [*Source*: Calculated by author from data published by the Reserve Bank of India (2012)]

Structural change in the Indian economy from agriculture to services and manufacturing has also impacted the settlement pattern and has raised the importance of urban issues in the national policy matrix. The combined contribution of urban centres to GDP increased steadily from 29 percent in 1951 to 46 percent in 1991 to 58 percent in 2008, and is projected to reach 70 percent by 2030 (Mckinsey Global Institute 2010). Recognising the importance of this trend, the central government launched a special programme called 'Jawaharlal Nehru National Urban Renewal Mission' (JNNURM) for infrastructure development of 63 cities, while the Eleventh Five Year Plan (2007–12) emphatically declared the cities as engines of economic growth, enhanced allocations for the sector and advocated urban governance reforms (Planning Commission of India 2006). These developments in many ways reflect not just a policy reversal, but more importantly a change in the political mindset, which acknowledges the role of the cities in economic growth (Kennedy & Zerah 2008; Shivaramakrishnan 2011).

Cities received only marginal attention from the Five Year national plans until the 1980s, leading to abysmally low budget allocations and incoherent policies. Scholars identify this neglect of urban issues as a carryover from the anti-colonial struggles (Luce 2006; Shivaramakrishnan 2011). Gandhi and most others held a romantic notion of the idyllic rural life, not corrupted by external or colonial influence (Luce 2006). During the 1950s and 60s several new state capitals (e.g. Chandigarh, Bhubaneswar) and planned industrial cities (e.g. Bhilai, Durgapur) did come up as part of Prime Minister Nehru's nation-building exercise through public sector investments in heavy engineering projects. But the political rhetoric of the post-colonial Indian state tended to prioritise the "rural over urban" as the Gandhian maxim of "India lives in villages" held sway (Shivaramakrishnan 2011 p.7). In the development planning arena, until recently, 'urban' was seen through a negative lens and efforts were mostly directed towards reducing urbanisation through rural development.

3.4   Changing pattern of urbanisation

India's urbanisation pattern depicts several paradoxical trends. With 286 million people living in cities, India has the second largest urban population in the world. There are 45 cities with million plus populations (Census 2011). The three largest cities, Mumbai, Delhi and Kolkata, each with populations over 15 million, are amongst the ten largest cities in the world. As per United Nation's projections, Mumbai and Delhi are going to be world's second and third largest urban agglomerations by 2025 (United Nations 2011). But on the other side, with nearly 70 percent of the people still living in the villages, India is the world's largest rural nation. Despite two decades of high economic growth, the urban population is just 31.16 percent of the total (Census 2011). Thus in percentage terms India's urban population is much lower compared to China and Southeast Asian countries as indicated in Figure 3.2.

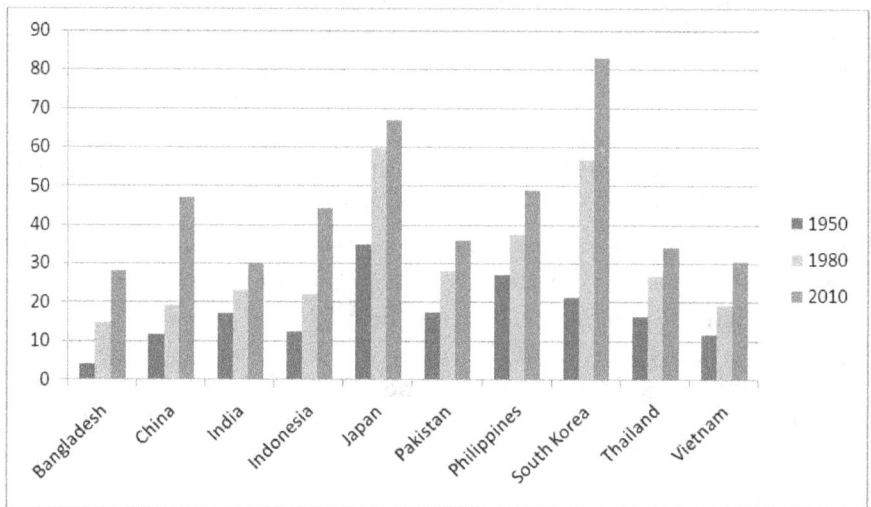

Figure 3.2 Urban population percentage in selected Asian countries
[*Source*: United Nations 2011]

However the recent census decade of 2001–11 marked, for the first time, higher population growth in urban areas than rural areas, while the decadal urbanisation rate of 3.35 percent also marked a substantial increase over the 1991–2001 census decades' urbanisation rate of 2.73 percent. These overall national figures, however, conceal major regional variations and a pattern of uneven spatial concentration of economic opportunities. As Kundu puts it,

> An analysis of the dynamics of regional development in the 1990s reveals that income growth has been uneven across states and so has the incidence of poverty. Despite significant growth in per capita income and the decline in poverty over the past decades, regional inequality in both has been accentuated. Rapid

income growth has occurred in developed regions as well as in and around Class I cities. (Kundu 2011 p.25)

Economically advanced states in southern and western India show higher rates of urbanisation, whereas depressed regions of north, central and eastern India depict higher overall population growth (Planning Commission of India 2012). However, even in these advanced states, growth is not happening in uniform patterns, but rather getting concentrated around the major urban centres like Mumbai, Pune, Bangalore, Hyderabad and Chennai. Economic opportunities in these cities are drawing in educated middle class, as well as unskilled construction labourers and wage workers from populous states like Bihar, Bengal and Uttar Pradesh. In the north and east, urban population is heavily concentrated around megacities like Delhi and Kolkata. All eight metropolitan regions, which are the locus of the new economic opportunities through globalisation, have witnessed high demographic growth as shown in Table 4.3 (Chapter 4). Bangalore and Hyderabad and the NCR area around Delhi have grown explosively. Growth of these three inland cities has brought down the primacy enjoyed at the macro-national scale by the colonial port cities like Mumbai, Kolkata and Chennai. But at a regional scale, growth is heavily concentrated around the big cities. The balanced regional development approach of the 1950s to 1970s, through central planning and public sector investments, has taken a back seat in the era of market-driven economic growth.

3.5   Decentralisation and urban governance reforms

Recognition of the importance of cities amongst the political leadership started to increase after Rajiv Gandhi (1985–90) became prime minister. Till then, "thinking in India on urban issues has been sporadic at best" (Shivaramakrishnan 2011, p.7), resulting in abysmally low budget allocations, split into myriad governmental programmes. Rajiv Gandhi's government initiated the National Commission on Urbanisation to investigate the state of the Indian cities, and also formed the National Capital Region Planning Board (NCRPB) to coordinate at a regional scale, development of Delhi and its surrounding areas. However, Rajiv Gandhi's attempts to revamp the local administrative machinery and improve delivery of central assistance through bottom-up planning met with stiff opposition from the state governments, fearing encroachment in their turf, as local government is a 'state subject' in the Indian constitution. Overcoming these reservations, the Narasimha Rao government passed the landmark 74th Constitutional Amendment Act (74CAA) in 1992, explicitly recognising urban governments as the third tier in India's federal structure, immediately after starting liberalisation of economic policies in 1991.

Political economic developments of the early 1990s, the advent of a multiparty coalition government at the national level, and the decline of central government's licensing and other regulatory controls over industrial investment yielded substantial autonomy to the state governments on economic issues and also unleashed a new era of sub-national economic competition. But the subsequent stage of devolution of power, by the state governments to the urban local bodies, did not follow the set course despite its constitutional mandate. This prompted the national government to attach a long list of mandatory and optional reforms for the state governments to undertake, when it launched the JNNURM programme in 2005, substantially increasing funding for urban infrastructure projects.

The 74CAA provided clear demarcation in the administrative powers of the local governments vis-à-vis the state governments; suggested new institutional arrangements for sharing of fiscal revenue; and ensured security of tenure for the local councils, against arbitrary dismissal by the state governments (Jain 2003; Shivaramakrishnan 2011). While elections to the local councils are regularly held and most states have constituted finance commissions to streamline revenue-sharing arrangements, the states have restricted the municipal domains to managing only the routine civic activities, citing capacity constraints (Shivaramakrishnan 2011). Urban planning functions in particular continue to be jealously guarded by the state governments through development authorities, or state town planning directorates, which not only report to the state governments, but are often directly headed by the chief ministers.

The reluctance of the states to devolve planning powers to the municipalities, even in the face of strong pressure from the central government, is neither out of ignorance about the economic role of the cities, nor due to administrative amnesia, but is rather calculated to maximise economic advantages to the governing regimes. There are no compulsive political pressures on the state governments to accord greater economic and administrative powers to the urban governments, as 'urban' still matters less in electoral terms than 'rural'. As has already been noted, India is amongst the least urbanised countries in the world, and despite two decades of high economic growth, the urban population is only 31.16 percent of the total (Census 2011). More importantly, even after the reconfiguration of the electoral constituencies in 2008, which substantially increased urban seats, rural seats continue to predominate. For example, in Maharashtra, which is the most urbanised amongst the bigger states of India with 42 percent of the population living in cities and having mega-urban agglomerations like Mumbai, Pune and Nagpur within its borders, only 35 percent of the Assembly seats are urban (Shivaramakrishnan 2011). Thus rural-centric political leadership holds sway over urban affairs, including urban economic policy issues.

Control over the urban affairs by the state administration has defeated one of the fundamental tenets behind the 74CAA, which was to institutionalise a more participatory planning process throughout the country. Although community consultation and public participation in planning in the Western sense are yet to be legally mandated in India, it was envisioned that transfer of urban planning functions from bureaucrat-dominated and state-government-controlled development authorities to elected urban local governments would make the planning process more inclusionary. However, resistance of the state governments has come in the way. Presently there are wide variations between the states regarding devolution of planning powers to the urban governments, as well as about encouraging public participation.

While participatory urban governance as envisaged by the 74CAA is yet to be fully realised, the engagement pattern between the local state and citizens in India has taken multiple dimensions in recent years. The vocal urban middle class, which has less influence in electoral politics because of the political dominance of the 'rural', has taken the 'apolitical' route of civil society activism to access the state, as Chatterjee (2004) observed. Civil society activism, in India, (as in other democratic countries) led to the emergence of several issue-specific NGOs (e.g. environmental conservation) and area-specific local resident welfare associations (RWA). However, in the Indian social context, most of the NGOs and RWAs are associated with the educated urban middle class (Chatterjee 2004). Particularly on issues related to urban governance, most NGOs and RWAs have espoused causes close to middle-class concerns, such as cleaner city environments and architectural heritage conservation—the areas which are often neglected by conventional politicians. On the other hand, civil society activism is yet to seriously embrace concerns of the peri-urban or rural areas.

Relatively more middle-class-dominated cities have institutionalised partnerships with civil society through program like the Bhagidari (Citizen engagement through neighbourhood associations) programme of Delhi government (Lama-Rewal, Stéphanie Tawa 2009) or more elitist alliances between the corporate sector, civil society elites and state government, as in Bangalore (Benjamin 2008). Both Delhi and Bangalore have seen enhanced engagement between the state and the civil society in workshops and seminars. However, the initiatives of Delhi and Bangalore are seen more as 'good practice' rather than as a mandatory requirement. The nature, scope and level of engagement vary, depending on the specific local context (discussed in detail in the case study chapters). Moreover, such consultations are usually restricted to the core city areas and do not cover peripheral areas.

Middle-class-dominated civil society activism, while opposing governmental action, has usually taken the legal route, by approaching the courts, through public interest litigation. For example, several NGOs and RWAs filed court cases against the growth of informal sector manufacturing activities within Delhi, in violation of the Master Plan. However, they usually avoided mass political agitation and have consciously sought to disassociate themselves from organised political parties. The 'political class' which runs the urban local bodies is seen by the middle class as corrupt, inefficient and backward, where considerations of the 'vote bank' predominate (Benjamin 2008). On the other hand, urban poor and slum dwellers, who earn their livelihood through the informal economy, and the people associated with the agrarian economy at the urban fringe, have tended to take the conventional political route to establish their claims on the city, by seeking protection and services from local party (and caste group) leaders (Benjamin 2008). In turn, the leaders try to mobilise people along caste groups to meet their electoral objectives. Thus, everyday issues and concerns of the urban poor and peri-urban communities are communicated through conventional political channels in elected rural and urban councils. However, discontents on highly emotive issues like land use conversion in fringe areas have frequently taken the form of street protests, demonstrations and political agitations.

Patterns of caste (and class) mobilisation frequently transcend the city and neighbourhood limits and extend over a larger geography. In this scenario the politics of urban transformation (through land use change), particularly in the peri-urban areas having a large rural population, becomes an appendage to the larger issues of state-level power equations played out between different caste and class groups over their political-economic interests.

3.6   Urban spatial restructuring and its discontents

3.6.1   First-worlding of Indian cities

The dominant narrative in the contemporary discussions on spatial restructuring of Indian cities centres on the issue of polarisation, between a small educated middle class tied to the globalised IT-BPO (Business Process Outsourcing) corporate economy and the vast majority of the rural and urban poor, who are peripheral to the process of economic globalisation. The popular press has termed this divide as 'India' versus 'Bharat' (Suri 2011). In this binary, 'India' represents the English speaking, educated elite. 'Bharat' the ancient name of India in native languages, represents the poor, tied to the rural agrarian economy and their urban counterpart, the migrants, slum dwellers and those tied to the informal bazaar economies. In this understanding, the increasingly neoliberal turn of the Indian state, since the 1990s, has been strongly reflected in the urban governance pattern, which has privileged the needs of the upper and middle classes, but in turn has marginalised the poor.

From the beginning of the 1990s, there have been several attempts by urban administrators and middle-class-dominated civil society groups to clean up the Indian cities, by relocating slums and polluting industries from core city areas. In most cases these movements had been packaged under the rubric of environmental conservation or architectural heritage conservation (Chatterjee 2004). At other times, powerful regional elites have attempted to make at least sections of their cities 'world class', by emulating foreign cities.

Thus planners in Bangalore strategise to turn the cyber city into another Singapore, while the elites of Mumbai clamour to emulate Shanghai. An alliterative slogan to turn Delhi from Walled City to World City, of the Chief Minister of Delhi ran for a long time before the Commonwealth Games (Miller 2009). Mamata Banerjee, the Chief Minister of West Bengal, has made several pronouncements aimed at regaining Kolkata's old glory by emulating London, and has started work on riverfront beautification (The Telegraph 2010, 2011c). According to Banerjee-Guha (2010), these elite-driven attempts at 'first-worlding' of Indian cities in the neoliberal era have increased urban fragmentation and hurt the interests of the poor through slum evictions and squatter resettlements. Research on restructuring of Bangalore (Benjamin 2010; Ghosh, A 2005; Nair 2000), Delhi (Dupont 2011), Mumbai (Banerjee-Guha 2007) further support this view.

3.6.2   Bypass urbanism

Another large volume of literature has emerged over the land acquisition issue, which is arguably the most contentious developmental debate in the post-liberal era. Availability of land on the fringe areas of the big cities is vital for the growth of the IT services sector. However, in recent years, land supply has become the greatest hindrance in India's growth trajectory, as agitation by the farmers against acquisition of agricultural land has stalled several major projects relating to the development of new townships, industrial estates, roads and highways.

Demand for land in the vicinity of the big cities has increased exponentially as India's economic growth surged following the deregulation of the early 1990s. Land at the proximity of the big cities having a large middle-class-educated labour supply are preferred by the IT-ITES (Information Technology Enabled Services) sector, which turned into the biggest growth driver of the Indian economy in the post-liberalisation era. In addition, there are pressures of outward expansion to meet the housing demands of the rising middle class urban population, which are also linked to the service-sector-led economic growth. To meet these twin demands for production and residential space by the new economy, the parastatal agencies started opening up the peri-urban areas through land acquisition and by providing new infrastructure. This strategy had been termed "by-pass urbanism" (Bhattacharya, R & Sanyal 2011 p.41). The parastatal agencies found it easier to build new growth centres in greenfield areas adjoining big cities, rather than undertaking the more challenging and time consuming tasks of tackling environmentally degraded yet commercially thriving inner city areas.

With fragmented ownership, regeneration of the congested inner city areas under the complicated Indian legal system would have entailed long and arduous negotiations with a vast number of small property owners and tenants.

To fast track economic growth and attract investments, in the face of intensified sub-national business competition, the parastatal agencies had been acquiring peri-urban agricultural land under a colonial era law, the Land Acquisition Act of 1894 (or its various state-specific variations), which empowers the state to acquire private properties by providing compensation (at a rate determined by the state), for purposes which serve the 'public good' (Ramanathan 2011). During the colonial period and the post-colonial phase of state-led development, 'public good' was usually associated with infrastructure projects like railway lines, roads, utility lines, schools, hospitals, public sector factories and power plants. But the role of the state started changing from direct provider to facilitator from the mid-1980s. The provisions of the original Land Acquisition Act were substantially modified in 1984 to allow the state to acquire land for private companies, to promote economic development (Ramanathan 2011). Demand for land, particularly in the vicinity of the large metropolitan centres, further accelerated from 2005 onwards, with the passage of the Special Economic Zone Act in 2005, which allowed 100 percent FDI investment in big real estate projects.

However, the growing involvement of the state agencies in facilitating private sector projects and particularly in the application of the Land Acquisition Act, to acquire rural agricultural land to facilitate industrial development or building of townships through private enterprise, has become highly controversial in recent years. The Land Acquisition Act (1894) has provisions for a single settlement of a compensation claim on the basis of the prevailing market rates for a similar land use. For example, compensation for acquiring agricultural land is determined on the basis of its existing agricultural usage. But the agitators demand higher payment (and/or jobs) on the basis of perceived escalation of land value, which the new development brings (Ram & Kakani 2009).

Widespread agitations (leading to protest marches, demonstrations and eventually blocking of access roads to the project site for several days) against land acquisition by the state in 2007–09 by the farmers, NGOs and political parties of West Bengal led to cancellation of a chemical industries cluster and relocation of an automobile factory to Gujarat. The protesters feared that the monetary compensation would soon disappear due to their lack of expertise in financial skills, while the loss of agricultural land would lead to permanent loss of livelihood (Nielson 2010). They also delayed several IT business parks near Kolkata (Banerjee, PS 2006, 2008; Nielsen 2010). Ripple effects of the agitation soon spread to other parts of India and affected Reliance mega SEZ projects at Navi Mumbai and Gurgaon amongst several others (Dohrmann 2008; Kennedy 2012). Starting off against private projects, the agitations also impacted several public infrastructure projects like the railways and the national highways.

Debate over the land issue has followed multiple trajectories of environmental and social justice. The provisions of the SEZ Act (2005) have come under much criticism, for accelerating the mechanism for 'corporate land grabs'. Questions have been raised about why the state agencies should facilitate SEZs, industrial estates or gated IT business parks, which are essentially private enclaves (Kasturi 2008, 2009). Scholars attribute the emergence of these privatised enclaves as a corollary to state restructuring and gradual insertion of Indian cities into the neoliberal global economic order (Banerjee-Guha 2008; Dohrmann 2008; Mukhopadhyay & Pradhan 2009). Recent decades have seen a gradual withdrawal of direct state involvement in planning and an increase in public–private joint ventures. Rather than directly building production spaces like IT business parks and SEZs, the parastatal agencies are facilitating private entrepreneurship in these areas. Acquisition of rural agricultural land through the power of the state is an intrinsic part of such facilitation processes, which in turn has increased vulnerabilities for the rural poor.

Others, however, see some sort of role for state agencies in the land acquisition process, even if for private companies, as impossible to avoid. Due to the fragmented nature of agricultural land holdings, unavailability of clear property title deeds, and lengthy registration procedures, land transactions in rural areas are highly complicated (Ram & Kakani 2009). It is argued that big projects, which require large parcels of contiguous land, will suffer enormous delays, if the private companies have to negotiate with individual small farmers. Even if most of the farmers agree to sell their land, a few persons can hold on and inordinately delay the project take-off, in turn hurting national economic growth. It is also feared that free market transactions in rural land would lead to the emergence of a land grabbing syndicate, which could only hurt the interests of the poor. They advocate for a more just land acquisition policy, with built-in provisions for resettlements.

The issue is currently being debated by the Parliamentary Standing Committee. According to the news reports, new legislation—Land Acquisition and Resettlement Act—is likely to replace the Land Acquisition Act of 1894. This would substantially increase compensation rates by taking livelihood impacts into account and would reduce the scope for acquiring land for private projects (The Telegraph 2012b).

3.7   New economic spaces

The literature discussed above situates the emerging macro pattern of urban restructuring in India within the overarching frame of state restructuring following economic globalisation. This helps us to see a broad brush picture of the ongoing contestations over urban space. It is undoubtedly true that Indian cities are extremely polarised between the rich and the poor, and pro-market reforms since the 1990s have further exacerbated the existing cleavages. However, beyond this rich–poor, 'India-Bharat' dichotomy, there are huge regional differences, which the existing literature has not investigated in depth. Moreover none of these studies has explicitly analysed the spatial implications of the IT outsourcing sector.

There are only a few studies which directly look at the influence of the IT services industry on the reshaping of urban space. Studies by Aranya (2008) on the intra-city location preference of the IT firms in Bangalore demonstrated a dual process: both to disperse from the city core and concentrate at other locations, based on operational requirements. In the start-up phase, when the firm size is small, with small number of employees and low business volumes, the firms tend to congregate in inner-city business districts, as the need for low transport cost predominates over the quality of infrastructure needed. In the second phase, when the business expands and the issue of data privacy between projects from rival clients gains importance, the firms establish 'development centres' in multiple locations within the city. In the third phase, with further growth in earnings, the issues of corporate image, high infrastructure and quality of physical environment become the dominant factors. At this stage firms tend to consolidate dispersed activities into the campus-like settings of the suburban business parks at the outer fringe of the city.

The suburban business park with big parking space became the preferred spatial model for the industry, as it started expanding from Bangalore to other cities, in turn beginning a process of urban transformation. Early research on changing peri-urban dynamics provided a broad overview of the new urban landscape in metropolitan cities of India with the emergence of the new production and consumption spaces for the new IT-driven globalised economy at the urban fringe (Dupont 2007; Dupont & Sridharan 2006). Secondly, they discussed the emergence of an intensely heterogeneous, complex and segmented settlement pattern at the peri-urban interface, in which the high-tech clusters and the planned settlements of the new digital age economy intertwine with congested rural settlements of an agrarian economy in the physical-spatial realm.

Subsequent research, mostly focusing on single cities, brought out different facets of this IT-led peri-urbanisation. For instance, research in the context of Delhi NCR linked this process of suburbanisation of the IT and other globalised services to the planning and infrastructure constraints in the core city areas. The IT-ITES sector's demand for buildings with large floor plates, huge parking lots and modern building services are almost impossible to meet in centre city locations due to paucity of land, high real estate prices, zoning and land use regulations (Chatterji 2007). Research on Hyderabad brought out intensive engagement of the state agencies in facilitating growth by providing land and infrastructure in planned townships for the IT and biotech companies and elite business schools (Kennedy 2007; Leclerc & Bourgignon 2006; Ramchandriah & Prasad 2008). This developmental process was linked to the strong desire of the local political elites to leapfrog the city's future growth trajectory into the knowledge economy. Analysis of the post-economic liberation growth process of Bangalore and Kolkata by Shaw and Satish (2007) also noted close engagement of parastatal agencies in the peri-urban transformation process to attract new economic sectors and as part of the sub-national economic competition. In addition, this research highlighted the cooperative role played by local and international finance in this restructuring process.

Expanding the urban footprint of Indian cities to meet the spatial demands of the globalised economy has increased contestations over peri-urban space. Much like their Southeast Asian counterparts, livelihood strategies of the households in peri-urban areas of Indian cities are constructed across rural and urban spaces, such as cattle rearing and the operation of taxi services or petty trading, but they face increasing threats due to rapid urban expansion (Hust 2005). Loss of land has necessitated change in livelihood strategies for the rural household, to cope with the new type of economic environment, without having the appropriate skills. This is causing severe socio-economic stress, as the planning policies of the cities have failed to take this situation into account (Hust 2005).

Studies at the peri-urban interfaces of the globalising urban regions of India, like Gurgaon in the Delhi-NCR area (Narain 2009; Narain & Nischal 2007), have documented growing discontent amongst the local agricultural communities whose lands were taken over by the state agencies to meet the needs of the growing city. As Narain (2009, p.51) put it, "the expansion of the city has altered patterns of rural natural resource use, created social, cultural and economic changes, and bred resentment among many peri-urban residents against urban authorities". Loss of cropping and grazing land has severely affected the occupational structure of the rural areas as a whole, not just that of the farmers. Livelihoods of potters, shepherds and farm labours, linked with the extended agrarian economy are also affected. Also, compensations, only in the monetary form as provided under the existing Land Acquisition Act, is inadequate to meet continuing livelihood needs, as people with low investments skills and few alternative livelihood options tend to fritter away the money. The inflow of quick money through land sales also leads to social vices, such as drinking and gambling. There are also long delays in releasing compensation payments, due to the complex bureaucratic hurdles involved. Based on these findings, Narain (2009) has suggested extending the scope of the Land Acquisition Act to include comprehensive resettlement packages and expediting compensation payments.

Studies at the fringe areas of the extended metropolitan belt of Bangalore, where the state agencies have acquired land to meet the infrastructure requirements of the expanding urban economy, have also faced rising discontent due to livelihood vulnerabilities, environmental degradation and differential provision of infrastructure services (CIVIC 2007). The study revealed that proceeds from the land takeover had benefitted farmers with larger land holdings, having more than two hectares of land. Relatively better educated and belonging to upper castes in the local social hierarchy, they had been better able to switch over to alternative livelihoods through trading or by constructing rental property. Whereas, small farmers, most of whom belong to lower castes, had suffered most. Without basic education, many of them had quickly spent the cash money on alcohol and other lifestyle choices. Bereft of earning, they had then been forced to take daily wage labour jobs in the construction industry. Environmental conditions in the village areas had degraded, as *Gomala* or village common lands, land-fills and waste disposal areas, etc., had been taken over (CIVIC 2007). Moreover, sanitary discharges from the new settlements are often haphazardly discharged towards the village areas. Roads and other new civil infrastructure are also primarily designed to meet the needs of industrial estates, IT parks and educated middle class residential areas. Many of the village areas are slums or unauthorised settlements and thus have been ignored by the formal planning regime.

Research by Benjamin (2008, 2010) attributed marginalisation of the poor to the elite-driven state policies of the post-liberalisation era. Small scale and often informal manufacturing and trading activities or old-fashioned industries like textile mills, which even now provide the bulk of the employment in Bangalore, are being systematically overshadowed in the planning agenda by IT, biotechnology and other high-end globalised sectors. Delivery of infrastructure, roads, power and other basic services privilege the areas associated with the new economy of globalised services. Revised planning norms call for relocation of old and polluting industries from the urban core to planned industrial clusters—which impact the job prospects of the lower end work force. The close association between the new economy elites and upper echelons of the state government has eroded the power of the local municipal politicians. This in turn has contributed to the marginalisation of the poor and local informal economies, which have stronger ties with the lower tiers of governance (Benjamin 2008). The gap between the rich and the poor has widened and the city has become more unequal. Kavi-Kumar and Viswanathan (2008) suggest this is due to the fact that the economic conditions of the middleclass in Bangalore has been improving at a much faster rate in the post-globalisation era—rather than the poor getting poorer.

Following a similar line to that of Benjamin (2008), Goldman (2011) observed that the governing elites of Bangalore are overtly focused on turning it into a 'world class' city, to match its reputation as a leading centre of the knowledge economy in the world. Pro-growth policies of the parastatal agencies which open up the fringe areas of the city for expansion to create production and consumption spaces for the IT sector have substantially increased commoditisation of the peri-urban land market and spurred speculative investments in the fringe areas of Bangalore (Goldman 2011). However, Goldman's research has not explored the political linkage of this speculative growth process. The question that is not answered is: who are the beneficiaries in this developmental mechanism and what are their connections with the IT industry and the local governing regime?

Most of the research linking IT services and urban restructuring centre on Bangalore. This is understandable, as the southern city is the global face of the Indian IT industry. However, over the years, the footprint of the IT-ITES sector has substantially expanded to other big cities of India. Apart from Bangalore, six other metropolitan regions of India (Hyderabad, Delhi NCR, Mumbai, Chennai, Pune and Kolkata) have attracted large volumes of IT investment (Khomiakova 2007; NASSCOM & A.T.Kearney 2009). There are crucial differences in the developmental trajectories of these regional IT clusters.

However, the existing literature neither provides a comparative perspective nor engages in analysing characteristics of the local governing regimes. The composition of the local governance coalitions, their objectives and priorities are not explored. More importantly, the existing literature on IT services has neither engaged in detail with the question of land supply, nor has it explored the impact of IT production spaces on the urban land market. The locational preference of the IT outsourcing industry in the fringe areas of the big cities and the ongoing contestations over peri-urban land have added a vital new dimension, which further reinforces the importance of investigating the local political contexts of these cities, as land issues are usually negotiated at the local realm.

The state governments in India enjoy a high degree of autonomy in pursuing their economic goals, including direct negotiations with international investors, but they are not fully autonomous and are bound by the rules established by the national government. Sinha's

(2005) study comparing the industrial development patterns of three Indian states—West Bengal, Tamil Nadu and Gujarat—showed that the governance regimes of the states responded to centrally established rules in vastly different ways. Study on the development of the software industry in three states of Southern India also showed unevenness in approach towards accessing global opportunities, even after the national government substantially liberalised the IT sector (Kumar 2009). But in each case the responses were calibrated with an eye towards the election cycle, to maximise political dividends for their ruling elites. However, research by Sinha (2005) and Kumar (2009), both focussed on state and national level political-economic factors and did not specifically address issues at the urban or metropolitan region scale.

Taking off from these understandings, this book compares the urban governance regimes of Bangalore with those of Kolkata and the Delhi NCR, to provide a more nuanced and fine grained understanding about the developmental pathways of the regional IT clusters in the peri-urban areas of the globalising urban regions of India. The comparative research adopts the integrated framework comprising structural and contextual factors for comparative governance evolved by DiGaetano and Strom (2003). The overarching macroeconomic environment of India, influenced by global economic processes, provides the backdrop of the research. Contestations over the peri-urban space between the globalised IT services sector and the local agrarian communities, is the integrating theme. Against this, mediations of the regional, state level political factors are analysed, to see how the local and global forces play out in transforming the urban fringe.

3.8   Summary

This chapter discussed how globalisation and macroeconomic changes are leading to urban transformation in India. From the 1990s onwards, IT-enabled back office services have become a principal growth driver of the Indian economy, while the proportion of agriculture in the national GDP has been consistently falling. But India's rate of urbanisation is still relatively low and an overwhelming 70 percent of the population still remain in the villages. Thus even though their economic significance is declining, the rural areas remain important in electoral terms, creating a huge disconnect between the political and economic spheres.

4

Research methodology

4.1   Introduction

This chapter includes a detailed discussion about the research design adopted for this book. The next section discusses why the primary thrust of the research is on qualitative analysis. Section 4.3 explains why this book adopted case study in a sub-national framework as the research method. Section 4.4 then provides the rationale behind the choice of particular case study locations. Section 4.5 discusses data collection strategies. Following that, Section 4.6 describes how data analysis was carried out. Section 4.7 highlights the constraints encountered during the research and limitations of the research. Section 4.8 concludes the chapter with a summary.

4.2   Qualitative research method

The main research objective of this book is to explore the interfaces between global and local actors in the land use transformation in the fringe areas of the metropolitan cities of India. The research involves exploring the roles of the major stakeholders, state, corporate and civil society and community organisations, to understand the character of the local governing regime and how the governing regimes mediate global economic forces. To understand the deeper local and global context in which the actions and strategies of the various state and non-state actors are embedded, it is pertinent to use qualitative research methods. Several scholars on research methods have stressed the usefulness of qualitative analysis in policy-related studies, where the primary objective is to gain deep insights into a process, which numbers cannot reveal (Gray et al. 2007; Punch 2008; Yin 2009). Previous research on other Asian cities such as Shanghai and Kolkata (Chen, Wang & Kundu 2009), Bangkok (Shatkin 2004) and Kuala Lumpur (Bunnell, Barter & Morshidi 2002), exploring local–global interfaces typically relied on qualitative analysis.

However, this research also uses a substantial amount of quantitative data, primarily to establish the background structural context, such as the growth of the IT outsourcing industry, relative economic growth rate of the Indian states, urban population growth, etc. All these quantitative indicators have been sourced from well-established international and national institutions, government and trade organisations, such as United Nations, World Bank, The Economist magazine, Census registrar, National Association of Software and Service Companies (NASSCOM), Planning Commission, etc.

4.3   Design of the case study research

Since the objective of the book is to enhance our understanding about the transformation of the fringe areas of the large globalising urban regions, through the interface between local and global forces, adaptation of a case study method, with an individual city as the unit of analysis, has been deemed to be the most appropriate. The case study research approach is an all-encompassing method and had been applied in several social science projects previously (Yin 2003). As Yin points out, case study is the preferred strategy in situations when the research attempts to explore a contemporary phenomenon in its real life context and when "boundaries between phenomenon and context" are not clearly evident.

The research questions for this book revolve around the characteristics of the urban governance regimes in pursuance of an economic development agenda. To compare and contrast the role of the urban governance regimes involving structural, agential and cultural parameters, an integrated theoretical framework, developed by DiGaetano and Strom (2003), has been adopted. However, comparative studies of economic governance regimes are inherently problematic. The economic bases of no two cities are exactly similar. The dependence of cities on particular economic drivers, whether in manufacturing or in the service sector, varies, and can have drastically different consequences, particularly in a macroeconomic environment dominated by global forces. Thus, British industrial cities Birmingham, Leeds and Glasgow all performed unevenly under similar economic contexts in the 1980s and 1990s. On the other hand, cities situated under different political and social contexts can have entirely different approaches towards global economic processes. Thus, the local governments of Shanghai, Mumbai and Sao Paolo, the main financial centres of large transitional economies like China, India and Brazil, have vastly different powers, priorities and capabilities to engage in economic development. Powers of urban governments and by extension their governing regimes are shaped by scalar relationships between multiple tiers of government within the nation-state. Thus city governments in China have far greater autonomy on economic issues compared to their Indian counterparts. Within a nation-state also, the powers of local governments vary considerably. Bigger cities generally have stronger local agencies with greater power and resources at their disposal, than smaller entities. The appropriate choice of case-study location therefore assumes critical importance.

To overcome the above difficulties, this book has adopted a sub-national framework to compare the governing regimes of three metropolitan regions of India over a single economic sector—that is the IT-ITES sector. These boundary conditions enable us to focus more closely and compare planning regimes, which have been functioning under the same constitutional and macro-economic framework, yet are moderated by differences in the political-economic dynamics at the sub-national level producing contrasting levels of economic development. India has a number of features which make it particularly suitable for sub-national comparative studies on economic development issues (Sinha 2005).

Firstly, it is a federal country composed of several states with a fairly high degree of political autonomy, which allows for some state-wise variability in economic policies. From the 1990s onwards, deregulation of economic and industrial policies and the advent of coalition politics in the national arena strengthened the roles of the state governments in economic issues and allowed them to seek international investments. Yet, at the same time, the state governments are not fully independent entities. They are bound by the regulatory environment established by the national government on import, export, currency valuation and national level corporate taxation.

Secondly, within the formal institutional power structure of the Indian national state, the provincial states show huge diversity in political-economic and socio-cultural practices. The sizes of the major states are similar, in terms of population and geographical extent, to that of several medium-sized countries (The Economist 2012a). Functioning under the overarching policy environment established by the national government, the state governments craft their own economic strategy based on the political interests of the governing regime. Sinha's research on the industrial development strategy adopted by the state governments established that even in the heydays of the public-sector-led developmental state era (from the 1950s to 1980s), the approach of the local governing coalitions was not purely guided by economic growth objectives but rather guided by the local political logic and by electoral prospects. In the Indian context, electoral calculi are often shaped by caste-based political alliances. But at the same time, they are not just about caste. As recent electoral trends point out, track records of the political parties in delivering developmental promises are increasingly gaining ground, particularly in the big cities. The approach and priorities towards development vary across the states, and economic development strategies in such situations are subjected to the interplay between caste and class-based regional political dynamics.

Thirdly, economic development in India had historically been highly polarised in certain mega-urban regions. In the colonial era, the three coastal cities Calcutta (Kolkata), Bombay (Mumbai) and Madras (Chennai), located in three corners of the country, held regional primacy. In the post-colonial era, centralisation tendencies of the national government turned Delhi into the fourth economic node, and the principal magnet of Northern India. The post-liberalisation phase of rapid economic growth saw the rise of Bangalore, Hyderabad and Pune. However, like Delhi, none of these are new cities and all have long histories. Political and economic changes have seen waxing and waning of their relative positions in the national hierarchy. Five of these cities, Mumbai, Chennai, Kolkata, Bangalore and Hyderabad are state capitals, while Delhi is the national capital. In the contemporary situation of economic globalisation and decentralisation, they further augmented their role in the national economy. Together, these seven cities account for 92 percent of the IT services exports (NASSCOM & A.T. Kearney 2009). Three out of these seven cities were selected as case study location, based on the rationale discussed in the following section.

Fourthly, the location pattern of the production and consumption spaces for the IT outsourcing industry around the big Indian cities shows remarkable similarity. Fringe areas of the big cities have emerged as the preferred destination for the industry, and most IT clusters have come up at the outer peripheries in new greenfield townships. The two prominent IT hubs of Bangalore, Electronic City and Whitefield, are located at the southern and south-eastern periphery (Aranya 2008). A third hub at Devanahalli near the new international airport has started to develop. Similarly in Chennai, most IT business parks are located at the south eastern edge along the Old Mahabalipuram Road. In Hyderabad, the IT firms are clustered in HITEC City, at the initiative of the TDP government (Kennedy 2007; Leclerc & Bourgignon 2006; Ramchandriah & Prasad 2008). In Delhi NCR, the major IT hubs are located in the suburban cities like Noida and Gurgaon, both of which are outside the administrative limits of Delhi (Maitra 2008). Similarly in Kolkata also, the two IT hubs are located in Sector V of Salt Lake City, and Rajarhat, near the airport at the north eastern fringe (Shaw and Satish, 2007). In Mumbai, scarcity of land at the urban core of South Mumbai has forced the IT companies to locate at Bandra Kurla complex and Navi Mumbai (Banerjee-Guha 2007; Nijman 2007), or in the Hinjewadi area in Pune along the Mumbai–Pune Expressway (Mahadevia & Parashar 2008).

The cities are comparable in terms of the structural context of economic governance. As discussed previously in Chapter 3, the locus of economic decision making in India rests with the concerned state governments (Shivaramakrishnan 2011; Sinha 2005). Thus even for megacities like Mumbai (population 16 million) and Pune (population 7 million), it is the Government of Maharashtra, which determines the incentive structure for the IT companies, not Brihan-Mumbai Municipal Corporation or the Pune Municipal Corporation—the elected local governments. Again, the floor area and zoning-related benefits provided under the state government's IT policies override the bylaws and planning guidelines of the city government. The elected municipal governments are primarily engaged in running routine civic services, while economic planning and related urban planning are handled by the state governments. Consequently, the game of urban economic competition between Indian cities, to attract IT sector investments, is essentially played out by the concerned state governments, each of which hold a similar degree of formal power under the Indian constitutional umbrella. This establishes the finite boundary condition for the selection of case-study location as specified by Yin (2009), while the contemporary phenomenon of IT outsourcing provides the real life context. The following section compares seven major IT clusters of India: Bangalore, Chennai, Delhi NCR, Kolkata, Mumbai and Pune, in terms of economic and population growth patterns, followed by a discussion about the local political context of the growth, to justify selection of the case study locations.

4.4   Selection criteria for case study locations

4.4.1   Urban economic growth

Several scholars have shown a strong synergy between globalisation and the acceleration of spatial polarisation, as economic growth under the neo-liberal regime has increasingly concentrated in certain strategic locations, as opposed to the policies of balanced regional growth in the earlier decades (Brenner 2004; Castells 2005; Sassen 2006). Similar trends are visible through the economic geography of the IT outsourcing industry. But at the same time, growth in this new economic sector is reconfiguring the national economic hierarchy. Growth in the IT services industry is accelerating the growth of these cities, which are already the most advanced cities in India. Mumbai, Delhi and Kolkata, the three largest cities of India, are also the major economic growth engines. Mumbai, which has the largest stock exchange, busiest air and sea ports, and maximum number of bank headquarters, is India's main articulation with the global economy and a major international financial hub. However, at a sub-national level, the economic power equation is changing. Delhi has replaced Kolkata as the second largest commercial city of India; while, powered by growth in the IT sector, Bangalore has overtaken Chennai as the leading economy of South India. Refer to Table 4.1 for a comparative ranking of the Indian cities in terms of GDP.

Table 4.1 Urban agglomeration GDP ranking

Urban agglomeration	2008	
	Estimated GDP (in USD bn.)	International rank in city GDP
Mumbai	209	29
Delhi	167	37
Kolkata	104	61
Bangalore	69	84
Chennai	66	87
Hyderabad	60	93
Pune	48	108

Note: City GDP based on Purchasing Power Parity. [Source: City GDP from Citymayors.com]

If we now locate these seven big IT clusters, with their respective State Gross Domestic Product (SGDP) and per capita SGDP, as indicated in Table 4.2, then we see that growth of the IT industry is mostly concentrated in the richer part of the country. Mumbai, Pune, Bangalore and Chennai are located in states where per capita GDP is higher than the national average. Similar is the case of Gurgaon in Haryana where most IT firms of the NCR are located. Kolkata and Hyderabad are located in relatively poorer states where per capita GDP is close to the national average.

Table 4.2 State GDP of select Indian states

IT cluster	State	State GDP 2011–12 (in billion USD)	Per capita state GDP, March 2012 (in USD)	Average state GDP growth rate between 2003 to 2012 (in percentage)
	India	1,850	1,329	8
Bangalore	Karnataka	90	1,507	8
Chennai	Tamil Nadu	125	1,853	9
Delhi NCR				
Delhi	Delhi NCT	62	3,637	10
Gurgaon	Haryana	61	2,361	9
Noida	Uttar Pradesh	135	666	6
Hyderabad	Andhra Pradesh	133	1,557	8
Kolkata	West Bengal	106	1,181	7
Mumbai and Pune	Maharashtra	232	2,158	8

Note: All GDP are on the basis of purchasing power parity basis. Source:(The Economist 2012c)

4.4.2   Urbanisation pattern

Concentration of economic growth opportunities in select regions led to the formation of several megacities in India. Mumbai, Delhi and Kolkata, the three largest urban cities of India, are amongst the ten largest cities in the world (United Nations 2011). Whereas, the urban population of India, even after two decades of rapid economic growth, is just 31.16 percent (Census 2011). Economic momentum in recent years has further intensified the process of uneven growth as the cities with the seven major IT clusters are amongst the eight largest cities of the country as indicated in Table 4.3. Out of these, the Delhi metropolitan region has recorded an astronomical growth rate, and is amongst the fastest growing urban regions of the world (United Nations 2011). Amongst the southern cities, Bangalore, Hyderabad and Pune have witnessed rapid growth in recent years, much of which is driven by the IT sector. Amongst the top Indian cities, Kolkata has recorded the lowest population growth rate, which is reflective of its relatively lesser economic growth rate.

Table 4.3 Urban agglomeration population growth rate

Urban agglomeration	Total population (in millions)			Decadal population growth (in percentage)	
	1991	2001	2011	1991 to 2001	2001 to 2011
Greater Mumbai	12.6	16.4	23.3	29.9	40.9
Kolkata	11.0	13.2	16.6	19.9	25.7
Delhi NCR	9.8	12.8	23.9	51.9	86.9
Chennai	5.4	6.4	8.9	18.5	38.6
Bangalore	4.1	5.7	8.0	37.8	41.0
Hyderabad	4.3	5.5	7.7	27.4	45.3
Pune	2.5	3.7	5.5	50.6	46.7

[*Source*: (Census 2011)]

If we now superimpose these mega urban regions on the national map, showing state-wise variation in urbanisation pattern (see Figure 4.1), we get the picture that most IT clusters are located in the relatively more urbanised states. Karnataka, Tamil Nadu and Maharashtra, which host the IT clusters of Bangalore, Chennai, Mumbai and Pune, are amongst the most urbanised in India, with urbanisation levels over 35 percent, against the national average of 31.16 percent. Kolkata and Hyderabad lie in relatively less urbanised regions, where state urbanisation levels lie in the 30–35 percent bracket. Haryana, which includes Gurgaon, the main IT hub of the NCR area, also falls in this bracket.

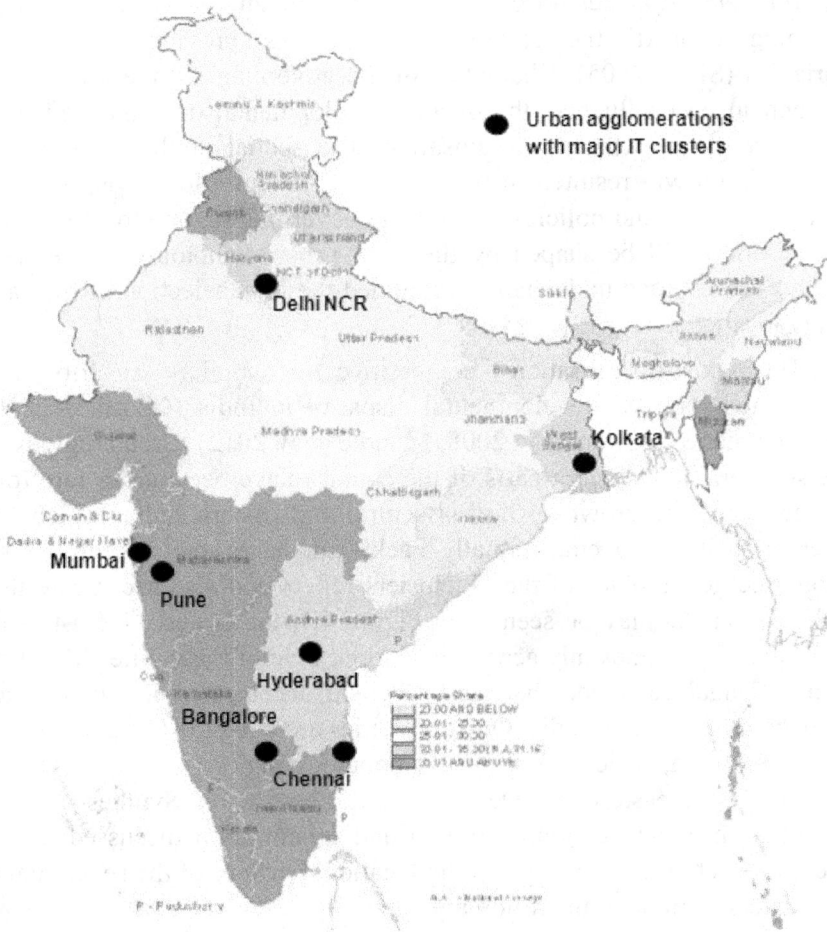

Figure 4.1 Urbanisation level in Indian states [*Source*: Census 2011]

4.4.3   Selection of case study cities

Central research questions for this book revolve around the interface between the local and global forces in transformation of the fringe areas of the big cities in India. In this process of urban transformation, the character of the local governing regime assumes crucial importance. The theoretical framework adopted for analysing the character of the governing regime emphasises drawing contrasting patterns, based on local political and cultural context, within similar structural environments (DiGaetano & Strom 2003). In an Indian development planning context, the state-level differences provide the crucial variables (Sinha 2005). Characters of the governing regime are shaped by, and in turn influence, the overall developmental outcome, reflected by economic growth and urbanisation. The spatial implications of the economic growth resulted in extensive peri-urbanisation. It is assumed that the attitude and policies of the local governing regime towards peri-urbanisation will be shaped by the rural–urban dichotomy in the state polity. These broad understandings guided the final selection of the case study locations.

The post-liberalisation competitive economic scenario has heightened regional developmental disparity in India (Ghosh, J 2010; Kavi-Kumar & Viswanathan 2008; Mundle et al. 2012). Urban regions of the southern and western parts of the country have been at the forefront of the economic growth, whereas central and eastern India, which are over populated and educationally backward, have lagged behind. The economic geographies of the IT clusters reflect and also accentuate this polarisation. As may be seen from Figure 4.1, the largest IT clusters of India are spread unevenly across the nation. Five of these cities Mumbai, Pune, Bangalore, Hyderabad and Chennai are located in the Deccan peninsula of southern India. Only two cities are from the Gangetic plains of Upper India, which are the most populous regions of the country— Kolkata in the eastern and Delhi in the northern flank. Synthesising the information about economic growth and urbanisation discussed in the previous sections, we can group the locational pattern of the seven major IT clusters of India in the following way:

- Four of the IT clusters, Bangalore, Chennai, Mumbai and Pune, are located in the states having high per person GDP, matched by high urbanisation levels.

- Two IT clusters, Kolkata and Hyderabad are located in relatively less urbanised states like West Bengal and Andhra Pradesh. But West Bengal's economic growth rate and GDP per person are both lower than that of Andhra Pradesh.

- The IT cluster of NCR in northern India is located in a region of high economic growth and rapid urbanisation. But the region had been predominantly rural, before the advent of economic liberalisation.

Three case study cities were identified, by drawing one city from each of the three categories, to reflect maximum contrasting pattern in governance arrangements. From the first group of four cities, Bangalore was selected. It is not only the largest IT cluster of India but also the global face of India's IT outsourcing industry. No discussion about the IT industry can possibly progress without referencing Bangalore.

From the second group, Kolkata was selected. In terms of growth in the IT sector, Hyderabad is much ahead of Kolkata. However, Kolkata was preferred as a case study location for the following reasons. West Bengal has a distinct leftist political culture. In recent years it faced a high degree of conflict over conversion of rural agricultural land to urban and industrial usage (Banerjee, PS 2008; Nielsen 2010). These conflicts have not only caused a lower economic growth rate in West Bengal but have also influenced national debate on the role of the state in acquiring land for private industrial enclaves. Thus, the Kolkata scenario has greater impact on shaping developmental trajectories. Being located in eastern India, it also provides greater regional diversity, at a pan-Indian scale, compared to Hyderabad.

The NCR area was selected as the third case study location. The region has experienced rapid economic growth as well as hyper-urbanisation. Although the core of the NCR had been urban for a very long time, unprecedented urban spatial expansion since the 1980s had led to growth spilling over into suburban satellite towns. Gurgaon, the prime IT hub in this region, has experienced extensive peri-urbanisation.

The three case study regions, Bangalore, Kolkata and the NCR, thus not only reflect diverse patterns of economic growth, but being located in three corners of India—south-west, east and north—they provide maximum geographical diversity. All three of them have experienced extensive urban spatial expansion in the post-liberalisation era, due to IT-driven growth. Thus the transformation of the fringe areas of these cities reflects tensions and contestations between local and global actors.

4.4.4   Selection of focus area within case study cities

The three selected case study cities are all big cities surrounded by extensive peri-urban areas and multiple IT-ITES hubs. However, as Sassen (2012) noted, even in 'top of the tier' global cities, the impacts of globalisation are not equally spread across the entire city. In these

Indian cities, the spheres of global exposure are unevenly concentrated in a few specific localities. For the sake of in-depth research, within the time and budgetary constraints, this book focuses on one such location in each of the case study cities. The choice of the focus area was guided by the research interest, which seeks to explore the tensions and contestations between global and local forces in the process of urban transformation. Thus, the areas with a greater degree of exposure to the external environment and areas undergoing change at the current juncture were preferred over localities less exposed to globalisation. Similarly, the newer areas currently undergoing change were preferred over more settled areas, where transformation has already taken place.

For instance, in Bangalore, there are three prominent IT hubs. The first cluster came up at the southern fringe of the main city, at a planned township developed in the early 1990s, called the Electronic City. Since then, a second hub formed at the south-eastern fringe from Koramangla to Whitefield. Now, the third cluster has recently started developing at the northern fringe in Davanhalli, near the new international airport. In the Delhi NCR area, there are two major IT clusters—Noida in Uttar Pradesh and Gurgaon in Haryana. Noida, a planned industrial township which started developing from the mid-1970s, has a large cluster of public sector companies and has also attracted IT investments. However, most IT companies in the NCR, particularly the larger business parks and SEZs, are predominantly located in Gurgaon, near Delhi airport (Maitra 2008). Similarly in Kolkata, there are two IT hubs. The first hub, which started to develop in the late 1960s, has formed in Sector V of Salt Lake City, a planned township. The second hub which started to develop in 1998 is situated in Rajarhat New Town, adjoining Salt Lake City and near the airport at the north eastern fringe. While the centre of Salt Lake City has the relatively smaller IT offices, larger business parks and IT SEZs are located in the newer Rajarhat area.

For focused attention, three of the IT hubs, the Koramangla-Whitefield area of Bangalore, Rajarhat new town of Kolkata and Gurgaon in the Delhi NCR area were selected. To further highlight the dynamics of global processes on the transformation of these areas, one particular IT business park / SEZ was selected from each of these areas. However, the choice was somewhat constrained. Although many SEZ projects have received approval in these areas, under the SEZ Act of 2005, only a few had reached operational maturity at the time of fieldwork in 2011. Post-2008 global financial crisis and the market slump had severely slowed down the construction. Secondly, the SEZs have become politically controversial, over the issue of land acquisitions, labour rights and interface with the neighbouring rural communities. In this context the developers are reluctant to entertain outside researchers, particularly from planning and social science related disciplines. Thirdly, the operating IT-ITES companies practice a strict regimen of access control. Thus gaining access inside the project areas was difficult. The author managed to gain access through his previous contacts in the real estate and IT industry.

4.5   Data collection

Primary data for the book were obtained through interviews and direct field observations. Based on the preliminary literature review, the following major stakeholders were identified: government planning agencies, IT corporate sector executives, real estate developers who are engaged in building IT business parks, civil society groups and NGOs active in the relevant area and the local community organisations. Different sets of questionnaires were prepared for the above five stakeholders (see Appendix). However, the interviews were conducted in a semi-structured manner, as they were to unearth underlying reasons and provoke detailed explanations from the respondents on complex urban policy related issues, rather than providing simple 'yes', 'no' type answers. Semi-structured interviews provide the necessary flexibility for the respondents to answer with a greater depth, yet remain within the framework established by the researcher for ease of comparison (Gray et al. 2007; Punch 2008; Yin 2009).

Again, as the research required information about higher level urban governance issues, 'key informant' method was the preferred mode for selecting the interview respondents. It is recognised in urban governance literature that there are three main stakeholder groups—the state, the market and the community (Minnery 2007). In the market category, however, it was realised that there are two distinct economic sectors—IT and real estate—and thus respondents from the two segments were separately categorised. Respondents in the 'community' category were also split into two, between urban middle-class-oriented civil society organisations, and local community organisations which represent rural people.

Following that, key respondents or top-level decision makers in the government agencies, private companies, civil society and local communities were approached for interview. For example, in the 'state' category, Secretaries of the Ministries of Urban Development and Information Technologies were interviewed. Being the highest ranking bureaucrats in the state administration, they were in a position to explain the government policies. In the IT and real estate corporate sector, the company directors, general managers and other such top executives, who were involved in the locational and investment decisions of their organisation, were interviewed. Similarly, at the local level, *Sarpanch* or heads of the village panchayet (council) were approached. A 'snow-ball' or chain referral technique was used and respondents were requested to provide the names of other knowledgeable persons for interview. Altogether 75 interviews were conducted. Table 4.4 below provides the detailed break-up of the composition of the respondents. In several cases, more than one respondent was present at an interview. For example, the top officers often called their junior staff to provide specific detailed information. This was most common when interviewing village community leaders. Most often they were accompanied by eight or ten persons. These secondary persons often provided additional information. However, these were counted as single interviews.

Table 4.4 Stakeholder interview matrix

Stakeholder groups	Bangalore	Kolkata	Delhi NCR
Government planning agency	5	4	4
IT-ITES corporate sector	5	5	5
Real estate developers	5	4	5
Civil society organisations	7	5	6
Local community groups	4	6	5
Total (75)	26	24	25
All India perspectives	4		

[*Source*: Author's fieldwork]

Fieldwork and interviews were conducted in two phases. The initial round was from December 2010 to March 2011. The next round was from December 2011 to January 2012. Almost all the interviews were carried out in the first round. During the second round, only some of the key informants were met to gather certain additional information.

Each interview lasted from 45 to 90 minutes. The long duration of the interviews (that too with top level executives) allowed for detailed discussions on the subject matter. The interviews with the village leaders were lengthiest, and often lasted up to 3 hours. This was because more people gathered at the interview, and many of them were keen to narrate their individual stories. Most of the interviews were conducted in English. But, interviews with the village people were conducted in local languages, Hindi in Delhi NCR, Bengali in Kolkata and Kannada in Bangalore. In the first two cases, the author's familiarity with the languages was useful. In the case of Kannada, a guide provided by a local NGO did the interpretations.

Apart from the primary data, the book also used an extensive array of secondary data, including IT policy documents, city-specific master plans, strategic policy documents of the concerned national and state government ministries and newspaper articles, etc. All these secondary documents were obtained from authentic sources, such as the websites of the state and national government ministries and planning agencies, and well-known newspapers such as the Times of India, The Telegraph, Business Standard and Deccan Herald.

4.6   Data analysis

There are five major analytical techniques for case studies, which are: pattern matching, explanation building, time series analysis, logic models and cross case synthesis. Since the primary objective of this research is to compare and contrast public policy in three Indian cities regarding IT clusters, the cross-case synthesis is the obvious analytic choice to draw the final conclusion. Data analysis was carried out through the use of the NVivo 9 software tool. All interviews and field notes were transcribed into electronic format. This also involved translation of several interviews into English from Bengali, Hindi and Kannada.

The data were then coded for traceability of location and stakeholders, as well as to maintain confidentiality about the identity of the respondent. An alphanumeric coding pattern was adopted in which the first two characters identified the stake holder category; the third character identified the location and the last two digits identified the number or sequence in which the person was interviewed. The following are the five codes for the stakeholders:

- PL – Planning agency and government officials
- IT – Corporate executives from software, engineering, BPO and other IT services companies
- RE – Corporate executives from real estate development companies
- CS – Civil society organisations, NGOs, individual activists, journalists,
- LC – Local community organisations, village panchayets, local political activists

The location codes are as follows:

- B – Bangalore
- K – Kolkata
- D – Delhi NCR

Thus for example, an IT executive interviewed in Bangalore is identified as IT-B-31, while PL-D-32 means a government official from the NCR area and CS-K-33 is a civil society activist from Kolkata.

The subsequent stages of analysis involved uploading of the coded interview records into the NVivo software for analysis, which included comparing linkages and patterns between the stakeholders and across the locations. As the interview followed a semi-structured pattern with the aim of extracting opinions and judgements from the respondents about public policy issues, the analysis necessitated placing the interview conversations in the overall context of the discourse, to bring out nuances of culture, metaphors and expressions, and go beyond merely expressed words, as suggested by Punch (2008). Thus, linkage, patterns, special gestures (which were noted down during interview), and interesting quotations were also identified for retrieval within NVivo.

Since the topic of research involves controversial public policy issues, detailed verification and triangulation of data was necessary (Yin 2009). This was done at the time of interviews, by asking similar questions to people belonging to different stakeholder groups. This was further buttressed through additional field observations and discussions with local academics. The additional field observations included visiting a couple of extra villages, apart from the target one, which had been directly impacted by the construction of the IT business parks. Moreover, basic findings of the case study were discussed with well-known local academics, who had already written or researched on closely related issues. These discussions were particularly helpful in getting additional contacts and leads.

4.7   Research limitations and constraints

Three possible constraints to the research were anticipated at the outset, which are: time and budget constraints, data limitations, and finally, reluctance to share knowledge with outsiders. Steps were taken in advance to mitigate the problems. As the case study locations are away from Australia, fieldwork involved expensive international travel. Multiple field trips could have strained budget resources. Thus the researcher tried to prearrange a maximum number of interviews through email. However, in spite of that effort, it was not possible to arrange all the interviews that way. Culturally, people in India are not very comfortable in scheduling dates far in advance. Thus most interviews had to be rescheduled or reconfirmed closer to the date. As the researcher had planned for a time cushion in each of the case study cities, such rescheduling was mostly possible. In two rare cases, the face-to-face interviews were not possible due to scheduling constraints and were substituted with telephonic interviews.

A major difficulty in obtaining reliable information through personal interviews is the possibility of bias of the respondents and also the researcher, stemming from preconceived notions and ideological orientations (Yin 2009). Respondents often reply in a way that they consider will please the interviewer, or provide a politically correct answer, rather than voicing their true opinion. As research in this book involves controversial political issues, this was major possibility. To overcome this, information obtained was triangulated. Moreover, additional field observations were carried out to get views from multiple perspectives.

The language barrier has also been identified as a key limiting factor in primary and secondary data (Yin 2009). However, this did not pose any problem, as English is widely spoken in India and is the language of all official communication. Secondly, the researcher is highly conversant in the local languages of Kolkata (Bengali) and Delhi (Hindi)—two of the three case-study locations. In Bangalore also, language was not an issue while talking with government officials, corporate executives and civil society activists. The only situation where interpreters were necessary was while talking with the rural communities, where a civil society activist acted as guide-cum-interpreter.

The major constraining factor encountered during fieldwork was gaining access to the SEZ projects. As the issue of land acquisition by the state agencies for SEZ projects is a highly charged political issue in India, this made it difficult to get access into SEZ projects. Most SEZ developers tend to avoid outsiders and particularly those researching on land transaction related issues. Developers also typically avoid discussing issues related to their political linkages. The IT companies operating in the outsourcing industry also follow extremely tight security regimens. As the author had worked as an architect-planner in India for several years, he utilised his contacts in the real estate industry to get access to some of the SEZ projects. Visits and information from a larger number of IT SEZ projects would have been helpful. However, to overcome these difficulties, the author triangulated and verified the information obtained from the limited visits through extensive discussions with the architects who designed the projects, real estate management consultants, members of industry chamber of commerce and academics.

4.8   Summary

This chapter discussed the research methodology adopted for the book. It outlined the justifications behind taking up a comparative study of urban governance in a sub-national framework and then discussed the criteria for narrowing down the choice of case study locations. Three metropolitan regions Bangalore, Kolkata and Delhi NCR were selected as case study locations. Within these regions, three specific locations were identified for focused attention and detailed research. As the research seeks to explore deep underlying factors in the interface between local and global processes in the transformation of these areas, a qualitative research method was adopted. Subsequently, the chapter discussed the approach to case study design, data collection and analysis strategies. Finally the constraints and limitations were discussed.

5

Socio-political context of the Indian IT industry

5.1   Introduction

This chapter analyses the structural context and the prevailing socio-political milieu within which the Indian IT industry is situated. The next section provides a brief overview of the growth of the IT outsourcing industry in India. Section 5.3 discusses various sub-segments of the IT sector; Section 5.4 situates the Indian IT sector in its socio-cultural context to understand how the class and caste composition of the industry influences its position in the public policy space. Section 5.5 then focuses on the major national- and state-level policy instruments impacting growth of the IT sector. Section 5.6 then discusses the spatial needs of the IT industry, then following that, Section 5.7 analyses how the recent changes in the policy environment are creating a synergy between the IT sector and the real estate sector, to meet the spatial needs of the IT sector. Section 5.8 concludes the chapter with a summary.

5.2   Globalisation and growth of the IT services outsourcing

The first stage of economic globalisation in the contemporary era was characterised by a shifting of blue collar manufacturing jobs from the West to low cost production centres in developing countries, particularly in East and Southeast Asia, while the cities of the developed world increasingly turned into hubs of white collar service sector activities. However since the late 1980s further advancement in Information Technology (IT) made possible outsourcing of lower order IT enabled service (ITES) functions to cheaper destinations, like Ireland, Philippines and India (Dossani & Kenny 2003; Srinivasan & Krueger 2005). Now an integral part of the business models of multinational firms, by 2010 outsourcing of office jobs generated USD 106 billion in global revenue, with India accounting for a 55 percent market share (NASSCOM 2011).

India's increasing attractiveness for sourcing of white collar office jobs is widely attributed to two major factors: availability of a large educated human resource pool which provides a 60–70 percent cost advantage over the developed countries, by adding over 570,000 technical graduates and another 3.3 million young graduates (and postgraduates) annually into the labour pool; and an enabling public policy environment and established business processes (NASSCOM 2011). A crucial attribute that sets apart the growth process of the IT services in India is that from the very beginning, Indian IT companies (e.g. Infosys, Wipro, Tata Consultancy Services) and the diasporic network of Indian engineers, working in the Silicon Valley (and other global centres), played a very strong role, along with investments in the sector by Western MNCs. Thus, unlike the Southeast Asian countries, where growth happened primarily due to investments by Western and Japanese companies, growth of the Indian IT services sector is a twin track process—of Indian IT companies expanding into the global markets as well as India attracting the global corporate sector to investments. In both of these global processes, of Indian entrepreneurs venturing out and international investors coming in, the diasporic network played a pivotal interfacing role (Guhathakurta & Parthasarathy 2007).

The Indian IT services sector started growing in the mid-1980s as private sector Indian companies began to penetrate the lowest end of the global services outsourcing value chain by doing routine coding work and supplying engineers to the American and other Western MNCs on short-term contracts—a practice that is commonly known as 'body-shopping' (Parthasarathy 2004). About the same time, reforms in India's regulatory environment and gradual reduction of import restrictions on computer hardware and software encouraged technology-oriented multinational companies like Digital Equipment, Texas Instruments and Hewlett Packard to locate a part of their R&D facilities in Bangalore, which had a large electronics and engineering talent pool (Vang & Asheim 2006).

During the economic boom period of the early 1990s, demand for UNIX and Mainframe professionals surged in the USA and the gap was filled by recruiting large numbers of engineers from India on a temporary basis. The technical credibility of these early engineers established India's reputation in the USA and Europe as a source of a high-quality human resource, which was further augmented during the

Y2K crisis and Euro conversion projects of the late 1990s (O'Connor 2003; Parthasarathy 2004; Srinivasan & Krueger 2005; Thite & Russel 2007). In later years, the economic downturn, after the 'dot-com' bust, tightening of immigration norms, advancements in telecommunication infrastructure in India, and increasing adherence by Indian companies to globally recognised quality standards (e.g. SEI—Software Engineer Institute and CMM—Capability Maturity Model certifications), encouraged several IT companies from the USA to seek further corporate cost optimisation by directly outsourcing work to India, rather than inviting more Indian software engineers to work in the USA.

With this change in industry practice from 'body-shopping' to 'off-shoring', the social capital of the expatriate Indian professionals played the catalytic role between the local and the global. From the mid-1990s, many Indian software professionals returned home on completion of their assignments (Chacko 2007; Parthasarathy 2004). When global corporations sought outsourcing opportunities in India, the fact that a large number of professionals with exposure, knowledge and skills from working in the West were already available in India, provided the necessary psychological comfort factor to Western companies about quality assurance in outsourced assignments (Vang & Asheim 2006).

From the lowly beginnings in the 1980s, over the next three decades, the nature and scope of outsourcing of services have changed. Shortages of skilled personnel in one location are being offset through sourcing of services from multiple locations internationally, and labour cost savings are no longer the only factor driving outsourcing decisions. A wide spectrum of complex services are now being outsourced as the corporate sector has started to leverage talent at a global scale (Booz Allen Hamilton – Fuqua School of Business 2006). Leveraging its vast human resource pool, India has now become not just the biggest, but also the most diversified destination for the global services sourcing market (A.T. Kearney 2009). The following section provides a snap-shot of the various sub-segments which comprise the IT services sector in India.

5.3   Industry structure

The generic term 'Information Technology sector' broadly consists of three segments: Information Technology software services, Information Technology enabled services and business process outsourcing, and

Information Technology hardware as outlined below (Chatterji 2013a; NASSCOM 2011):

- Information Technology software (IT Software): Software coding, testing and customisation, IT consulting, system integration, network infrastructure management, customer application development, etc.

- Business Process Outsourcing (BPO): This segment is also widely termed as Information Technology enabled services (ITES) and covers a wide array of back office jobs, starting from the lower-end functions like call centres and routine data processing (i.e. employee payrolls) to more knowledge intensive applications in engineering design, multimedia and graphics, medical and legal transcriptions, insurance claim processing, inventory management, etc.

- Information Technology hardware (IT hardware): Assembling of computers and peripherals etc. Although exports have started, this segment is still predominantly oriented towards the domestic market.

Compared to the domestic orientation of the IT hardware industry, the software and the ITES-BPO applications have been globalised and export-oriented from their very inception and contribute the bulk of the IT export earnings. On the whole, IT software and ITES–BPO services contributed 88 percent of the overall sector revenue of USD 108 billion in 2012 (NASSCOM 2013). Rapid growth of the software services sector and improvements in India's telecommunication infrastructure during the early 1990s set the stage for growth in the BPO and ITES segments from the mid-1990s. Taking their cue from the software industry, companies like GE Capital, British Airways and American Express began off-shoring lower end office jobs to India and now comprises a major component of the overall Indian IT services sector. Figure 5.1 shows steady growth in export earnings by both the IT services segments over the past several years. As may be seen from the figure, by 2012 the export earnings by the ITES–BPO segment accounted for 42 percent of the overall sectoral earnings by the Indian Services industry.

The engagement pattern of the global corporate sector with the Indian IT-ITES sector may be classified into three broad segments (Messner 2009). Firstly, there are specialised Indian IT software (e.g.

TCS, Infosys, Tech-Mahindra) and BPO companies (e.g. WNS Global Services, Quantro BPO Solutions). Big software companies have also diversified their operations by establishing separate subsidiary BPO entities (e.g. Wipro BPO, HCL Technologies BPO). Secondly, there are MNCs, who have established captive branch platforms in India, such as IBM, Microsoft, Oracle, Siemens, etc., to execute a part of the operation assigned by the parent company (e.g. Siemens Power Engineering in India provides engineering design services for turn-key power projects built by Siemens AG globally). Thirdly, there are joint ventures between Indian and foreign companies like TCS–Mitsubishi. But global–local differentiation is increasingly becoming blurred due to the fluidities brought in by crossholdings between Indian and Western corporate groups.

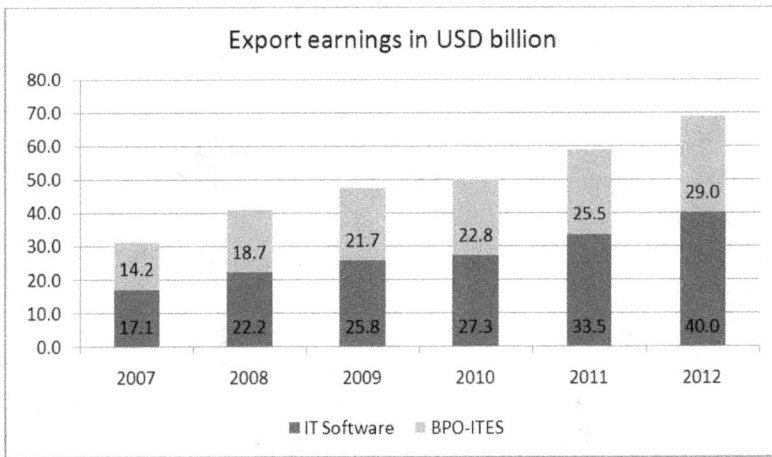

Figure 5.1 Growth in IT services
[*Source*: Prepared by author sourcing data from NASSCOM 2013]

5.4   Socio-cultural environment

Impressive economic performance at the international level over a sustained period of time has enabled the IT-ITES sector in India to acquire a high-profile global image amongst the people in Indian cities, due to projections by the popular media. Listings of Indian software companies in international stock exchanges or persons of Indian origin rising to top positions in the Silicon Valley companies are routinely touted by the Indian TV channels and newspapers as major national achievements. The point that many of the Indian IT entrepreneurs or global corporate executives have come up from ordinary middle-class backgrounds, as opposed to being born in traditional business families, has made them into middle-class icons. As Upadhya puts it,

> Most of the founders of software have come from the middle class, building on their cultural capital of higher education (usually in engineering) and social capital (knowledge and networks) acquired through professional careers. This class (and the IT industry itself) is also distinguished by its close integration into the global economy and its relative autonomy from the 'old' Indian economy dominated by the public sector and the nationalist capitalist class. (Upadhya, Carol 2004, p.5141)

Growth of the Indian IT industry through globalisation has produced a new 'transnational capitalist class' (Upadhya, Carol 2004, 2007). While IT entrepreneurs at the top of this class pyramid, such as Narayana Murthy (founder of Infosys), Vinod Khosla (co-founder of Sun Microsystems), or Suhas Patil (founder of Cirrus Logic)—have become high profile celebrities, thousands of engineers and MBAs in the middle rungs also pursue global careers.

The IT-ITES-BPO is now the largest 'organised' or 'formal' sector[1] employer in India in the private sector and directly employs 2.8 million people, besides generating another 8.9 million indirect jobs (NASSCOM 2012). But the formal and informal jobs taken together constitute only a miniscule percentage of India's total workforce (Joshi 2009). Several scholars have noted that the employment generated by the sector tends to benefit the educated urban youth but leave out people from the rural areas or from the lower social strata (D'Costa 2011; James & Vira 2012; Upadhya, C. & Vasavi 2006).

It is important to note here that from its very inception, the Indian IT services sector has remained overwhelmingly oriented towards the English-speaking countries, while the United States alone accounted for 65 percent of its export revenue in 2011 (NASSCOM 2012). Communication skills are particularly valued in the industry,

---

[1] Formal sector refers to registered business organisations. While there are no official figures, it is frequently assumed that between 60 and 80 percent of the jobs in Indian cities are in the informal or unorganized sector.

as it involves extensive dealing with foreigners at every level of the employment hierarchy (James & Vira 2012; Upadhya, C. & Vasavi 2006). Even the 'foot soldiers' of the industry, the call centre workers, engage in real time voice communication with external clients. At the upper tier, the software engineers frequently travel to client sites for assignments.

Thus, the IT-ITES-BPO workforce in India, even at the lowest rung, is mainly urban youth with at least a university degree. Most of them also come from educated families with at least one parent being a graduate (James & Vira 2012), which in the Indian social context, mostly correlates with the upper caste (Upadhya, C. & Vasavi 2006). Growth generated in the IT-ITES sector, which pays high salaries by Indian standards and has a decent work environment, has opened up huge career aspirations for educated urban middle-class upper-caste youth. This has enabled even those at the bottom—the call centre and BPO workers—to substantially improve their quality of life. A Secretary to the Government of West Bengal observed

> The IT growth has created a chain reaction in the middle and lower middle-class suburbs of Kolkata. Everybody aspires for an IT job. Boys and girls from middleclass families want to study engineering or management. But even the sons and daughters of drivers and maids want to study English, so they could get a call centre job. This was just unthinkable ten—fifteen years back. (Interview: PL-K-04, 20 Dec 2010)

PL-D-25, a top economist associated with national economic planning in Delhi, asserted during an interview on 20 January 2011, that due to their global scale of operations, the IT firms follow highly ethical corporate governance practices. The IT sector brings clean (as opposed to dirty manufacturing) and high-quality jobs to the urban areas, observed PL-D-33, the head of Gurgaon's urban administration when interviewed on 2 February 2011.

These optimistic views about the IT sector are however not uniformly subscribed to. Livelihood concerns of the rural population have emerged as a key issue in India and bring out a crucial dichotomy in the IT-ITES-driven growth model. The business model of the IT outsourcing industry requires the companies operating in the sector to be oriented to their Western clientele and linked through high speed telecommunications networks. But they are also disembedded from their immediate physical environment, having marginal local linkages. The enclaves create high-quality built spaces to meet global corporate specifications and provide jobs for the educated middle class, but have only limited direct spin-offs for the local communities. A politician from the peri-urban areas and a member of Gurgaon's newly formed Municipal Corporation observed that,

Jobs in these IT-BPO companies are for the city boys and girls, those who have studied in English medium schools. For our children, who had studied in Hindi medium, it is very difficult, even though they have studied English. Companies say their accent is not good. How can the children of the farmers have good English accent? (Interview: CS-D-62, 31 January 2012)

Nevertheless, the IT-ITES sector enjoys an overwhelmingly positive image amongst the bureaucratic and policy elites of India. PL-K-49, an advisor to the Government of Karnataka, explained during an interview on 17 February 2011 that, "The IT sector is seen as an agent of change and modernisation. It has opened huge global opportunities and increased aspirations for the large and vocal Indian middle class, after decades of economic stagnation. No policy maker can ignore this".

It is to be noted here that the post-liberalisation economic boom has sharply expanded the size of the middle-class[2] population from 1 percent of the population in 1985 to 5 percent (or about 50 million) people by 2005, and this is projected to reach 20 percent of the population by 2015 if the current growth trend continues (McKinsey Global Institute 2007). Understandably, most of this new middle-class population is concentrated around the biggest cities of India, which had witnessed a high economic growth rate since the beginning of the neoliberal reforms and the rolling back of centralised planning. Close association with the career aspirations of this new Indian middle class, along with the nation-building dreams of the bureaucratic and policy elites, has enabled the IT-services sector to favourably negotiate the policy space at the national and state levels over the past two decades, as discussed in the following section.

---

[2] Defined on the basis of real annual household disposable income of USD 23,530 to 117,650 at purchasing power parity (Mckinsey Global Institute 2007)

5.5   National and sub-national policy framework

5.5.1   National government policies

The IT-ITES sector has become a crucial stimulant behind India's national economic growth. Between 1998–99 and 2011–12, its contribution to GDP increased from 1.2 percent to 7.5 percent, while the contribution to exports increased from less than 4 percent to about 26 percent (NASSCOM 2012). Moreover, although the jobs created by the sector are numerically insignificant at the national scale, the IT-ITES employees have high 'spending capacities' and stimulate economic growth (Joshi 2009), and thus politically are very significant.

Growth of the IT services industry has run parallel to the process of economic liberalisation of India and is often seen as the biggest success story of the neoliberal reforms (Kumar 2009; Parthasarathy 2004). Supportive policy environments created by the national and state governments played major parts in creating this 'success story'. However, instead of direct intervention, the Indian national state has played a facilitative role in encouraging private entrepreneurship and foreign investments. National-level policy reforms in this sector, such as the National Telecommunication Policy and the Software Technology Parks of India (STPI) schemes, have been engineered through consensus between Congress, BJP and other leading political parties. As India has been run by fragile and fractious coalition governments since the 1990s, this is a particularly noteworthy feature.

The National Telecommunication Policy was first launched by the Congress government in 1994 but was substantially amended in 1999 by the BJP-led coalition. The telecom policy addressed the problems of poor communication infrastructure during the days of public sector monopoly, by gradually un-bundling the sub-sectors (e.g. basic telephony, cellular-mobile, Internet, satellite and cable TV) to the private sector and privatising the state-run Videsh Sanchar Nigam Ltd. (VSNL), which controlled international communication (Business Today 2007; Chowdary 1999). Improvements in telecom infrastructure have enabled the real-time data-transfer-oriented BPO sector to flourish.

The STPI scheme launched by the Ministry of Communications and Information Technology in 1991 was specifically designed to provide a thrust in software exports. The scheme created an institutional structure to bring the industry and the state on a common forum to facilitate and also regulate IT software and other IT enabled services export regimes. The key functions of the STPI are as follows (Chatterji 2013a; STPI 2010):

- *Policy development*—by acting as the platform for interface between the industry and the government departments at national and state levels. Regularly conducts workshops and seminars to bring the policy makers and the industry together.

- *Administrative and statutory services*—monitoring of tax incentives and export obligations of the companies registered under the scheme.

- *Entrepreneurship development*—encouragement to small- and medium-sized enterprises (SME) through incubation facilities, seed funding and project marketing strategies; export promotion through market analysis and segmentation strategies, organisation of specialised training, exhibitions, seminars, workshops; financial support through venture capital; development of business parks with high speed data communication facilities and other basic infrastructure to meet the spatial needs for SMEs. Beginning with Bangalore, 51 such facilities were developed across the country up to 2010.

The tax holiday under the STPI scheme helped the industry grow during its formative years. Although the IT sector lobbied hard for its further extension, the tax rebates under the STPI scheme ended in 2011. However, the central government has announced a new regime for tax exemptions under the Special Economic Zone Act of 2005, which envisages establishment of duty-free enclaves for export promotion, all over the country. The SEZs are considered as specifically delineated duty-free enclaves, deemed to be foreign territory for the purpose of trade, operations and duties, taxes and tariffs (Ministry of Law and Justice 2005).

The regional head of an STPI unit IT-K-12 when interviewed on 24 January 2011 observed that this approach towards clustering of industries was inspired by the success of the SEZ is China in attracting foreign investments. As India suffers from acute infrastructure deficiencies, it was felt by the policy makers that developing these zones with world class infrastructure will accelerate economic growth, rather than trying to develop the whole country. However, unlike China, where SEZs are owned by the state agencies, India adopted a more market-driven approach, and allowed private companies to establish SEZs. Moreover, given the domination of IT and other service sectors in the Indian economy, service-sector-oriented SEZs were visualised. According to the STPI official,

> Clubbing of IT-ITES services within the SEZ Act was done basically to simplify the tax administration system. Since the IT-ITES sector had been getting tax exemptions, it was felt that locating them in a zone will make it easier to monitor" (Interview: IT-K-12, 24 January 2011)

Under the Act, the IT-ITES (including electronic hardware) is considered as a unique classification and requires to be established on a minimum 10 hectares of land. Up to December 2012, 588 Special Economic Zones have been formally approved, out of which 355 are in the IT-ITES category (Government of India 2012). To ensure smooth transition for the IT companies from the STPI scheme to the SEZ scheme, the regional directors of the STPI were designated as development commissioners of the IT-ITES-oriented SEZs. As development commissioner, the STPI regional directors are required to facilitate development of IT SEZ projects by certifying duty-free movement of building construction materials and equipment (e.g. steel, cement, batching plants, cranes, etc.) as well as operational requirements for the IT companies (e.g. computer equipment and software). They are also required to ensure proper coordination with the central and state governments and monitor performance of SEZ developers and operational IT units in their zone.

In a major departure from the STPI scheme, the SEZ Act (2005) has introduced a spatial dimension in the office location policy for the export-oriented IT-ITES firms (Chatterji 2013a). The main differences between the STPI scheme and the SEZ scheme are as indicated in Table 5.1:

To qualify for tax benefits, the IT companies are now required to be physically located within a notified SEZ territory. The minimum land area stipulation of 10 hectares for the IT-ITES-oriented clusters, though much smaller than other categories of special economic zones, is in construction terms, much larger than what the software and BPO companies normally deal with; and most IT-ITES-oriented SEZs are being promoted by real estate developers having expertise in managing large scale construction projects.

Table 5.1 STPI scheme versus the SEZ scheme [*Source*: Business-Standard 2011b; Ministry of Law and Justice 2005]

Software Technology Parks of India (STPI) scheme	Special Economic Zone (SEZ) scheme
100 percent export-oriented units	Units located in SEZ are required to achieve net foreign exchange surplus every financial year, but need not be 100 percent export-oriented.
No minimum area stipulation	Minimum size for IT-ITES-oriented services is 10 hectares (25 acres)
Corporate income tax exemption up to the financial year of 2010	1st 5 years—100 percent of the profit exempted from income tax 2nd 5 years—50 percent of the profit exempted from income tax 3rd 5 years—50 percent of the reinvested profit exempted from income tax
Minimum Alternative Tax (MAT) at 10 percent	MAT at 18.5 percent
No exemption from service tax	Exemption from service tax
No exemption from local tax	Exemption from local tax
Only the IT-ITES units are entitled to the tax benefits	Real estate developers of the SEZ projects are also entitled to the tax benefits in addition to the operational IT-ITES units

The switch-over from the STPI scheme to the SEZ scheme is resented by small- and medium-sized firms (Business-Standard 2011b). The small enterprises have not only lost the tax holidays they enjoyed under the STPI scheme, but now need to physically shift office locations to SEZ enclaves to avail new tax benefits. This involves higher rental out-goings. Since office space availability under SEZ enclaves is much less, therefore opportunities for rent seeking are proportionately higher for the promoters.

The SEZ project promoters who provide leased spaces to the IT-ITES firms also get tax benefits under the SEZ scheme. The real estate sector is the net gainer in change-over from the STPI to the SEZ scheme, observed IT-K-12, the regional head of STPI, when interviewed on 24 January 2011. And this has brought about a close tie between the IT and the real estate sectors, with profound implications for urban land transformation—an issue that is discussed in more detail under Section 5.7. But before we go there, we need to take into consideration the facilities and support the IT sector receives from the state governments, as discussed below.

5.5.2   State government policies

Under the Indian federal structure, the sub-national states enjoy a large degree of autonomy in economic matters. The scope of this autonomy has substantially expanded since the economic and political developments of the early 1990s. The rolling back of the national government's industrial regulatory regime has considerably strengthened the role of the state governments in pursuing private investments. The industrial investors, in most sectors (including IT-ITES-BPO), are no longer required to seek approval of the national government agencies and are only required to deal with the state and municipal governments, to sort out basic needs like land, water, power, etc.

Moreover, since 1989, India has seen the advent of multiparty coalition governments at the national level, due to the weakening of the Congress party. The decline of a strong centralising political power has created a void, which is increasingly being filled by the small political parties, having influence in specific regions and/or states. These developments have increased the political importance of the centripetal forces, regional political leaders and the state governments in the economic domain. As The Economist (2012b p.6) puts it, "Regional parties fill the [power] gap. Usually built around a charismatic individual who becomes a state's chief minister, they matter, wielding near presidential power over a territory that often has a country-sized population". There is also increasing regional economic competition between the states to attract the high profile IT-ITES sector investment.

The state-level IT policies articulate the vision of the concerned governments towards the IT-ITES sector. These documents usually contain incentive schemes for increasing IT-ITES investments in the state; plans for development of IT clusters at major cities; and programs for increasing use of IT in routine administrative and developmental works. The Government of Karnataka, whose capital city Bangalore is the global face of the Indian IT industry, took the lead amongst the Indian states, in framing a state-specific IT policy in 1997, which subsequently became the guiding template for other states to follow.

The Millennium IT Policy of Karnataka asserts the state's intention of retaining its front ranking position in the IT sector (Government of Karnataka 2000). To further consolidate the advantage, it proposed to develop Bangalore as a knowledge capital, by prioritising investments in biotechnology, aerospace technology and other technology intensive areas. Karnataka's IT policy also seeks to increase synergy between technology domains and between hardware and software production. For example, it envisages a strategic clustering potential between aerospace and defence-related electronic manufacturing and the software companies in Bangalore. Karnataka's IT policy also outlined the need to expand business ties with non-English-speaking countries and has sought to facilitate establishment of foreign trade missions in Bangalore.

The West Bengal government also followed an aggressive state-led growth strategy to attract IT investments to Kolkata. It is a much bigger city and has a longer tradition as a centre for education than Bangalore or Gurgaon. But in comparison, Kolkata lagged behind in attracting knowledge economy jobs and suffered a brain-drain of the educated middle class. In order to fight back, the West Bengal IT Policy has set a target of reaching number three position nationally by capturing 15 percent of the market by 2020 (Government of West Bengal 2012). The policy has identified a strategic priority to increase trade with Japan and Taiwan, by leveraging Kolkata's location in eastern India and take advantage of the Indian national government's 'Look East' foreign policy initiative which seeks to enhance ties with Southeast and East Asia. In the functional domain, the main emphasis of the West Bengal IT policy is towards multimedia, animation and the gaming industry. West Bengal has a strong artistic heritage and Kolkata has a vibrant cultural industry, including the Bengali film industry. Understandably the IT policy seeks to build on these strengths, by emphasising visual arts-related software development and training facilities.

In contrast to the functional thrusts in Karnataka and West Bengal's IT policy, 'land' is the cornerstone of Haryana's IT strategy. The IT policy pledges simplified land-use conversion procedures for agricultural and industrial lands to IT business parks (Government of Haryana 2000). Haryana's liberal land policies enabled property developers to acquire vast land parcels in Gurgaon, to build high-quality business parks and associated facilities. Gurgaon's favourable location adjoining Delhi airport and with an abundant land supply turned it into an attractive destination for the IT-ITES sector.

In their 'race to the bottom' to attract the IT-ITES sector, the state governments offer a range of fiscal and non-fiscal benefits, which include: rebates in property registration fees and stamp duty exemptions; entry tax and sales tax exemptions; and reduced power tariffs, as detailed in Table 5.2. Mega projects in all states receive additional incentives but definition of such projects varies. Projects bringing in investments worth USD 18.6 million are classified as 'mega' in Karnataka, whereas in West Bengal it is only USD 4.65 million. IT-ITES projects also receive several additional exemptions from city-level zoning regulations as outlined in Table 5.2, which includes the ability to locate irrespective of local area Master Plans, additional building heights or extra Floor Area Ratio.

Table 5.2 Fiscal benefits under state IT policies [*Source*: Government of Haryana 2000; Government of Karnataka 2000; Government of West Bengal 2003, 2012]

	Haryana	**Karnataka**	**West Bengal**
Property registration fees and stamp duty	45 to 90 percent exemptions	All units creating more than 250 jobs in Bangalore and 100 jobs in other cities in the first year of operation get a rebate of 15% of the cost of land from state agencies or 15% of stamp duty if set up on privately acquired land	100 percent exemptions
Other tax incentives	100% exemption of sales tax	100% exemption of entry tax	100% exemption of sales tax
Loan from state financial institutions	Priority sector for lending assistance from state-level financial institutions		Lower interest loans for mega projects and those that create jobs for more than 750 people in first year
Special incentives for mega projects	Special incentives for projects investing INR 300 million (USD 5.58 million)	Special incentives for projects investing INR 1000 million (USD 18.6 million) or creating 1000 jobs	Special incentives for projects investing INR 250 million or (USD 4.65 million)

Contd...

Contd...

	Haryana	Karnataka	West Bengal
Training subsidies			50 percent reimbursement for getting ISO / ISO 9000, SE-CMM Level 5 or similar quality certification
Zoning regulations related benefits	Liberal conversion of existing manufacturing industries to IT Parks	IT units with 5 kVA power requirement can be set up anywhere irrespective of Master Plan in residential / commercial and industrial areas	
Floor Area Ratio (FAR) benefits	FAR relaxation up to 100%, increased building heights permitted	FAR relaxation up to 50%	IT policy 2012 has indicated that FAR and building heights will be increased to maximise land utilisation.
Land allocation	Preferential allocation to the IT-ITES sector		Land allocation through WBEIDC and local government agencies

Almost all states have extended certain regulatory exemptions related to labour and environmental laws to the IT-ITES sector, which enable them to run 24×7 schedules for 365 days on a shift basis, to serve their clientele spread across several time zones on a real-time basis. Going a step further, West Bengal has classified the IT-ITES sector as a 'public-utility service' and it has thus been exempted from labour unions and industrial strikes (Government of West Bengal 2003, 2012). As West Bengal has a history of militant trade unionism, the government sought to reassure the IT sector investors through such a clause.

Similarly states like Karnataka and Haryana which frequently suffer electrical power outages seek to assure productivity through pledges of uninterrupted supply and exemption from power outages. Almost all states have classified the IT-ITES as a non-polluting or 'green' category industry and exempted from inspections under pollution control acts.

Permits for installation of diesel generators for emergency power supply (required due to frequent power outages in Indian cities) have also been simplified for the IT-ITES industry. Additionally, the sector enjoys reduced electricity tariff rates, in line with bulk industrial consumers, which are much lower than office or commercial rates.

Several state governments in India have developed institutional structures not only to fast-track IT-service investment approvals, but also for supporting the investors for getting land, buildings and other facilities (Chatterji 2013a). There are moves to streamline regulatory approvals through 'single window' clearance, where all approvals are processed concurrently by a single nodal agency. For instance, in Karnataka, initially IT investments used to be promoted through Karnataka Udyog Mitra—the general purpose agency for industrial promotion. However, a new agency, Karnataka Biotechnology and Information Technology Services (KBITS), was created in 2010 for exclusively channelizing IT and biotech investments. West Bengal also provides a similar 'single-window' clearance and through West Bengal Electronics Industries Development Corporation (WBEIDC). At other places, investors are also provided with dedicated 'escort officers' to expedite approval procedures from various regulatory agencies (Chatterji 2013a).

Apart from streamlining administrative procedures, the state agencies are also attempting to expand the spatial footprint of the IT-ITES services beyond the metropolitan regions by establishing business parks in smaller towns. Thus, KEONICS of Karnataka has set up incubation facilities and IT-services-oriented SEZs in Mangalore, Mysore and Hubli (Interview: IT-B-47, 15 February 2011). West Bengal's new IT policy also has a similar emphasis on building IT services production facilities in smaller towns like Durgapur and Siliguri. Entrepreneurs who establish new business ventures in small towns away from the metropolitan regions get special incentives in the form of land and rent subsidies, as well as extra grants for providing technical training for their employees (Government of West Bengal 2012). In recent years there has been a growing trend where back-end operations call centres and data-processing services, particularly those serving the Indian domestic market, have started moving to these smaller cities, due to high rental values and employee salaries in the big cities. High labour attrition rates have emerged as a significant challenge confronting the Indian IT-services sector in recent years (A.T. Kearney 2009; James & Vira 2012;

NASSCOM 2012). Software engineers and even call centre workers frequently jump companies to fast track their careers. Since most IT-ITES-BPO companies provide a relatively flat organisational structure, the scope for rapid promotion in the career ladder is relatively slow within the same organisation. Employees circumvent these barriers by job hopping (James & Vira 2012). The scope for such employee mobility is naturally higher in big cities, which offer greater options.

On the other hand, companies spend large sums of money in training new employees. High labour attrition, in which employees take with them key domain knowledge, is a major challenge for the IT-ITES corporate sector. Moreover, cities like Bangalore or Gurgaon, which have witnessed rapid economic growth in recent years, have also witnessed sharp increases in land values and property rental rates. In this situation, gradual dispersal to smaller and cheaper destinations, which in India are called Tier II and Tier III cities, has become an attractive option for the corporate sector, explained IT-D-26, the research head of the IT-ITES-BPO industry chamber NASSCOM (National Association of Software Service Companies), when interviewed on 21 January 2011. By facilitating development of Tier II and III cities within their states, the state IT policies are trying to prevent this process of geographical dispersal from leaving their state altogether and also trying to meet their balanced spatial development objectives.

However the bulk of the operations and the export functions are still overwhelmingly concentrated in big cities (NASSCOM & A.T.Kearney 2009). The smaller cities also suffer problems due to the non-availability of skilled professionals, as ambitious workers prefer to work in big cities which offer greater career choice. The state governments are aware of these trends and are trying to encourage a 'hub-and-spoke' kind of an arrangement between the primate cities and the Tier II or III cities (Interview: IT-D-22, 29 January 2011).

It is evident from the above discussion that there is a high degree of similarity in the IT policies and incentive packages of the different Indian states. This has come about due to the fact that framing of these policies is mostly done in consultation with the industry bodies like NASSCOM, or central agencies like the STPI. In this scenario, availability of land, on a sufficient scale, near big cities having a large educated workforce has become the key differentiator, determining the economic geography of the industry. The following section discusses the spatial requirements of the industry.

5.6   Production of work spaces

As discussed earlier in detail (in Section 3.7), earlier research on intra-city location preference of the IT firms in Bangalore showed that well-known and established IT companies in India, for whom the issues of corporate image and quality of infrastructure are the most dominant concerns, tend to prefer the campus-like settings of the suburban business parks at the outer fringe, such as Electronics City or Whitefield (Aranya 2008). Research in other cities, where the growth of the IT services sector, was later compared to Bangalore, found that big companies typically favoured the suburban business park model from the outset. Thus in the Delhi-NCR area, most software and BPO firms are concentrated in either Gurgaon or in Noida, outside the borders of the core city (Chatterji 2007; Maitra 2008). In Kolkata, the IT clusters are located in the Salt Lake City and the Rajarhat New Town area, not within the municipal limits of Kolkata (Chen, Wang & Kundu 2009; Shaw & Satish 2007). Evidence from Hyderabad (Kennedy 2007; Ramchandriah & Prasad 2008), Pune and Chennai corroborate this as a pan-Indian pattern, where the production spaces of the Indian IT-ITES industry are almost entirely in the form of gated enclaves in the fringe areas of the big cities.

Research on the spatial preference of the producer services sector has shown that firms tend to cluster in CBD or downtown areas, due to the need for frequent face-to-face communication with their clients (Sassen 2001). Even though many of the Indian IT-ITES-BPO companies operate in such producer services related vertical domains, such as legal, advertising, financial, engineering or management consulting, that they cannot be called producer services in the truest sense—as they mostly operate for overseas clients on specific assignments. Most of their communication requirements are handled through telecommunication networks. The need for face-to-face communication is minimised by stationing liaison persons. Thus Indian IT-ITES companies post a representative in their client offices, and vice versa. CBD locations have no specific functional advantage for the IT-ITES sector (Chatterji 2013a). Moreover, inner-city areas of almost all Indian cities are congested, face severe infrastructure constraints and are unable to meet the volume and quality specifications of this globalised economic sector. By-passing the inner-city squalor, parastatal agencies are facilitating greenfield developments at the urban fringe to generate production space for the new economy (Bhattacharya, R. & Sanyal 2011). The SEZ Act (2005), which prescribed 10 hectares of contiguous land for the IT-ITES SEZ, has given further impetus to such by-pass urbanism, as it is almost impossible to find such land areas otherwise (Chatterji 2013a).

Almost all the IT-ITES executives interviewed by the author (between December 2010 and March 2011) also expressed a preference for the sprawling campus-like settings, as opposed to multi-storeyed office blocks. Many of them, even those in cities like Kolkata and Gurgaon, frequently pointed out the campus of Infosys Technologies in Bangalore as an 'ideal campus.' The lush green Infosys campus, located within Bangalore's Electronic City, is itself a mini-city for 20,000 workers, spreads over 17 hectares and even includes its own golf course. The principal of a renowned Bangalore-based architectural firm, which designed this famous campus and several other such IT office complexes informed,

> When I began the project, the company's head told me, 'every evening I see my capital assets [software engineers] walking away at 5 pm. The design of the complex should be such that the employees should feel relaxed and comfortable to spend long hours.' That's why we provided so many recreational facilities and created a college campus like ambiance. (Interview: RE-B-40, 9 February 2011)

Seventy-four percent of India's IT workforce is less than 30 years of age, and many of them join work fresh from college (NASSCOM 2011). The IT executives insist that these young staff members feel at-home in such campus-like settings, and this in turn improves productivity. Work in the IT outsourcing industry is highly demanding. Software developers and others in managerial positions are frequently required to stay back after regular office hours—either to communicate with their overseas clients (or in-house counterparts) or meet demanding project schedules.[3]

---

[3] This does not include the call-centre workers who work fixed hours but in shifts according to the time zone of their clientele.

Due to the nature of their business, IT-ITES-BPO companies regularly receive foreign visitors. Many companies also have a few Western expatriates in their regular workforce—to coordinate projects, train Indian staff and for other managerial functions. In such situations, a high-quality ambiance, as well as rigorously adhering to safety and security standards assumes high importance—issues which are often compromised in the commercial buildings in the older areas of the city. While golf courses, as on the Infosys campus, are exceptions, business parks located at the urban fringe do offer high-quality infrastructure matching Western standards (Figures 5.1 and 5.2 show the contrasting landscape inside and outside an IT business park).

Figure 5.2 Well-maintained landscape inside an IT business park, Bangalore
[*Source*: Author]

According to the chief architect of the real estate major DLF Group, which has built more than thirty such technology parks and IT-ITES SEZs all over India, these complexes typically include: large floor plates (in modules ranging between 1500 to 2500 square metres); central air-conditioning; full power back-up through diesel generators (as a precaution against erratic electric power supply), 24-hour video surveillance and rigid access control; on-site ambulance facilities; cafeterias served by reputed fast-food chains; gymnasiums, large underground parking spaces and aesthetic landscaping (Interview: RE-D-19, 12 January 2011). To avoid commuting problems for their employees to these suburban business parks, IT-ITES companies normally arrange to-and-fro transport by chartered buses and pool cabs.

Figure 5.3 Messy bazaar streetscape outside an IT business park, Bangalore
[*Source*: Author]

While a few big Indian IT firms, such as TCS, Wipro, Infosys and Cognizant, have developed their own campuses, most other business parks and SEZs are built by real estate developers having expertise in managing large construction projects. RE-D-24 who heads the strategic consulting division of the international real estate consulting firm Jones Lang LaSalle's India office informed when interviewed that,

> The multinational IT companies typically prefer to lease rather than own office space. This provides the flexibility of scaling up or down as the global market situation changes. The IT companies prefer to operate in their core area only and they want to get started quickly. For them it is very difficult to get into construction and building activities—which are messy areas. (Interview: RE-D-24, 19 January 2011)

To meet the needs of a diverse range of customers, the developers of the IT-ITES SEZ offer several customisation options (Interview: RE-D-19, 12 January 2011). Thus big companies like IBM, Microsoft, Google, and Yahoo can get their own buildings, customised to their specific requirements, built within the boundary walls of the SEZ. On the other hand, smaller companies, or even big companies when moving into new locations, frequently prefer 'plug-n-play' facilities, which minimise their set-up times. Over the years, a close synergy has developed between the IT-ITES sector and the corporate real estate sector, as is discussed in the next section.

5.7   Link between IT and real estate sectors

Demand for IT-ITES office spaces and associated facilities has emerged as the main driver behind the urban land market in India since the mid-1990s. According to research by a global real estate consultancy, the IT-ITES sector directly accounted for 48 percent of the 3.8 million square metres of office space demand in 2010 and is the foremost stimulant behind premium residential townships, hotels, shopping malls, educational institutes and specialty hospitals (Jones Lang LaSalle 2010). While initially the relationship between the growth in the IT services sector and its cascading impact on the real estate industry followed the normal market principles, from 2005 onwards, when the SEZ legislation came into being and restrictions on FDI in real estate were lifted, the relationship between the two sectors underwent a paradigmatic shift.

As previously discussed under Section 5.5.1, the SEZ Act prescribes a minimum 10 hectares of land area for establishment of IT-ITES-oriented SEZs and has also extended the tax concessions to the project promoters in addition to the operating IT-ITES units. These two provisions of the Act encouraged real estate companies, having expertise in managing large construction projects, to aggressively enter into the field, and promote IT-ITES SEZs. Large-scale construction activities at the scale of an SEZ are beyond the core strength of most IT-ITES companies. Thus, big domestic IT companies (e.g. TCS, Wipro, Infosys, Satyam, etc.) have set up their own SEZ projects in several cities, but most of the IT-ITES category SEZ are being developed by large real estate companies (e.g. DLF, Unitech, Shapoorji Palonji, etc.), and these projects typically include multiple clients. As discussed in the previous section, the buildings are designed in modular fashion, so as to accommodate spatial needs of different companies. According to the chief architect of India's largest real estate company DLF,

> A 10 hectare SEZ has the potential to generate between 200,000 to 300,000 square metres of built space, as most Indian cities allow FAR between 2 to 3 for IT business parks. This is much larger than the needs of individual software or BPO companies. Typical SEZ projects include a two or three anchor tenants and many small tenants, just like in shopping malls (Interview: RE-D-19, Interview 12 January 2011).

It is also important to note here that the construction and building sectors in India are amongst the most corruption-ridden. To complete a sizable project, a builder is required to complete about 175 documents and get approval from 40 different sources, which causes delays and leads to corruption. Multinational IT companies want to avoid these hassles and typically prefer to lease, rather than own space in India which also allows greater flexibility in scaling up or down in response to the global economic climate. (Interview: RE-D-24, 19 January 2011)

The SEZ Act thus came as a boon for the real estate sector, which seized the opportunity and launched a series of IT SEZ projects. Almost simultaneous liberalisation of the FDI norms enabled global investors to enter the Indian market. The combined impact of the two soon began to be realised. Within 2 years of the promulgation, India's land and property market attracted USD 11.36 billion in FDI, and the proportion of foreign investments in the real-estate sector went up from 0.7 per cent in 2005–06 to 11.1 percent in 2009–10 of the total foreign investments in India (Jones Lang LaSalle 2010, 2012b).

Real-estate-related FDI into India has predominantly taken the route of mutual funds (Wadhwani 2009), leaving out the messier side of the business—direct involvement in construction and building activities—to Indian companies with appropriate local knowledge. But as the inflow of FDI into the real estate sector started in 2005 with global fund managers like Merrill Lynch, JP Morgan and Morgan Stanley starting to buy real-estate-oriented equity funds, India's banking regulator, the Reserve Bank of India (RBI), began to tighten its control over bank lending in the sector. Bank lending for purchase of vacant land was stopped altogether. According to a senior economist associated with the Planning Commission of India,

This was a necessary step by the RBI to protect the Indian banking sector from over exposure into the volatile real estate market. Inflow of speculative investments like mutual funds added fuel to an urban land market which was already on fire. If the RBI had not tightened the money supply then, Indian banks would have been saddled by now with bad debts like the American banks." (Interview: PL-D-25 on 20 January 2011)

As the RBI stopped the banks from lending money for purchase of vacant land and imposed stricter norms for loans to the real estate sector, that void was filled by the private equity funds. Interviewee RE-D-24, Vice President (Strategic Consulting) Jones Lang LaSalle, explained when interviewed on 19 January, "The mutual funds started picking up equity stakes in investment grade real estate—mostly IT SEZs, prestigious office buildings and townships. Equity became the main route to project finance as the debt option dried out". Understandably, these investments flowed into the commercially oriented multi-tenant IT SEZs and business parks promoted by real estate companies, rather than the SEZs built by IT companies for their own internal use.

After 2009 the flow of FDI substantially slowed down as most of the initial mutual funds reached their "maturity life and reached exit phase", while the onset of the global recession slowed down new inflows (Interview: RE-D-24 on 19 January 2011). From 2011 onwards, the markets slowly started bouncing back again. The ebbs and flows of the FDI in India's property market have moved with the global economic scenario. According RE-B-41, a real estate market analyst, a crucial factor here is the dependence of the Indian real estate market on the IT-ITES sector—which itself is vitally dependent upon the external global market (Interview: 10 February 2012).

The growing bond between the IT-ITES and the real estate sectors may be gauged from the fact that out of the 355 IT-ITES category SEZs approved—283 are being developed by real estate companies, 43 by parastatal agencies and the remaining 29 by big Indian software companies (Government of India 2012). Partially this linkage is due to market logic, but to a large extent it is because of the requirements of the SEZ Act (Chatterji 2013a). Recession in the global market has substantially impacted these SEZ projects. Visits to the project sites during fieldwork in 2010 and 2011 revealed that substantial land in the projects is lying vacant. Construction schedules have slowed down, due to slackening of demand and none of the projects are complete. But the developers are holding on to the land they acquired at the peak of FDI inflow, while the property prices in the neighbourhood have substantially appreciated.

The synergy between the IT-ITES sector and the real estate sector has formed a powerful growth machine, driving spatial expansion of the Indian cities towards the outer fringe. While these onward urban expansions are creating new economic opportunities for the local agrarian communities, they are also creating new threats and vulnerabilities over loss of agricultural land. The negotiations between these two opposing forces take place at the local level and are contextualised by place-specific socio-political factors, as will be explored in later chapters.

5.8   Summary

This chapter discussed the overarching socio-economic and political context within which the Indian IT-ITES sector is situated. Starting off at the bottom tier of the outsourced office services value chain, India has become the leading global player in this segment. IT-ITES companies are clustering around the big cities and growth in this sector has opened up huge career opportunities for an educated middle-class workforce. However, the downstream benefits of the IT-ITES sector are questionable. Nevertheless, impressive growth of the sector through globalisation has led to it being perceived in a particularly favourable light, in the imagination of the middle class and the political elites of India.

Economic policies and institutional structures, both at the national and sub-national levels, have significantly facilitated the development of the IT-ITES sector. Initially, tax holidays and other incentives under the STPI scheme helped the sector to mature and grow in scale. The SEZ Act further extended the tax benefits. But the SEZ Act also institutionalised a linkage between the IT-ITES sector and the corporate real estate sector, in the production process for work spaces, extending the tax benefits to the project promoters and specifying a minimum land area threshold. In terms of work space, well-established and big IT-ITES companies have a preference for suburban business parks, which provide high-quality infrastructure and security within gated enclaves. However, to avail themselves of tax benefits, they are now required to be physically located within the designated SEZ premises.

Apart from the national schemes, the IT-ITES sector also receives subsidised land and a range of incentives under state-level IT policies, due to increasing competition between the states to attract the sector. However, the incentive packages in the state IT policies are designed through consultations with the industry chambers, and this has brought a large degree of uniformity in the state-level IT policies. In this scenario, the availability of *land* of sufficient scale near big cities having a skilled *labour* force have become the crucial determinant driving the economic geography of the industry.

The synergy between land and labour is leading to the formation of IT clusters in the fringe areas of the big cities. Rapid expansion of the urban footprint, to make production and consumption spaces for the new economy, is bringing new growth opportunities but also new tensions and contradictions. The interface between these opposing forces is negotiated on the local terrain and mediated by place-specific political dynamics, as the case studies of the IT clusters in three cities—Bangalore, NCR and Kolkata—bring out in the following chapters.

Case study I: Bangalore IT cluster

6.1   Introduction

This chapter contains a case study about the IT clusters in Bangalore, capital of the Karnataka state in southern India. Bangalore's emergence as a global hub for software development and high-tech research has drawn much attention in recent years. Studies by Parthasarathy (2004), Vang and Asheim (2006) and O'Connor (2003) focused on the social embeddedness of the software industry and the thick international network connecting Bangalore with Silicon Valley and other global regions. Narayana (2010) analysed impacts of such global processes on Bangalore's economy and demographic growth. Chacko (2007) discussed how increasing job opportunities have prompted reverse migration of skilled Indian professionals to return from the West. Resultant spatial impacts, rapid peri-urbanisation, spiralling land values and rising trends of speculative real estate investments were discussed by Aranya (2008) and Goldman (2011). Shaw and Satish (2007) discussed the close linkage between global and local capitals in urban restructuring. Benjamin (2008, 2010) examined the flip sides of globalisation: marginalisation and livelihood vulnerabilities of the poor due to elite-driven policies of the state. Small-scale local economies, which provide the bulk of the employment, are being systematically overshadowed in the planning agenda, by the advanced services-driven new economy (Benjamin 2010). Taking off from here, this chapter explores the nature of the governance regime that had moulded Bangalore's developmental landscape in particular ways. The following section provides a brief background of the growth of the IT-ITES industry in Bangalore. Section 6.3 then discusses the state-level political-economic culture of Karnataka, which nurtured the development of Bangalore's IT industry. Section 6.4 then takes up the spatial implications of the IT-ITES industry and the urban development pattern of Bangalore. Section 6.5 includes illustrative examples of one IT business park in Bangalore. Section 6.6 analyses the roles of various stakeholders associated with the growth of Bangalore's IT cluster and its urban transformation. Section 6.7 concludes the chapter through a summary.

6.2   Development of IT services sector

Bangalore is one of the largest technology clusters in the world. Studies by global management consulting firms have consistently rated Bangalore amongst the top five global IT outsourcing destinations along with Delhi NCR, Manila NCR and Dublin (A.T.Kearney 2009). There are 2084 IT-ITES companies in Bangalore, which provide employment for about 500,000 people (Government of Karnataka 2011). Apart from IT software and business process outsourcing services, Bangalore is also India's largest hub in biotechnology, aerospace engineering and defence-related electronic hardware.

The seeds of Bangalore's knowledge economy were planted back in the 1950s, by then Prime Minister Jawaharlal Nehru's decision to locate the strategic defence and electronics industry in the city through the public sector (Nair 2005). Nehru was influenced by the city's deeply rooted culture of nurturing institutions of higher learning and its pleasant urban environment.

During the colonial period and till the 1950s, Bangalore was essentially a provincial town with a large military cantonment and a few well-known academic institutions (e.g. Indian Institute of Science). Between the 1940s and 1950s, four large manufacturing industries owned by the national government were located at the outskirts of the city. These were: Hindustan Aeronautics Ltd. (aircrafts and helicopters), Indian Telephone Industries (telecommunication equipment), Hindustan Machine Tools (metal forming and die casting etc.) and Bharat Electronics Ltd. (weapons and communication equipment) (Nair 2005). Several large research laboratories in the areas of electronics, communications and avionics were also established around these production facilities in the following years (Nair 2005).

With big investments pouring in from the national government, particularly in defence-related fields, Bangalore, the city of future in Nehru's imagination, was developed by the 1970s, as India's largest agglomeration in the aeronautics and electronics industry (Parthasarathy 2004). Bangalore's higher altitude, pleasant climate and dust-free air were found particularly suitable for high precision-oriented production facilities in the electronics and communication sectors (Vang & Asheim 2006). Its long legacy, since 1864 as a garrison town and its location, deep inside southern India, far away from the troubled borders with Pakistan and China, also no doubt played a role in deciding the location for strategic defence-related laboratories and production facilities.

The concentration of large numbers of research and development facilities in the era of state-led development turned Bangalore into India's prime hub for engineers and scientists. Later, with the neoliberal turn of the Indian state in the 1980s, this human capital pool was leveraged by Indian private sector software companies to aggressively expand in the international arena, and also attracted global corporations to locate their R&D centres to the city (Parthasarathy 2004; Vang & Asheim 2006). Thus, during the 1980s, when the trend of outsourcing started catching up in Silicon Valley's IT industry, Bangalore already had a dense organisational network in the electronics and telecommunication technology in place, and had a head start over other Indian cities.

From the mid-1980s onwards, the process of global and local IT companies clustering around Bangalore ran almost concurrently. Digital Equipment, soon followed by Texas Instruments, started the trend by locating their first R&D facilities outside the USA, in Bangalore (Vang & Asheim 2006). Around the same time, Bangalore-based Indian IT companies like Wipro and Infosys began to penetrate the global market (Parthasarathy 2004). Success of these early ventures established Bangalore's reputation as a software engineering talent hub. Later on, from the mid-1990s as the 'outsourcing' in the USA's software development industry gathered momentum, the links between the expatriate Indian professionals working in the USA and Bangalore's IT community turned the city into the preferred destination (Parthasarathy 2004).

While the national government's industrial locational decisions during the era of state-led development provided Bangalore with a head-start, and social connections amongst the expatriate Indian professionals had become the link between the local and global, the Karnataka state government also contributed significantly in consolidating Bangalore's position as the leading knowledge economy destination of India in the post-liberalisation era, through pro-active policies, as discussed in the following section.

6.3   State and local socio-political culture

Karnataka is a large state, having a population of 61.1million, that is comparable with the UK (Census 2011). It is one of the more economically developed and urbanised states of India. Karnataka's per capita state GDP of USD 1507 is higher than the national per capita GDP of USD 1329 (The Economist 2012c). Similarly, Karnataka's 38.57 urban population percentage is significantly higher than the 31.16 percent national average (Census 2011). It is considered as one of the better administered states of India, with a long embedded culture of state-led development, going back to the late nineteenth century (Kadekodi, Kanbur & Rao 2007). It has been amongst the front ranking states, in adopting market-oriented policy reforms in the post-globalisation era.

Political power in Karnataka had always swung between major national level political parties (Shastri 2009). Starting from its formation and until the 1980s, politically Karnataka was considered as a Congress party bastion. Since 1983, however, in every assembly election, the incumbent government was been voted out and power has rotated between Janata Dal (S) and Congress (Assadi 2004; Shastri 2009). Gaining popularity since 2000, the Hindu nationalist Bharatiya Janata Party (BJP) came to power in 2008 and remained so till 2013.

However, along with the influence of the mainstream political parties, caste affiliations play vital roles in shaping the electoral politics of Karnataka. Vokkaligas and Lingayats, two landowning farming castes, lead rival caste coalitions which dominate the state politics (Assadi 2004; Breeding 2011; Shastri 2009). Lingayats account for about 15.3 percent of the population, while the Vokkaligas account for about 10.8 percent (Shastri 2009). "Power tussles between these two castes more than any other factor are what makes and breaks governments", informed CS-B-64, a local journalist (interview: 8 February 2012). Political parties have accommodated the caste coalitions within their ranks, but this in turn has also increased the scope for corruption (Breeding 2011; Kadekodi, Kanbur & Rao 2007). Caste vote banks come with their sets of obligations and reciprocity. Leaders are expected to provide particularistic favours to their supporters, in exchange for support. In recent years, Karnataka has witnessed large numbers of political scams, particularly on issues related to mining and real estate contracts. Thus,

Ramachandra Guha, one of India's most distinguished historians and political commentators observed,

> I know that we may be speaking here of a race to the bottom, but I would still like to claim that the political culture of the state where I live, Karnataka, is more degraded than that of any other state of the Union ... Across party lines, the legislators and ministers of Karnataka now tend to privilege the interests of mining and real estate lobbies above the concerns of the ordinary citizens of the state (Guha 2012 p.10).

Corruption and caste-oriented sectarian considerations compelled the incumbent BJP government to twice change its Chief Minister, since coming to power in 2008. Frequent changes in government and the non-ideological (on economic issues) nature of Karnataka politics, has provided much policy space for the bureaucratic elites. Until the recent surge of corruption charges had somewhat dented the state's image, it was often considered as a "model developmental state" where senior bureaucrats enjoyed more autonomy in policy framing compared to most Indian states, and this resulted in the state having "better crafted policies and more policy continuity" (Kadekodi, Kanbur & Rao 2007, p.650). These policy initiatives were most evident in two areas: promoting technology-led development and local governance reforms. In both these cases, the state's administrative apparatus demonstrates long-term path dependencies, which could be traced back to the policies of the former princely state of Mysore.[1]

On economic matters, governments headed by different political parties, Congress, Janata Dal (S) and BJP, had more or less followed pro-growth economic policies from the 1990s onwards. However, considering the fact that the rural population constitutes about two-third

---

[1] During the colonial period, Mysore (which now forms the core of Karnataka) was often held out as the model developmental state. Advised by visionary technocrat dewans (ministers) like, Sir M. Visvesvaraya and Sir Mirza Ismail, the feudal state vigorously took up the cause of promoting scientific and technical education along with building industrial infrastructure through state support. Back in 1905, the Maharaja of Mysore took proactive steps by providing land grants and capital subsidies, to locate the Indian Institute of Science in Bangalore, which was conceptualised by Swami Vivekananda, a monk from Calcutta and Sir J.N. Tata an industrialist from Bombay. For details refer (Kadekodi, Kanbur & Rao 2007) and (Nair 2012).

of the electorate, all political parties consider it expedient to temper their support for urban-centric economic growth policies with a liberal dose of pro-rural rhetoric (Scoones 2003). Regarding the IT-ITES sector, Congress and BJP are seen as more supportive. The Congress government under S. M. Krishna (Chief Minister of Karnataka 1999–04, Foreign Minister of India, 2009–12) had been particularly proactive in supporting the new economy-driven urban development. Whereas, previously Janata Dal (S) under the leadership of H.D. Deve Gowda (Chief Minister 1994–96, Prime Minister of India, 1996–98) had been lukewarm and eager to project his image as a protector of rural interests.

In recent times, several mega projects such as the Bangalore–Mysore Infrastructure Corridor and Bangalore's new international airport have become controversial because of the acquisition of agricultural land and resettlement issues. The new airport is located in the Devanahalli area about 40 km north of Bangalore and was developed through a public–private joint venture, involving a state government enterprise, a central government enterprise, an Indian private company and Siemens of Germany. The project was strongly supported by Congress government under S.M. Krishna as commensurate with Bangalore's rising global profile. But launching of the project was delayed by several years due to opposition from H.D. Deve Gowda (Benjamin 2008, 2010) and was finally completed in 2008.

Likewise, the progress of the Bangalore–Mysore Infrastructure Corridor, which was originally conceptualised in 1995, has been slow due to land-related problems and court cases (Raghuram & Sundaram 2009). The project envisages building a tolled expressway connecting Bangalore and Mysore. Five private townships and other high-end residential and commercial projects are proposed along the way. PL-K-46, Chief Planner of the project, informed when interviewed on 15 February 2012 that the project was initially conceptualised on a PPP model between the state government and Indian and American private companies when Deve Gowda was the state's chief minister. Later, however, when the party of Janata Dal(S) returned to power, and his son H.D. Kumaraswamy became chief minister, the project was temporarily suspended. Its revival in 2008 by the BJP government was termed by Deve Gowda as India's biggest real estate fraud (The Hindu 2008). According to local press reports, Deve Gowda's opposition to the IT and high tech economy of Bangalore is driven by his personal rivalry with Congress leader S.M. Krishna (The Hindu 2005). CS-B-35, a civil society activist felt that,

> Deve Gowda and Kumaraswamy are trying to remain relevant in Karnataka's politics. Deve Gowda's opposition to IT and big projects of Bangalore are actually for the consumption of the rural vote bank. He fears that his party will be squeezed out by the rising BJP and Congress. (Interview: 7 February 2011)

While such political exigencies of Karnataka's politics, driven by rural–urban dichotomies have occasionally caused road blocks, the political leadership as a whole have been following pro-growth strategies. However, more than the political leadership, activist state bureaucracy played a prominent role in Bangalore's 'take-off' and insertion into the global knowledge economy by creating dedicated institutional arrangements and framing industry-friendly policies, after the beginning of economic liberalisation by the national government. Karnataka government played a key role in the establishment of Electronic City, which was India's first planned IT-oriented business park, in the southern fringe of Bangalore in 1995. The project was initiated through a collaborative mechanism, where state government agencies provided land and civic infrastructure while central government established a satellite earth station for high speed data communication, for private companies to set up operations (Parthasarathy 2004).

As already discussed in Chapter 5, Karnataka was the first state to frame an IT policy in 1997. From the late-1990s, Bangalore faced increasing competition from other metropolitan regions in attracting IT investments. In response to the competition, the state government revised its IT policy. The new document asserts the state's intention of retaining its front ranking position in the IT sector; to further consolidate Bangalore's position as a knowledge capital by encouraging hi-tech investments; and to expand the scope of IT outsourcing from non-English-speaking countries by facilitating the establishment of foreign trade missions in Bangalore, and by promoting language skills (Government of Karnataka 2000).

To implement the IT policies and actively promote investments, the Karnataka government has created special institutional arrangements. Initially, IT investments were routed through Karnataka State Industrial Development Corporation (KSIDC), the state's all-purpose industrial promotion agency. However, now there are two different agencies involved in the IT sector, which are KBITS (Karnataka Biotechnology and Information Technology Services) and KEONICS (Karnataka State Electronics Development Corporation). KBITS was formed in 2000 to provide a 'single-window' interface between the industry and the government for quick approval of projects. KEONICS promotes small-sized software and BPO units through incubation facilities, venture capital and development of business parks. It also runs more than two hundred training centres all over the state, to build up the computer skills of the people. In spatial terms its focus is outside Bangalore. A General Manager of KEONICS explained the government's strategy regarding IT services when interviewed:

> Bangalore is facing huge competition. It has become very expensive. Employee salaries and (*employee*) attrition rates are both very high. Land prices are also extremely high. Only the top-end IT companies can afford to set-up office here anymore. We need to create alternative arrangements. Otherwise they (*IT companies*) will move to Hyderabad or Pune. That's why we are promoting smaller cities like Mysore and Mangalore to create hub and spoke arrangements. Companies, who find Bangalore expensive, can relocate their back office in these cities. Infosys has already relocated their training facilities to Mysore. It has already started shaping that way, but the future will be more and more hub and spoke. (Interview: PL-B-47, 15 February 2011)

Bangalore's lead in the high tech industry is facing strong regional challenges, from Chennai, Hyderabad and Pune. In this scenario, Karnataka government's strategic vision towards the development of Bangalore has moved beyond the IT outsourcing sector and now includes the biotechnology and aerospace industries. In IT services, it is trying to climb up the value chain. The top echelons of the state bureaucracy work closely together with the industry in crafting the state's economic strategy. PL-B-42, a key policy advisor to the Chief Minister, articulated the vision for Bangalore as,

> The IT software sector in Bangalore has kind of reached a plateau. Almost all the top global companies are already here. If you want routine software bug testing etc. you no longer come to Bangalore. You'll go to Chennai or Pune. New investment in IT will gradually taper-off, unless we move up towards more specialised services. We also need to diversify,

to hedge our risks. Biotech and aerospace are two fronts where we've competitive advantage, and we should build on to these strengths. Growth in these areas will also help the IT sector. (Interview: PL-B-42, 11 February 2011)

Bangalore is already India's leading centre in the biotechnology area. The Karnataka government also pioneered in launching a biotech policy to attract investments (Scoones 2003). Similarly, in recent years, the Karnataka government has sought to capitalise on Bangalore's existing strength in aeronautical and defence electronics, to woo new investments in these sectors by promoting an aerospace-oriented SEZ adjoining Bangalore's new international airport (Deccan Herald 2011).

Apart from facilitating investments through favourable fiscal policies and land supply, Karnataka had also actively ensured a skilled labour supply—another key ingredient in success in the knowledge economy sector. Along with its neighbouring states Karnataka has been in the forefront of liberalising norms for the establishment of private sector engineering, management and medical colleges since the 1980s, ensuring a steady stream of technical labour supply to the region's growing economy (Parthasarathy 2004). There are 158 engineering colleges in the state and similarly large numbers of medical and management institutes (Government of Karnataka 2011). Most of these institutes are privately owned and charge high tuition fees (Gupta 2008). While some of the new private colleges are good, the quality of many is suspect. Nevertheless, they have been able to attract students from all over India, capitalising on the demand for higher education amongst the burgeoning Indian middleclass.

There are strong links between the Karnataka's political class and the mushrooming education industry. Many of these institutes are de-facto owned by the politicians. As academic-cum-policy advisor PL-B-42 informed,

> These private colleges help Karnataka draw young talent from far-flung eastern states like Bengal and Bihar and are also big money spinners. Most of these are actually owned by MPs and MLAs, but run in the name of religious trusts or NGOs. This is easy money and politicians of all parties are involved in this game. (Interview: PL-B-42, 11 February 2011).

Similarly, IT-B-37, a professor in one of the better known institutes, informed when interviewed on 8 February, "Our institute is run by a religious trust. But the daughter of a former minister is the chairperson of the trust and most other members of the governing body belong to the extended family". However, rapid growth of these private educational empires has created an unexpected strong bonding between Karnataka's caste-centric, rural-rich dominated political system and the globalised knowledge economy of Bangalore. The IT-ITES and biotech sectors are the main consumers of the education industry, just the same way as they are fuelling the demand in the real estate sector. Driven by the direct personal interest of the political class, support for pro-growth policies in Karnataka runs across party lines of Karnataka, which has turned its capital, Bangalore, into one of India's top three cities for attracting global investments. The next section discusses how these economic developments have impacted Bangalore's urban growth pattern.

6.4   Urban development pattern

6.4.1   Location

Bangalore is located at the top of the Mysore plateau (at an elevation of about 900 m above sea level) at the southeast corner of Karnataka (refer Figure 6.1). Most of the city lies within the Bangalore Urban District.

The Bangalore Urban District directly adjoins the state of Tamil Nadu to its east, while the borders of Andhra Pradesh are also very close.

Bangalore's high altitude has endowed it with a pleasant climate and impacted favourably on the city's initial growth as a centre of the knowledge economy (Vang & Asheim 2006). However, Bangalore's close proximity to Tamil Nadu and Andhra is an issue of concern for the state's present day political elites. There are worries about cross-border economic competition. ELCOT, a Tamil Nadu government undertaking, has built a large IT SEZ at Hosur, just 10 km from Bangalore and on the Bangalore–Chennai Highway and advertises its proximity to Bangalore amongst the main advantages. A top bureaucrat of Karnataka expressed his worries,

> The Hosur SEZ is clearly aimed at Bangalore. They (Tamil Nadu government agencies) are very aggressive. They want to ride on the success of Bangalore, by poaching companies with lower tax rates, by building so close. Now imagine what can happen if they start constructing a new airport. We've just built our

new international airport. But we can't do anything if they build another. (Interview: PL-B-47, 15 February 2011)

Figure 6.1 Location map of Bangalore [*Source*: http://www.mapsofworld.com (Accessed 9 January 2013)]

There are also concerns about speculative real estate investments. For example, CS-B-35, head of an NGO, informed that the rich and powerful agricultural communities had been investing heavily since the 1970s in the land market in the extended fringe areas of Bangalore. The land purchases were "not for cultivation, but for investment" (Interview:

7 February 2011). Bangalore's rapid economic growth over a long period of time and resultant spatial expansion made such investments a potentially very lucrative proposition.

6.4.2   Growth pattern

Supportive state policies and economic growth have contributed to the rapid spatial and demographic expansion of Bangalore, especially since the beginning of the IT-ITES-induced construction boom in the 1990s. As per the records of the Bangalore Development Authority (BDA),

Between 1983 and 1990 the urban area of the city increased from 202 sq km to 283 sq km. In 2003 the city's area increased to 565 sq km, indicating a 100% increase in 12 years and an annual progression of 2200 ha with a growth rate of 5.4%. This is a considerably significant growth rate and is the highest in the country. (Bangalore Development Authority 2005, p.11)

> The BDA's planning envisages expansion of the city to cover 1307 sq km by 2015 with a 107 km long peripheral ring road encompassing the area. The scale of this growth can be gauged by the fact that in 1949 the administrative limits of the city covered only 69 sq km. "In the absence of a defined natural boundary, the city has spread in all directions and along the major roads" (Bangalore Development Authority 2005).

From the 1950s till the 1980s, Bangalore expanded in concentric circles. The core area includes the original settlement or 'Petta' which is now a retail and wholesale trading area. To the north of this is Cubbon Park, the administrative heart and the Cantonment area, which developed during the colonial period. Self-contained townships for public sector aeronautical and electronics factories and research laboratories are located further to the north. The western part of the city includes residential and small-scale manufacturing industries. Since the early 1990s, Bangalore's outward expansion has been driven by the IT-ITES-led new economy (Bangalore Development Authority 2007).

There are three major IT hubs in Bangalore as shown in (see Figure 6.2). The first hub is located at the southern fringe of the city along the Hosur Road (NH-7) and Electronics City. Development of Electronic City in the early 1990s spurred the growth in this area.

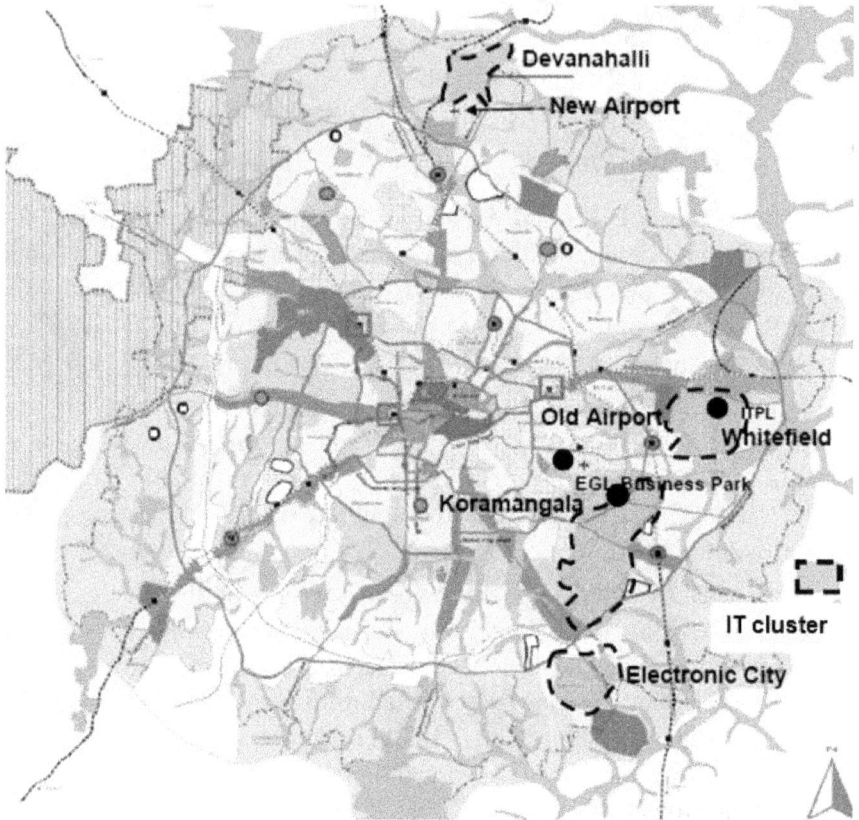

Figure 6.2 Location of IT clusters in Bangalore Metropolitan Region [*Source*:
Bangalore Development Authority]

The second hub started taking shape from early 2000, at the eastern
fringe, from Koramangla to the Whitefield area along the Inner Ring
Road and Outer Ring Road. In this stretch, development of International
Technology Park (ITPL) at Whitefield acted as a catalyst. The third and
the newest hub started forming since 2008, around the new International
airport at Devanahalli, at the northern fringe.

Until the mid-1990s, the land development process in Bangalore was
almost exclusively state led. That is, the state-planning agencies would
first acquire land in the peri-urban areas, prepare a master plan, create
land sub-divisions and then either allocate or sell to private enterprises.
Since then to speed up land supply for new urban and industrial projects,
the Karnataka government encouraged land development by private real

estate companies and simplified procedures for conversion of agricultural land to urban usage. According to a senior planner with the BDA,

> Land acquisition by government is a lengthy procedure. Problem is, most often it lands up in court, as people are never satisfied with the compensation payment. Once the issue goes to court, it takes years—you know how the system works. To get around this, the (state) government decided to allow private developers to purchase agricultural land and then apply for land use conversion. A circular was issued in 1999 which very much simplified this procedure. They (the developers) still have to prepare a Master Plan and get approval from the local development authority. But it is all very easy now. (Interview: PL-B-46, 15 Feb 2011)

With the Karnataka government encouraging private sector investments in land development, Bangalore's growth has increasingly followed a twin-track or two-stage process. For example, the state government developed an iconic project on the distant periphery (ITPL or the new airport) and built connecting roads. This in turn encouraged private developers to develop residential and commercial projects around that area and along the connecting road, by directly purchasing the land from the local people. This twin-track approach substantially speeded up urban land supply, keeping pace with economic growth.

Bangalore's population has rapidly increased over the years, as it has been amongst the fastest growing regions of India. The city population was only 1.21 million in 1961, which increased by more than three times over the next three decades to reach 4.13 million in 1991. Since then, in two post-reform decades the population has more than doubled. Bangalore's population increased to 6.68 million in 2001 and 9.59 million by 2011 (Census 2011). This astronomical growth, however, has not been matched by a proportionate increase in civic infrastructure facilities. Because of these shortcomings, the urban governance structure has come under intense scrutiny. It has also been the subject of new experiments, as discussed below.

6.4.3   Institutional structure of urban governance

Bangalore was a divided city during the colonial period. The military cantonment area, which included most of the European settlements, was under direct British control. The rest of the city and the industrial outskirts were under the Maharaja of Mysore. The twin cities were merged in 1949 to form a single municipal administration, known as Bangalore Municipal Corporation (BMC) (Nair 2005). The unified city first became the capital of the State of Mysore, and then from 1956, the enlarged State of Karnataka. The need for planned urban development of Bangalore with its augmented status was realised at an early stage. Bangalore Development Committee (BDC) was constituted in 1952 and entrusted with preparation of the Outline Development Plan (ODP) (Bangalore Development Authority 2005). The first ODP was prepared in 1963 and approved in 1972, after inordinate delay at both stages. As in the post-colonial era of rural-centric political culture, urban development was no longer a priority. Meanwhile Karnataka passed the Town and Country Planning Act in 1961. The BDC was superseded by the Bangalore Development Authority (BDA) in 1976 which functions directly under the Government of Karnataka. It is a nodal planning agency with jurisdiction extending beyond the core city and covering the entire metropolitan region. BDA prepares Comprehensive Development Plans (CDP) with 10-year time horizons as per the requirements of the Town and Country Planning Act. The first CDP was launched in 1985, followed by the second in 1995 and the third in 2005. The third or current CDP (2005–15) spans a 1306 sq km area, and includes seven city municipal councils, one town municipal council and 387 villages (Bangalore Development Authority 2005).

However, planning has failed to keep pace with economic change. Problems like traffic congestion along with power supply are especially highlighted by the popular press on a regular basis. Growth in the post-1990s era happened along with rapid growth in middle-class consumerism. Thus the vehicle ownership rate increased from 58 vehicles per 1000 population in 1981 to 365 vehicles per 1000 in 2006; and the number of registered vehicles more than quadrupled from 0.63 million in 1990 to 3.13 million in 2006 (ABIDe 2010). Physical land-use-oriented planning practices and inadequate funding for civic infrastructure compounded the crisis.

During the late 1990s, IT corporate 'czars' like Narayan Murthy (Infosys) and Azim Premji (Wipro) were at the forefront of criticism about the infrastructure deficiencies of Bangalore (Times of India 2003). S.M. Krishna, who became the Chief Minister after the Congress party returned to power in 1999, took major steps to address these concerns, by building partnerships with the corporate and civil society actors and thus departing from the previous state-led planning mould. Krishna was keen to showcase his modern tech-savvy image to his party's central leadership (Scoones 2003). He also faced stiff competition from neighbouring Hyderabad in retaining IT investments. A former Chief Secretary of Karnataka and urban policy advisor to successive state governments, noted when interviewed:

> During that time (late 1990s) Bangalore faced real threat. Our infrastructures were crumbling under growth pressure. On the other hand, Andhra Pradesh under Chandra Babu Naidu's leadership was aggressively wooing IT companies. He succeeded in wooing Microsoft to locate its first campus (in India) in Hyderabad. It was a big jolt. (Interview: PL-B-49, 17 February, 2011)

Krishna aspired to turn Bangalore into a 'world class' metropolis, like 'Singapore' (Nair 2000). He launched a task force called Bangalore Agenda Task Force (BATF) under the leadership of Nandan Nilekani, CEO of Infosys, thus charting a new course in public–private partnerships in urban governance in India. The task force included top IT and biotech corporate 'czars', civil society elites (e.g. Ramesh Ramanathan of Janaagraha) and top bureaucrats like PL-B-49 (Benjamin 2010; Ghosh, A 2005; Goldman 2011). The government order constituting the task force claimed that "the vision of the government is to make Bangalore as India's best city in next five years". (as quoted in Ghosh, A 2005, p.4016)

BATF attempted to address the developmental challenges through technocratic means by introducing digital mapping and a management information system for efficient delivery of urban infrastructure and revenue generation. BATF was also instrumental in bringing in external expertise to guide the planning process of Bangalore. Thus a French consortium called Groupe SCE was brought in under an Indo-French collaborative program. The CDP (2005–15) bears strong imprints of this initiative. Backed by the task force, which had strong political backing from the chief minister, the French consortium was given wide liberty in its approach.

However BATF's involvement in planning came under much criticism. Ghosh (2005) and Benjamin (2010) have argued that the involvement of BATF, comprising of corporate and civil society elites in the planning process of Bangalore, undermined the democratic principles of the 74th Constitutional Amendment Act of 1992, which visualised a larger role for elected representatives in planning. But Bangalore's municipal councillors were sidelined in BATF workshops, as typically meetings were held in five-star hotels and all deliberations were in English. Interviews conducted during the fieldwork for this book also revealed strong reservations about the BATF. For instance, CS-B-35, head of CIVIC (Citizens Voluntary Initiatives for the City), one of Bangalore's most respected NGOs working in the area of participatory governance, vented her strong disapproval about BATF's approach. She observed,

> During the BATF days we had governance by corporate big-wigs. Their focus was on aesthetics and beautification—how to make Bangalore look good to the foreigners. Infosys Foundation built public toilets in the CBD areas, but not in the slums, where toilets are most needed. They spent money on new and improved bus shelters, but that money could have been better spent by introducing new buses. (Interview: 7 February 2011).

According to PL-B-39, a senior urban planner working for Groupe SCE and closely associated with CDP (2005–15), when interviewed on 9 February 2011, termed this as 'outsourcing of planning' resulting in a focus on frivolous issues, and in this, BATF was driven by a desire 'to showcase, to compete and to make statements' (Interview: 9 February 2011).

The influence of BATF waned with the end of Krishna's tenure as Chief Minister in 2004. However, the BJP government, which came to power in 2008 under B.S. Yeddyurappa, has also constituted a task force along similar lines called Agenda for Bengaluru Infrastructure Development (ABIDe), consisting of representatives of the IT (and biotech) corporate sector (e.g. Dr. Kiran Mazumdar-Shaw, MD Biocon, T.V. Mohandas Pai, HR head Infosys) civil society elites (e.g. Anita Reddy, Director AVAS) and senior bureaucrats (e.g. PL-B-49). But unlike BATF which had a corporate executive at the helm, ABIDE is headed by Ananth Kumar, M.P., a former central government minister and a senior politician, while Rajeev Chandrashekhar, M.P., an entrepreneur turned politician, is the Convenor. Civil society activist CS-B-35 felt when interviewed on 7 February that these subtle differences place ABIDe in a more favourable position than BATF to negotiate the government machinery and local political system.

ABIDe has prepared a vision document, 'Plan Bengaluru 2020', which projects the emergence of Bangalore as a mega-urban region of 8000 sq km. It has also drafted a Bangalore Metropolitan Regional Governance (BMRG) Bill to coordinate planning and infrastructure development at the supra-urban scale, a pioneering attempt in urban rescaling in India. The BMRG has proposed creation of a large regional authority headed by a powerful directly elected mayor[2]. PL-B-42, a member of ABIDe, explained,

> Bangalore is one of the fastest growing cities in the world. Unless we plan in advance, it will be a big mess. And for that to happen, we need to think big. But more importantly, we need a really strong body to be in charge of that. This can only happen if we have a directly elected mayor. Otherwise, there are too many vested interests at the state and local level to scuttle the regional plan. (Interview: 11 February 2011)

However, the BMRG bill has faced strong opposition from the Legislative Assembly. There is a feeling that such a strong civic government will usurp its power and become a parallel power centre against the state government. This opposition has hindered progress of the bill in the state legislature (Deccan Herald 2012). According to CS-B-64, a local journalist and environmental activist, the BMRG bill is also being strongly opposed by the politicians from the rural areas of Karnataka, who apprehend that the BMRG will be dominated by a middle-class and elitist agenda (Interview: 9 February 2012).

According to Nair (2005), the absence of strong social movements and the concentration of large numbers of an educated middle class have come to dominate the planners' imagination of Bangalore over a long period of time dating back to the pre-colonial days. Rapid growth of the IT–biotech economy over the past two decades has further strengthened these forces. The next section takes a look at how the requirements of the new economy are reconfiguring the urban space of Bangalore, through an example of the Embassy Golf Links Business Park.

---

[2] Mayors in India are usually elected indirectly, by the elected municipal councillors

6.5   Illustrative case study: Embassy Golf Links Business Park

Starting in 2002, the Embassy Golf Links (EGL) Business Park has developed over the years to become one of India's landmark corporate addresses. The project was designed by RSP Architects and Planners of Singapore, and was promoted by the Embassy Group, a prominent Bangalore-based real estate company. Apart from this project, the Embassy Group has built several other high-end IT office parks, SEZs, residential and retail projects in Bangalore and Pune, and has now started venturing internationally, by developing projects in Malaysia and Serbia.

Spread over 24.3 hectares, the EGL office complex is located at Challaghatta village in east Bangalore, on Inner Ring Road near the old HAL Airport (which was Bangalore's main airport until 2008). It adjoins a golf course to the east, Inner Ring Road to its north, and Challaghatta village to its south and west, as shown in Figure 6.3. The area is located in between Koramangala and Indira Nagar, two prime sub-business districts, and is part of the extended IT hub of eastern Bangalore.

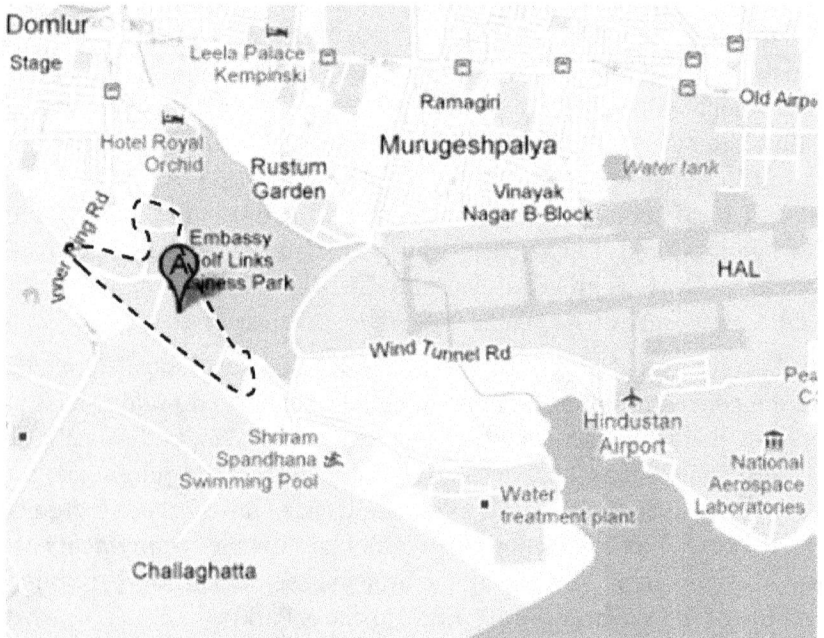

Figure 6.3 Location map EGL Business Park [*Source*: Googlemaps.com (Accessed 9 January 2013)]

Land for the project was directly purchased by the developers from the local villagers. Subsequently, the land was vested with the local government agency and leased back. It is important to note here that during the socialistic turn of the Indian state in the 1960s, upper limits were imposed on the plot sizes in the urban areas owned by individuals and private companies, to reduce speculative land holdings and free up the surplus land to build housing for the poor. However, the legislation did not meet its aim and led to a large number of litigations as people sub-divided the plots amongst family members (Shivaramakrishnan 2011). Most states repealed the Urban Land Ceiling Act in the mid-2000s. However, in the intervening period, a practice developed to get around the legislation, where land acquired in excess of the permitted limits was vested by the private parties to the parastatal agencies, who in turn leased back the land to the private developers. Land assembling for the EGL followed this practice. The business park includes 6.33 million sq ft (588 thousand sq m) of office and ancillary spaces in 20 buildings, where over 45,000 people work. A 250 room business hotel, to be managed by the Hilton group, is under construction at the time of writing. A large number of global corporate firms have leased office space in this complex, as indicated in Table 6.1.

RE-B-48, a senior manager of the Embassy Group, mentioned "Mercedes R&D centre is located here. This is the only R&D centre of Mercedes outside Germany. LG and Huwai also do product development here for mobile phones" (Interview: 16 February 2011). The developer built customised buildings for major tenants like IBM, Microsoft, and Goldman Sachs. Smaller tenants are located in modular office blocks.

Table 6.1 Occupants' list: Embassy Golf Links Business Park [*Source*: Project Manager, Embassy Group, Bangalore, personal correspondence 13 September 2011]

Company	Functions and activities
IBM	Implementation and maintenance for software like SAP, Oracle, Peoplesoft etc., Research in Linux products, business analysis
Microsoft	R&D for Data Protection Manager, RFID Platform Technologies, Office Mobile, Windows SFU, Visual Studio, Office Live Meeting, multilingual systems and GIS
Goldman Sachs	Investment banking, business strategy analysis, accounting

Contd...

Contd...

Company	Functions and activities
Yahoo	Development of algorithms for web page clustering, classification and ranking, pattern matching, database mining
Net App	Application development for data management, cloud computing
InMobi	Software development for mobile phone advertising
Huawei	Product development for telecom and networking solutions
Digicaptions	Digital cinema, graphics and 3D animation software development
LG Soft	Mobile handset applications, digital video broadcast, biometrics software development
ANZ	Operations and technological support for shared administrative services, payroll management, etc.
CSC	Remote IT infrastructure network, security and web hosting management
Misys	Banking and capital markets risk management solutions
Fidelity	Database management, IT support and BPO services
Vodafone	Corporate management and marketing
24x7 Customer Care	Software development for predictive customer servicing
Target Corp.	Statistical modelling for market research and asset protection
Daimler Chrysler	Research in data encryption, telematics, finite element modelling
Synergy	Project management, architecture and engineering consultancy
Stylus	Software customisation for enterprise resource planning, customer relationship management and healthcare management
Cushman and Wakefield	Real estate and marketing research consultancy
Price Waterhouse	Audit and accounting, business transformation strategy analysis
Sasken	Software services and solutions in 3G, wireless broadband, signal processing and IC design
Continuous Computing	Development for 3G and 4G wireless infrastructure and Trillium protocol software
Retail Full-Serve	IT support and software applications for retail chains
Indegene	Marketing strategy for pharmaceutical industry and cloud computing
RCI	Database management and IT support
McAfee	Anti-virus and intrusion prevention software development

To cater to the above offices, the business park provides several additional amenities, including: two multi-cuisine food courts; banks; convenience shops; a Hindu temple and a church; a large open air amphitheatre and several landscaped water bodies and green courts (see Figures 6.4 and 6.5). There is a multi-level underground parking lot for about 7500 cars. For going around within the complex, there is a battery-operated shuttle bus service. Ambulances and fire tenders are also stationed in the complex for 24 hours a day. IT-B-45, a Vice President of a multinational software company, informed when interviewed on 16 February 2011 that, "EGL follows best corporate practice on occupational safety and health standards. Otherwise we wouldn't have opened shop here".

Figure 6.4 Church inside EGL Business Park [*Source*: Author]

The EGL business park provides a high level of security infrastructure. The whole complex is surrounded by a high perimeter wall. Access is restricted through two manned security gates. Both the gates are also provided with motorised traffic spikes, to shred tires of intruder vehicles. Entry of visitors is only through prior appointment. There is a security control room for 24×7 camera monitoring. Apart from this overall campus security, each building has its own bar-coded security. According to RE-B-48,

Figure 6.5 Recreation space in EGL Business Park [*Source*: Author]

> Security infrastructure is the key which helps us to win the trust of our corporate clients. We've some of the best known companies in the world located in our premises. There are so many expats working here. They are very sensitive on security issues. (Interview: 16 February 2011).

The upper floors of the office towers in the EGL complex provide a sweeping panorama of vast open spaces, which is a rare luxury in a fast-growing Indian metropolis. The view includes the KGA golf course, HAL airport tarmac, and extending over the small cluster of Challaghatta village settlements, stretches all the way to Bellandur Kere, Bangalore's largest lake. The presence of the airport prevented high-rise buildings in the vicinity till the EGL came up. But development of the prestigious business park and closing down of the airport has increased real estate pressure on the Challaghatta village area and also on Domlur on the opposite side of the Ring Road.

A large number of shops and commercial developments have come up in the Domlur side, which until recently was a middle-class residential neighbourhood. These changes are particularly visible along the Ring Road. Expensive restaurants like TGIF (Thank God It's Friday), trendy bars, cafe, music shops and other retail shops are coming up along the ground floor, while the upper floors are getting converted to small offices and service establishments. LC-B-44 (local councillor and owner of an electronic goods shop) appeared upbeat,

> Coming up of the EGL Park and other IT offices in Koramangala and Indira Nagar have helped us. Earlier this was only a residential area. But now it is becoming a fashionable commercial area. Property prices have increased more than ten times in last 10 years. The problem is traffic and finding parking space. Otherwise, it is a great location. (Interview: LC-B-65, 24 January 2012)

While Domlur had long been an established urban neighbourhood, the southern side of the Ring Road had been mainly rural, except for the HAL Airport. Land in this area was mainly used for cultivation of vegetables like brinjal, peas and tomatoes. But development pressures have now converted Chelarghatta village to a lower-middle income residential neighbourhood. The village residents have informally added extra floors, converting single-storied houses to three-storied tenements, renting flats to people working in EGL and other offices. A former postal clerk and part-time vegetable farmer, who sold his land to EGL and now earns his living through house renting informed,

> Land prices in this area started going up from the mid-1990s with all these fancy IT offices coming up. Prices jumped three, four times. My brother and I jointly had about 3.5 acres of land. We decided to sell off, as the money that we were earning by cultivating tomato and brinjal were very less. Our children were also not interested in farming. They are educated and want to do only desk job. Working in the field is tough, younger generation want the easy way out. But in retrospect I think, I should have waited bit more. I wanted to, but my brother was in a hurry. Now land price here is INR 12000 to 15000 per sq ft (about USD 24 to 30 per sq m) but those days it was less than INR 150 per sq ft (about USD 0.30 per sq m). (Interview: LC-B-66a, 24January 2012)

The major problem for Chelarghatta is access. Construction of the EGL business park has blocked the front part of the village and it is now accessible only through a narrow winding road running along the business park. LC-B-66(b), a lawyer and an original resident complained,

> Our access has become very difficult. The EGL Road is narrow and one side is always parked with cars. They don't have visitor parking. All visitor cars are parked on the road. It is difficult for two cars to pass side by side. The problem is particularly acute during morning and evening rush hours when the chartered buses come to drop and pick up EGL employees. About thirty buses come daily and that time it is impossible to go out. We have told this to EGL, but they don't listen. (Interview: LC-B-66b, 24 January 2012)

LC-B-66(a), the former postal employee turned landlord, concurred,

> Because of narrow road property prices are not going up. I get only INR 9000 to 10000 (about USD 36 to 40) a month for a 1000 sq ft (90 sq m) three-room set (a unit with bed rooms and a living room). But in Domlur it is more than double. (Interview 24 January 2012).

LC-B-66(c), a third resident, a tenant originally from distant Manipur in Northeastern India, and working in the EGL complex as a receptionist, blamed the civic authorities.

> It is all BDA's fault. They have blocked a long stretch of the Ring Road for underground pipe works for more than one year. So where can the visitor's park? We can only allow cars with EGL parking stickers to park. There had been so many cases of car bombs. How can we take the risk? They (BDA) should have planned for this. (Interview 24 January 2012).

On the whole, it appears that the development of the EGL Park has generated several downstream economic opportunities and improved the living conditions of the local residents. But civic facilities have worsened and their requirements are being ignored by the parastatal agencies. The next section looks at the roles of various stakeholders in the transformation of Bangalore's fringe areas.

6.6   Stakeholders in transformation of the urban fringe

6.6.1   Role of state and local government

Karnataka government's proactive policies have played a pivotal role in sustaining Bangalore's position as India's pre-eminent IT and biotech services hub. As discussed in Section 6.2, the Karnataka government took the lead amongst the Indian states in articulating a vision for supporting the IT-ITES sector by pioneering policies like the Karnataka IT Policy (1997) and the Millennium IT Policy. The state agencies showed similar dynamism by making available land to meet the spatial demands of the sector.

Since the late 1990s, deterioration of Bangalore's physical infrastructure due to exponential growth over the decade became an issue of concern. Karnataka started facing increasing challenges in retaining the footloose IT outsourcing sector from Andhra Pradesh (and other states) offering better fiscal incentives and better physical infrastructure. In response, the Karnataka government adopted a two-pronged strategy. Firstly, it started developing alternative growth centres in the smaller cities in the state. Secondly, it entered into partnership with the IT corporate sector and civil society, to improve the competitiveness of Bangalore. Inclusion of the non-state actors like BATF and ABIDe has brought in greater synergy between the economic objectives (that is to retain Bangalore's lead in IT, biotech and knowledge economy sectors) and its manifestation at the city-level master plan, through arrangement of production and consumption spaces.

Initial impetus for Bangalore's peripheral expansion to accommodate the spatial demands of the new economy, was laid by the state government itself. KEONICS, a Karnataka government enterprise, laid the foundation of India's first IT business park by developing Electronics City over 1.3 sq km of land at the southern fringe of Bangalore. Land for the project was directly acquired by the state under the Land Acquisition Act in 1978, informed PL-B-47, a top official of KEONICS, when interviewed on 15 February 2011. The original intent of KEONICS was to develop the area as an electronics hardware manufacturing zone, but it was not successful. Later on it persuaded the national government's Department of Electronics to establish advanced satellite communication infrastructure, which encouraged software and other IT services exporting companies to locate there. It is a self-contained mini city, having a large number of offices, management institutes, residential and commercial facilities. Big names like Infosys, Wipro, Hewlett Packard, Bosch and Siemens established their own campuses within the Electronics City, which subsequently set the trend for the independent suburban business park model for the IT-ITES sector in India (Aranya

2008). The development of Electronics City exemplifies the partnership between state and national government agencies, which paved the way for attracting private investments. It is now managed as a cooperative by the organisations operating from there.

Similarly, formations of IT hubs at the northern and eastern flanks of Bangalore were also initiated by the state government, acting in tandem with the corporate sector and the national government. The ITPL project was conceptualised in 1992 through a bilateral cooperation agreement between the then Prime Minister of India P. V. Narasimha Rao and the Prime Minister of Singapore Goh Chok Tong. About 28 hectares of land for the project was acquired by the Karnataka Industrial Areas Development Board (KIADB). The project was developed and managed by Ascendas, a Singapore-based property developer. Like the Embassy Golf Links, ITPL is also a premium category business park. According to RE-B-44, Director at the Bangalore office of Jones Lang LaSalle,

> Development of the eastern fringe of Bangalore took-off with the launching of ITPL (International Technology Park Ltd). ITPL and EGL are like two anchors at either end and spurred the growth of a whole range of IT business parks, SEZs and independent office developments at Whitefield, Surjapur Road and Outer Ring Road, stretching all the way up to Koramangala. (Interview: 11 February 2011)

Bangalore's third and newest IT hub has started forming at Devanahalli near the new Bangalore International Airport (BIAL), about 40 km north of the CBD. Just like ITPL, land for development of the BIAL airport and the adjoining Bangalore Aerospace Park spread over 398 hectares of land (including a 102 hectare SEZ) was acquired by the KIADB. The state government holds minority equity stakes in these projects (Bangalore Aerospace Park 2012).

As the ITPL project spurred development of the eastern fringe, development of the airport and adjoining areas by the state government has a catalytic effect in attracting private real estate development at the northern fringe of Bangalore. A large number of office parks, educational institutes, shopping malls and gated apartment complexes are coming up, including Manyata Embassy Business Park, spread over 45 hectares of land, one of India's largest IT-ITES SEZ projects, developed by the Embassy Group.

But unlike the projects like Electronic City, ITPL and the Bangalore Aerospace Park where the state government directly acquired the land for setting up of the business park, in the case of Embassy Tech-Zone, Manyata Embassy Business Park and all such privately developed projects, the state is acting as a facilitator rather than direct provider of land. Rural lands are directly purchased by the project developers. The state government then facilitates the legal procedures to convert the land use to set up IT business parks and other usage as discussed in Section 6.5.

If the land is already located in an urban area and earmarked for certain other usage in the Master Plan, such as residential or industrial, the state IT policy enables the conversion to IT business parks (including SEZ), as it has overriding power over the local zoning regulations (Government of Karnataka 2000). But if the land is 'agricultural' then it first has to be converted to 'non-agricultural' zoning—a cumbersome procedure in most Indian states. In this context, the Karnataka government's move in 1999 to simplify the land use conversion procedure, paid rich dividends. As RE-B-44 put it,

> Karnataka acted at the right time. Simplification of land conversion procedure ensured land supply to meet economic demand and spurred the land market. A large number of IT offices and tech-parks have come up through private venture, like EGL. Otherwise these investments would have gone to Hyderabad or Chennai. (Interview: 11 February 2011)

While the Karnataka government's enabling policy measures helped to open up newer production and consumption spaces for the IT-related services, by expanding the footprint of Bangalore towards the peri-urban fringe, it has also attracted large-scale speculative real estate investments (Goldman 2011) and corruption in land use conversion as well (Guha 2012). According to RE-B-44, these are an "unavoidable spill-over of economic growth". The political class of Karnataka, the thriving private education industry and the real estate sector have all become part of a huge growth machine (Logan & Molotch 1987) in Indian context, whose engine is the IT-ITES sector.

This growth machine has occasionally hit road blocks and delays in acquiring rural land, settling compensation claims and negotiating with the rural-centric political interests, as exemplified by the case of the Bangalore–Mysore Infrastructure Corridor or the BIAL airport project.

But in the end, the state managed to get its way. High volumes of private investments pouring into Bangalore and the city's rapid expansion testify to this.

This growth was largely due to the fact that the IT-ITES sector opened up profit opportunities through real estate development and setting up of private educational institutes. The Vokkaliga- and Lingayat-dominated, landed-farmer-led political class of Karnataka are directly involved in this process. The big farmers-turned-rural political elites, particularly in fringe areas of Bangalore, have now become stakeholders in the IT-driven spatial expansion of the city, by investing their agricultural surplus into urban property markets and in the education sector. Thus the growth of the IT sector has created an alliance between the urban middle-class-dominated IT corporate sector and the rural elite-dominated political system.

6.6.2   Role of corporate sector

The IT-ITES corporate sector enjoys a high profile and plays a major role in shaping the spatial expansion of Bangalore to generate new production and consumption spaces, through its active participation in the task forces like BATF and ABIDe. As discussed in detail in Section 6.4, the task forces, institutionalising public–private partnership in urban governance, were set up in the first place due to criticisms of Bangalore's deteriorating civic infrastructure by the IT 'czars'. BATF, the first task force, was headed by Infosys CEO, Nandan Nilekani and included representatives from IT, ITES and biotech sectors, in addition to civil society and government departments. ABIDe is also structured along similar lines, though headed by a senior politician.

The influence commanded by the IT services sector over Bangalore's governance issues is unprecedented in the post-colonial history of major Indian cities. Mumbai and Kolkata, with older, more established business houses, had occasionally roped in the corporate sector to support city beautification initiatives, but their influence had never extended into setting strategic planning directions in the way BATF influenced CDP 2005–15 (Benjamin 2010; Ghosh, A 2005) or ABIDe is attempting to do now with Plan Bengaluru 2020 or the Regional Governance Bill. In Bangalore itself, there had been corporate houses, which had been rooted in the city for nearly one hundred years, such as United Breweries and

Binny's Textiles (Nair 2005). But these old-economy-linked concerns never enjoyed the power and influence that the IT sector does today.

The enhanced influence of the IT sector is certainly not due to the number of people it employs. After all, the 500,000 people who are directly employed by the sector is far smaller than the textile sector (Benjamin 2010). It is partly linked to the IT sector's economic contribution, but more importantly to its global image. It is due to the growth of the IT outsourcing industry that brought international attention to Bangalore. As the head of Bangalore's oldest architectural firm and a founder member of BATF, observed,

> Growth of the IT sector is the biggest success story of India's economic liberalisation and Bangalore is its most visible image. Bangalore and IT have become synonymous, in the global media. It is the most visible symbol of new India. (Interview: RE-B-40, 9 February 2011)

This globalised image of the IT-ITES sector, constantly circulated by the business press and satellite TV channels, and its association with the high-tech and knowledge economy, has a strong influence on India's urban middle class. The growth of the IT outsourcing industry, and the new opportunities it has brought about for career advancement, foreign travel and a high-quality domestic work environment (as in Embassy Golf Links Business Park) fired the imagination of educated urban Indians as we discussed in Chapter 5. To a great extent, the emergence of the new Indian urban middle class is directly linked with the growth of the globalised IT services sector. Consequently, the urban middle class is the most vocal supporter of policies favouring IT-ITES services and other policies which support economic globalisation. While this IT-led future imagination cuts across the whole Indian middle class, it is in Bangalore that it finds maximum support from the political class. Compared to all other Indian cities, educated middle-class citizenry wield greater power in Bangalore. As academic Balaji Parthasarathy mentioned, "Middleclass is much stronger in Bangalore than elsewhere in India. It has a cosmopolitan character, which allows educated middle class from elsewhere in India to gravitate towards Bangalore". (Interview: 8 February 2011)

From the days of the Mysore royalty, Bangalore deliberately privileged advanced learning and knowledge. The middle class dominated the planners' imagination of the city (Nair 2005). It is this middle class domination which enabled the IT corporate sector to play such a strong role in urban governance, and in recent times, it found its most vocal proponent in S.M. Krishna, when he became the chief minister in 1999. RE-B-40, prominent architect and part of the city's establishment observed,

> At last we found a person like us. A sophisticated and educated politician, who would listen to the voice of the modern educated people—about the city—not just the villages. He understood the needs of Bangalore in the global age and formed the task force (BATF) to accomplish the task, which the government alone is not capable of doing. (Interview: RE-B-40, 11 February 2011).

Since then, the corporate sector has sought to transform Bangalore as a 'modern' and 'global' city, as the image of the new India through new experiments in urban governance, an opportunity which it is unlikely to find in any other Indian city.

6.6.3   Role of civil society and community organisations

While it is difficult to establish any direct relationship between the civil society groups and Bangalore's urban spatial expansion, the civil society groups do enjoy a high profile in the overall urban governance framework of the city. This may be attributed to the long established tradition of debates in local council and the essentially middle class character of Bangalore. The Janata Party government of the early 1980s took pioneering steps in ensuring participatory governance by empowering local bodies and encouraging debates (Guha 2012; Kadekodi, Kanbur & Rao 2007). In recent times this translated into a high degree of civil society activism in urban governance. Academic Balaji Parthasarathy also concurred with this view. As he put it,

> Bangalore has a long culture civil society activism over heritage conservation and to save the natural environment, like parks and lakes. There is strong educated middle class base here. So these issues are more popular here than other big cities. (Interview: 8 Feb 2011)

In recent years, the civil society groups have expanded their activities beyond natural and built heritage conservation issues and started to address wider issues in urban governance. There are NGOs like CIVIC and Janaagraha, which are actively engaged in policy research and activism for greater implementation of participatory planning practices, as prescribed under the 74th Constitutional Amendment Act. For example, CIVIC have launched a public awareness campaign about the need for devolution of power from the Karnataka state government to the Bangalore city government. Janaagraha has gained national prominence for suggesting the formation of sub-municipal level units like ward councils and neighbourhood-level area councils to better channelise voices of urban residents in the political forums and thus expand the scope for public participation.

The NGOs of Bangalore regularly organise seminars and workshops—sometime in association with the civic agencies—to discuss the city's urban future. Even while opposing the moves of the government, the civil society activists have confined themselves to submitting petitions and organising public awareness campaign through electronic and print media and not taken the routes of direct obstruction or street agitations. According to the director of CIVIC,

> Probably, we in Bangalore debate more than any other Indian city over planning issues. We had been trying to raise awareness amongst the people about urban issues by organising seminars and workshops. We try to bring representatives from BDA and other planning agencies and the response is encouraging. People at least the middleclass has started taking interest. (Interview: CS-B-35, 7 February 2011).

The urban governance mechanism of Bangalore has institutionalised the participation of civil society groups, by forming task forces like BATF and ABIDe. BATF included Ramesh Ramanathan, director of Janaagraha. Similarly, ABIDe also includes Anita Reddy of AVAS, another prominent NGO. Both the task forces also included well-known local academics. Some of these forces, for instance PL-B-42, have actively pushed for expanding the spatial limits of the city, through their advocacy of the Regional Governance Bill, as discussed in Section 6.4.

Most of the civil society organisations that are not formally part of the BATF or ABIDe, while generally supportive of the IT sector, consider its link with the real estate sector to be a major cause of concern. Commenting on the rapid expansion of Bangalore into the peri-urban areas during interview on 7 February 2011, CS-B-35 observed that "Karnataka government had provided lot of incentives to the IT sector and they created lot of growth opportunities. But slowly the distinction between IT and real estate is getting blurred". CS-B-43, head of another NGO, was more forthright, as she said,

> IT is being used as a facade. More and more (*agricultural*) land is being converted in the name of setting up IT SEZ and business parks. How much percentage of the land is actually being used for IT and how much are getting into simple real estate market? Nobody knows. (Interview: 11 February 2011)

When asked about the lack of any major protests or agitations in Bangalore over the land acquisition issue, as compared to West Bengal, she blamed the prevailing political culture of the state: "Politicians of all parties are involved in this (real estate). Much of the land in the rural areas of Bangalore is owned by them. That's why they can't launch strong protests" (Interview: CS-B-43, 11 February 2011). In the absence of proper debate in the legislative chambers over the urban governance issues, the civil society groups in Bangalore have taken upon themselves the task of voicing these concerns about the rapidly changing urban landscape.

6.6.4   Characteristics of the governing regime

Based on the role of the different stakeholders in the transformation of the peri-urban landscape of Bangalore discussed above, the following section identifies the main characteristics of the local governance regime, using DiGaetano and Strom's (2003) framework.

- *Governing logic* – In the case of Bangalore the governing logic is a combination of 'exclusionary negotiations' and 'particularistic personalised exchange'. The state bureaucracy and higher echelons of the political leadership have a long tradition of supporting higher education and modern technological development. In recent times they have privileged high-tech and knowledge-intensive development. They are also acutely conscious of retaining Karnataka's leading position in garnering knowledge economy investments. IT-ITES (also biotech and aerospace) have brought global name recognition for Bangalore and thus are placed on a high pedestal compared to more labour-intensive low visibility industries. However, growth of the IT sector has also opened up avenues for direct personal gain for a section of the state's political class. Growth in the IT services is creating more opportunities for speculative real estate development and the private education industry—the sectors in which the state's rural rich-led political elites are deeply involved. Consequently, Bangalore has seen huge rise in land-related corruption cases.

- *Governing relations* – Governing relations are based on consensus and also reciprocity. Faced with threats of regional economic competition and capital flight, the top leadership of the state has formed a partnership with the IT-ITES corporate sector and civil society elites to restructure the governance arrangements of Bangalore, improve infrastructure and also to generate new growth spaces. There is an attempt to turn Bangalore into a 'world class' city through a compact between the higher echelons of the state bureaucracy, top political leadership, the IT-ITES corporate sector and civil society elites. In this process, the IT industry has come to be seen as a principal cog in an economic growth machine. This has helped to mobilise support from the political class in the state, as the IT sector has directly benefitted a large number of the politicians by generating demand for additional real estate and education, in which they are commercially involved. However, in the process, it has run into occasional road-blocks in land acquisition and resettlement measures. Several civil society activists, when interviewed (between 7 and 13 February 2011) claimed that powerful political families of Karnataka own vast land tracts around Bangalore, and often development plans are modified to suit rent-seeking objectives of these political elites. Planning in Bangalore has co-opted the politically powerful big farmers for spatial expansion to generate production and consumption spaces for IT-driven economic growth. Thus, growth in Bangalore is driven by a strong alliance between the political elites, IT corporate sector, upper echelons of the state bureaucracy and civil society elites.

- *Key decision makers* – Political support of the state chief ministers and the strong bureaucratic machinery of the state have played crucial roles in furthering development of the IT-ITES sector. However, instead of acting in a top–down fashion, the administrative leadership of the state has included the non-state actors in corporate and civil society in the governance network. The task force system has created opportunities for decision making through deliberations amongst the elites. However, at the same time, this excluded the urban poor and even the political leaders of the elected local government.

• *Political objectives* – The dominant political objective in Bangalore is to turn the city into a global hub in the knowledge economy and sustain its leadership position in India, in this area. The spin-off benefits of this growth objective have created an alliance between the rural-rich led political system and the educated urban middle-class-led economic system. Politics in Karnataka is polarised along caste lines, in which landed Lingayat and Vokkaliga agricultural lobbies are dominant. A big section of this rural-elite has aligned with the middle class to create new production and consumption space for an IT-led new economy in the fringe areas of Bangalore. Growth in IT has created new investment opportunities and scope for direct material gains for these rural political elites. This in turn has led to formation of an alliance between the rural elites and the urban middle class. Secondly, growth in the IT sector most directly benefits the educated upper and middle-class people living in big cities like Bangalore. Thus, the support to the IT sector has brought two apparently opposing groups (powerful rural rich and urban middle class) into an alliance.

Overall, the characteristics of the local governing regime may be termed as 'corporatist'. But at the same time there are signs of it turning towards 'clientelistic'—with the political elites increasingly benefitting from the land-related transactions. This corporatist nature of the governing regime is resulting in rapid expansion of Bangalore's urban footprint through the planning machinery, which is ultimately leading towards hyper-urbanisation at a regional scale requiring new governance arrangements.

Table 6.2 contains a synopsis of Bangalore's urban governance characteristics discussed above, following DiGaetano and Strom's framework.

Table 6.2 Characteristics of Bangalore's urban governance regime
[*Source*: Compiled by author based on DiGaetano and Strom's framework]

Parameters	Bangalore's urban governance characteristics
Governing logic	Combination of 'exclusionary negotiations' and 'particularistic personalised exchange'.
	Long tradition of supporting higher education and technology-led development. This translated into support for the IT and other knowledge economy sectors.
	But in recent years close link has developed between the IT-led growth machine and rural land conversion process.
Governing relations	Governing relations are based on consensus and also reciprocity.
	Close cooperation between the political leadership, IT-corporate sector and civil society elites, to turn the city towards a global hub in knowledge economy
Key decision makers	Elite task force consisting of the political, bureaucratic, corporate and civil society elites.
	Particularly, strong collaboration between the state bureaucracy and the IT-corporate sector. State-level political and civil society actors have been co-opted into this compact.
	However the elitist decision-making system excludes the urban poor and also the lower, municipal-level politicians.
Political objectives	To turn Bangalore into a global hub in the knowledge economy.
	The spin-off benefits, in the form of land development has created an alliance between the rural-rich driven political system and educated urban middle-class-led economic system

6.7   Summary of case study findings

This chapter analysed how the emergence of Bangalore as a globally acknowledged centre of internationalised IT services is transforming its urban development pattern and triggering rapid spatial expansion. There is a strong compact between the state's political leadership, upper echelons of the bureaucracy, IT corporate executives and civil society elites in transforming Bangalore as a knowledge-economy-driven 'world class' city.

Karnataka's governing regime, which is facilitating growth of the IT sector, is essentially 'corporatist' in character. The state has a long legacy of promoting higher education and has a technology-led development philosophy (Kadekodi, Kanbur & Rao 2007). Since the post-1990s period, this translated into extensive support for IT services. Proactive policies of the state government helped it to retain Bangalore's leadership position as the pre-eminent knowledge economy hub of India, in the face of growing competition from other Indian cities. In doing so, the state has expanded the urban governance framework and formed partnerships with the non-state actors in for-profit and non-profit sectors.

Urban policy framing in Bangalore largely revolves around middle-class concerns. Its position in the global knowledge economy has come to dominate the planners' imagination of the city. The middle-class-led planning machinery has created opportunities for development of production and consumption spaces for the IT-services-driven new economy, by facilitating rapid expansion of Bangalore's urban footprint into its rural hinterland. This urban expansion process occasionally encountered stiff opposition from the rural population and strong rural–urban dichotomies which characterise the political culture of Karnataka (and most other Indian states).

However, despite occasional delays and bottlenecks which slowed down iconic projects, by and large, the IT-driven urban growth process has continued unabated. This has been possible because the growth in the IT sector has created spin-off benefits for the rural rich in the fringe areas of Bangalore, by increasing land values. From 1999 onwards, simplification of procedures for conversion of agricultural land for development of IT business parks and periodic expansion of the city's territorial limits, not only enabled timely land supply to meet the demands of the industry, but also created greater opportunities for commoditisation of land. A rapid increase in land prices has enabled the rural rich to cash in and convert the proceeds into speculative real estate investments. Arguably, this has benefitted a large section of the political elites. The process of Bangalore's spatial expansion is thus happening through an alliance between the urban middle-class-dominated IT services economy and the rural rich-dominated political system.

Case study II: National Capital Region IT cluster

7.1   Introduction

This chapter contains a case study about the IT clusters in the extended metropolitan region of Delhi, called the National Capital Region (NCR). As previously discussed under Chapter 1, within the NCR belt, IT companies are clustered in three locations, falling under the administrative domains of three different state governments, which are: Delhi (Delhi NCT), Gurgaon (Haryana) and Noida (Uttar Pradesh). However Gurgaon, located at the southern fringe of Delhi, has not only the largest concentration of IT firms in the region, but has emerged as the leading location for the ITES-BPO segment nationally. It has therefore been selected as the case study location.

Geography is a hugely important factor in the development of Gurgaon. Its economic growth, to a large extent, is due to its proximity to Delhi, but it is being mediated through the political and administrative machinery of Haryana, the state under which it formally belongs. Section 7.2 traces the developmental trajectory of the knowledge economy in Delhi and its eventual spill-over into the suburban satellite towns like Gurgaon. Section 7.3 provides a brief overview about the local political-economic culture. Section 7.4 then takes up the spatial implications of the IT-ITES industry and the urban development pattern of Gurgaon. Section 7.5 includes detailed illustrative examples of one IT business park in Gurgaon. Section 7.6 then discusses the roles of various stakeholders associated with the process of urban transformation of Gurgaon and then analyses the characteristics of the local governing regime through the lens of DiGaetano and Strom's (2003) framework. Section 7.7 concludes the chapter through a summary.

7.2   Development of IT services sector

As may be seen from Table 5.1 in Chapter 5, the National Capital Region is India's second largest IT services cluster, in terms of export earnings, number of operating companies in the sector and number of employees. However, unlike Bangalore which has large concentrations of software companies, the NCR belt is known as a stronghold for call-centres, BPOs and engineering companies and is the leading location in India for the ITES segment (NASSCOM & A.T.Kearney 2009).

The growth of the engineering services outsourcing business in the NCR area bears much similarity to the public-sector-led growth trajectory of Bangalore. During the 1950s and 1960s a large number of power plants, steel, petro-chemical and other heavy industrial and infrastructure projects were started all over India through the public sector, under Nehru's modernisation drive. In most cases these big projects were undertaken through foreign technical collaboration. However, to coordinate the technical aspects of these projects, manage the timelines, award tenders, negotiate with foreign counterparts and eventually to indigenise the technical knowledge, several large public sector engineering organisations were established. For most of these ventures, engineering offices, dealing with project management, procurement and contractual matters were located in Delhi for ease of coordination with the concerned ministry in the Government of India (Interview: PL-D-29, 26 January 2011). Thus, project management and engineering coordination functions of large public sector conglomerates like the National Thermal Power Corporation (NTPC) and Bharat Heavy Electricals Ltd. (BHEL) were all located in Delhi, even though their production and operation networks were spread all over the country.

This centralisation process gained further momentum during the time of Indira Gandhi (1965–77, 80–84), as more and more industrial sectors came under the orbit of governmental control (Interview: PL-D-29, 26 January 2011). In the course of time, Kolkata- and Mumbai-based consulting companies, which provided detailed engineering design, also opened major branch offices in Delhi, for better coordination of design issues with their clients, as public sector projects gradually gained importance in the developmental state era. Centralising tendencies of the national government changed the character of Delhi, from being a sleepy administrative capital in the 1940s to a major economic centre by the 1980s. Hosting of mega events like the Asian Games in 1982 and Commonwealth Games in 2010, which required building of several new roads, flyovers, stadiums, hotels and other urban infrastructure projects further added to Delhi's economic attractiveness. Growth of employment opportunities was matched by a concurrent rise in educational opportunities and several well-known tertiary institutions were located in the city.

The pull factors through expansion in economic and educational opportunities in Delhi ran concurrently with the push factors of economic decline in several north Indian states during the 1980s, turning Delhi into a catchment for migrants from a vast region. In this decade, terrorist violence peaked in Punjab and Jammu and Kashmir, while the economies of the densely populated north Indian states like Uttar Pradesh, Bihar and West Bengal deteriorated. The population growth rate of Delhi started accelerating from the 1980s. During the census decade 1981–91, the city recorded a high decadal growth rate of 46.9 percent, which increased to 51.9 percent during census decade 1991–2001 and then further increased to 86.9 percent during the census decade 2001–11—the fastest amongst the metropolitan regions of India (Census 2011).

By the kick-off stage of India's economic liberalisation in 1991, Delhi had turned into the most attractive economic magnet in the whole of northern India for educated youth, leaving Kolkata far behind. The post-liberalisation decades have further intensified the NCR area's economic gravitational pull. Thus, vast numbers of youth from the distant northeastern states now flock to Delhi and Gurgaon for call-centre and BPO jobs (McDuie-Ra 2012). Availability of large educated human resources encouraged Western MNCs to locate their outsourcing offices in the Delhi–NCR area. These also included several top of the line global engineering companies like Bechtel and Flour Daniel of the USA, Lurgi of Germany, and ABB of Switzerland.

One of the pioneers of this trend was the German electrical engineering giant Siemens. While Siemens had been operating and manufacturing in India since the 1920s, it took a major step in 1998 by setting up its global competence centre for design of thermal power plants in Gurgaon. For this, Siemens opened a 100 percent subsidiary, called Siemens Power Engineering Pvt. Ltd. (SPEL). Starting-off with just 40 engineers in 1998, SPEL now has over 600 engineers and provides 'plant layout engineering' for projects handled by Siemens globally, while overall coordination with client, vendors and construction site are handled from Germany. Largely similar working strategies are followed by other firms outsourcing engineering design to India. A top executive of Siemens PG, who was closely associated in setting up of

SPEL, explained the rationale behind the choice of the NCR when interviewed,

> When we decided to relocate our global design engineering facility from Kuala Lumpur to India, we had several locations in mind, Bombay, Bangalore, even Goa. Siemens Indian head office is in Bombay, so it was an obvious choice. Bangalore is the head office of Siemens Information Systems, so that was another choice. Then we studied pros and cons of each location in detail. Bombay was too expensive for housing, and difficult to get new employees to locate from other parts of India. Bangalore was good, but we are not so much into software. We needed people with power plant design background. These were available mainly in two places, Delhi, which had companies like NTPC and BHEL, and Calcutta, which has DCL. The final choice was between Delhi and Calcutta, but we ultimately zeroed in on Delhi. We recruited our top managers from NTPC and BHEL, as they have better contract and project management background. They did not want to go to Calcutta. Also, Delhi has got better airport and international schools for the children of the German expatriates. We recruited many junior engineers from DCL Calcutta, who were willing to relocate to Delhi. (Interview: IT-D-16, 11 January 2011)

Along with the highly specialised engineering sector, the NCR area also has the highest concentration of call-centres and general purpose BPO firms in India. The large pool of educated youth from throughout Northern India has turned the NCR into an attractive location for these jobs. The call-centre BPO growth in the region was kick-started with the decision of GE Capital to locate its facility in Gurgaon in 1997. IT-D-19, who was involved in the starting of GE Capital's Gurgaon operations, explained the logic behind the location choice:

> We needed smart young English educated boys and girls for the call-centre business. Till then almost entire outsourcing work was going on from Bangalore, which was mostly related to software development and other hardcore technical things. But we were in voice-calling field, which required real time interaction with customers based in USA, but mostly on simple, non-technical issues, like credit card billing, or ticket booking. We required people with basic education but excellent

communication skills and those who can work at night shifts to match US time zones. So we preferred Delhi over Bangalore. We felt that Delhi girls and boys are better in talking. We also felt that the South Indian accent will also be a big negative factor. Another reason was cultural. We feared that girls in South India would face opposition from home in working at nightshifts. Now of course things have changed. But ten-twelve years back, those were major problems. (Interview: IT-D-19, 12 January 2011)

Taking-off from this lead established by the GE Capital (now hived off as a separate company called Genpact, with Gurgaon as its global headquarters), a large number of call centres and BPOs have opened up in the NCR belt, such as IBM-Daksh (now renamed as IBM Global Services), American Express and British Airways.

Till the 1980s, most public and private companies used to be located within the administrative boundaries of Delhi. However, since then, planning constraints and cheaper real estate have encouraged growth of the suburban townships like Noida and Gurgaon (Maitra 2008). Most public sector companies have tended to locate to Noida (Interview: PL-D-28, 26 January 2011), but the multinational and Indian corporate sector tended to prefer Gurgaon as discussed in the following sections.

7.3   State and local socio-political culture

Haryana is small, but one of the most prosperous states of India, with a per capita GDP of USD 2381, which is much higher than the national average of USD 1329 (The Economist 2012a). Since its formation in 1966 by dividing the state of Punjab, political power in Haryana has changed several times between the Congress party and an opposition alliance led by regional parties like Indian National Lok Dal (INLD) or Haryana Vikas Party (HVP). The Hindu nationalist Bharatiya Janata Party (BJP), which has pockets of influence in the urban areas of the state, often joined such coalitions as a junior partner. Since 2004, the Congress party under the leadership of B.S. Hooda has been in power. But, more than the party labels, politics here is characterised by charismatic leaders who head political dynasties and caste lobbies. INLD is identified with Devi Lal and his son O.P. Chowtala, both former chief ministers of the state. Similarly, Haryana Vikas Party is identified with the family of Bansi Lal who had earlier led Congress governments at the state, but later on fell out with the party's central leadership.

Haryana was at the forefront of the Green Revolution during the 1960s and 1970s, which not only influenced the economic formation of the state, through bumper agricultural productivity and rural prosperity, but also impacted urban and rural socio-political relations, through a strong caste-dominated structure. The political landscape of the state is dominated by the Jats, a conservative, land-owning farming community (Jodhka & Dhar 2003; Yadav 2000). Constituting about 22 percent of the population, the community had held the chief minister's position for 30 of the 45 years of the state's existence. Lower caste Dalits are almost equal to the Jats in numerical terms, but lack political and economic clout (Jodhka & Dhar 2003). Other politically important (and land owning) castes are the Gujjars and Ahirs (Yadavs).

Successive political leaderships of Haryana have sought to project their rustic, son of the soil image. These rural-centric politics have paid rich dividends due to the fact that the state lacked any major urban centre within its jurisdiction (Chatterji 2013b). Even its capital, Chandigarh, is outside the administrative domain of the state. Haryana's largest town, Faridabad, is more commonly recognised as an industrial suburb of Delhi, than as a city in its own right. This sharp rural–urban divide has started getting blurred of late (Kennedy 2012). Haryana's urban population has increased from 24 percent in 1991 to 29 percent in 2001 to 35 percent in 2011 (Census 2011). Rapid growth in recent decades has catapulted Haryana amongst India's most urbanised states, from amongst the most rural. But urbanisation is predominantly concentrated in the Gurgaon, Faridabad and Sonepat districts (see Figure 7.1) which are part of the NCR planning framework. In socio-cultural terms, the state is still considered backward, due to caste-centric politics, a high degree of female foeticide and atrocities against Dalits (Jodhka & Dhar 2003; Yadav 2000).

Haryana played a pioneering role in India, in facilitating the entry of private developers into large-scale urban development through conversion of rural agricultural land from the late 1970s onwards— long before the advent of economic liberalisation on the national stage. The land development policy of the state operates under two legislative frameworks (Chatterji 2013b; Joardar 2006). The Haryana Urban

---

[1] Chandigarh, designed by Le Corbusier, is the joint capital of Haryana and Punjab. It is administered directly by the national government as a Union Territory.

Development (HUD) Act of 1977 empowers the state agencies to acquire agricultural land for developing residential townships and industrial estates, and to contract out development to the private sector. Under the Haryana Development and Regulation of Urban Areas (HDRUA) Act of 1975–76, licences are awarded to big private developers to acquire, assemble and develop a minimum contiguous 100 acres of land. These legislations were initiated by the Congress government headed by Bansi Lal. According to a former Chief Secretary of Haryana,

> Chaudhariji (Bansi Lal) was a moderniser. He realised the need to diversify the economy and reduce dependence on agriculture. But in those days, industrialisation was difficult (due to controls in place). Haryana also doesn't have much mines and minerals. So he put thrust on other options like tourism and housing, which can develop easily because of our proximity to Delhi. But companies like DLF and Ansals also made big efforts. Basically they took the initiative to convince the government that in near future Delhi would feel population pressure and that Haryana will benefit from that. Honestly, nobody of us in the government thought on those lines. (Interview: PL-D-59, 4 January 2012)

Economist Bibek Debroy also credits the lobbying effort and foresight of the big developers in creating the land market of Gurgaon,

> This is largely because of the people like K.P. Singh (DLF Chairman) and Sushil Ansal (Ansal Group Chairman). They had the foresight and realised that Delhi will soon face huge pressure, and that will be a big opportunity for them. They also realised the potential of Gurgaon, which was otherwise a God-forsaken place. Faridabad and Noida (in Uttar Pradesh) were far more important in the 1970s. They took the initiative to convince the Haryana government and are reaping the profits now. (Interview: 21 January 2011).

This early liberalisation initiative of the Haryana government did not, however, attract much public or academic attention in the initial days, as the impacts only began to be felt after two decades—from the mid-1990s, when Gurgaon started growing at an astronomical rate. As Debroy mentioned, it was indeed a huge opportunity for the large real estate companies as they amassed large land banks in the state, particularly in the NCR areas near Delhi. Property development in Haryana received a further boost with the enactment of the SEZ Act by the central government in 2005. Haryana was the first state to enact a matching state-level legislation (Kennedy 2012). Location patterns of these projects indicate complete predominance of the southeast corner of the state, near Delhi. All 47 SEZ projects in the state are located in this region, with Gurgaon district alone accounting for 39 SEZ projects. (Government of India 2012). Being within the extended metropolitan belt of Delhi and part of the National Capital Region framework, the area enjoys better industrial infrastructure, road, rail and air connectivity, access to the market of Delhi and skilled labour supply, compared to the rest of the state, which remains largely rural.

Land development is also the cornerstone of Haryana's IT policy (Government of Haryana 2000), which pledges preferential land allotment for the IT-ITES sector, and liberal land use conversion procedures for the industrial manufacturing units located in urban regions to change to IT offices and SEZs. Most of these projects are being developed by big real estate firms. This property-led growth approach has produced an extremely chaotic and unsustainable urban pattern, but the Haryana brand of market-driven urbanism has increasingly drawn attention across the country for generating rapid urban economic growth, while at the same time ensuring a 'fair' or 'market' price for acquiring rural agricultural land. From mid-2000 onwards, large scale acquisition of agricultural land by the state agencies to facilitate private-sector-led projects had become hugely controversial in India, generating several conflicts. In this scenario, Haryana's neoliberal model, which permits direct purchase of agricultural land by private companies, with minimal state intervention, has become attractive to other state governments (Kennedy 2012).

This is not to suggest that Haryana has been immune to farmer agitations or that there are no resentments in the rural areas over land acquisitions—far from it. Farmers complain of collusion between private developers and state-planning agencies, which artificially lowers land values. It is alleged that in several cases, state agencies issued legal notices for land acquisition, and determined compensation rates. At this stage, private developers stepped in, offering proportionately higher prices, which most farmers accepted as a better option under the 'pressure' of forced acquisition. After the developers purchased a substantial amount of land, the legal notices were withdrawn (Interview: LC-D-28, 31 January, 2011). Local discontent (along with the global financial crisis) delayed and scaled down the ambitious multi-product

SEZ planned by Reliance Industries in association with Haryana State Industrial Infrastructure Development Corporation (HSIIDC), spread over 100 sq km in area spanning across the Gurgaon and Jhajjar districts (District Administration Jhajjar 2011; Kennedy 2012). Narain also observed tensions in several peri-urban villages of Gurgaon over the loss of agricultural land and water resources (Narain 2009).

But the intensity of the protest movements in Gurgaon and elsewhere in Haryana has been at a lower scale compared to other Indian states. Kennedy (2012) attributes this to caste-centric polarisation. The protest movements were led by upper caste landed farmers, belonging to the Jat and Gujjar communities, but excluded the landless Dalit peasants, thus failing to build an effective rural coalition. Additionally, social scientist Madhu Kishwar (Interview: 14 January 2011) pointed out that rapid economic growth in NCR draws in landless rural youth to the urban informal economy. To meet the agricultural labour shortage, Haryana's farmers depend on seasonal migrants from Bihar and eastern Uttar Pradesh. This in turn adds to the complications of organising protests.

Rapid urbanisation and economic growth in the NCR area is gradually blurring the sharp edges of the rural–urban divide in Haryana's polity. The Hooda-led Congress government, which was re-elected a second time, has accelerated urbanisation and industrialisation. A large number of farmers have moved from dependence on the agrarian economy and have become stakeholders in the new urban economy (Kennedy 2012). To create spaces for the new opportunities, brought in by closer integration of the Indian economy with global capital, the landed rural elites of Haryana have forged partnerships with big real estate firms.

From the late 1990s, declining agricultural productivity, an increasing debt burden, aspirations of the younger generations for an urban lifestyle and the lure of money from the private developers, made many of the farmers in the peri-urban areas of the NCR belt sell their land holdings. Several farmers invested their money into retail, transport, construction and property businesses. For instance, the taxi cab and chartered buses serving the BPO companies are run by ex-farmers. Most others invested in the property business, building cheap rental housing and shops in the village areas, which get engulfed due to urban expansion, thus building links with the new economy, a phenomenon most pronounced in Gurgaon.

7.4   Urban development pattern

7.4.1   Location

Gurgaon district (and the town of the same name) of Haryana is located to the south of the Union Territory of Delhi and is just 15 km from Delhi airport. Gurgaon is a part of the National Capital Region, an extended metropolitan planning region which consists of the city of Delhi at its core and the adjoining districts belonging to the neighbouring states (see Figures 7.1 and 7.2). The older part of the town, centring around the rail station had been in existence for a long time. Modern Gurgaon largely grew along the Delhi–Jaipur national highway (NH-8). In 2010, Delhi Metro railway line was extended to Gurgaon.

Figure 7.1 Location map of Gurgaon
[*Source*: http://www.mapsofworld.com (Accessed 9 January 2013)]

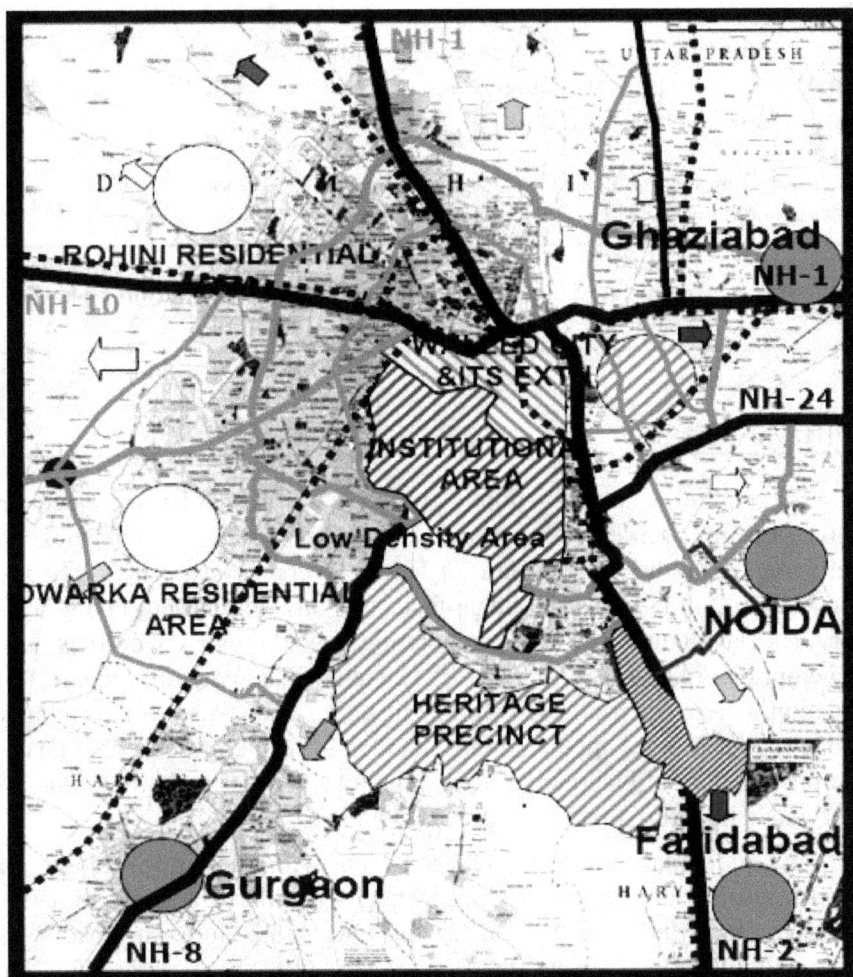

Figure 7.2 Delhi and its satellite cities in the NCR [*Source*: City Development Plan (2006), Government of the National Capital Territory of Delhi]

Gurgaon continued to remain a backward agricultural town until the mid-1980s. Since then it has grown exponentially, not only overtaking other suburban towns, but Delhi itself, in attracting higher-end domestic and international investments. This growth happened in two phases. Between the mid-1980s and the mid-1990s, Gurgaon developed as Delhi's industrial and residential suburb. From then onwards, the growth momentum further picked up, as Gurgaon turned into a major IT-BPO hub. The economic pull of Gurgaon has drawn a large number of migrants. As Table 7.1 shows, between 2001 and 2011, the population of the Gurgaon district increased by almost 74 percent. The urban population increased by a staggering 283 percent, while the formal urban limits also expanded by almost six times.

Table 7.1 Population increase in Gurgaon between 2001 and 2010
[*Source*: Census of India (2011)]

Census year	Population of Gurgaon district	Population of Gurgaon Municipal Area	Decadal growth percent	Urban area (in sq km)
2001	870,539	228,820	73.9	35
2011	1,514,085	876,824	283.2	207

The largely laissez faire growth, however, has created a heterogeneous settlement pattern along with stark deficiencies in delivery of public infrastructure. Three layers of the city's history, rural-agricultural, industrial manufacturing and globalised ITES–BPO services, have come to coexist, generating new claims and conflicts. The development of Gurgaon reflects the tensions of its particular geographic location, where economic growth is happening due to its close proximity to Delhi, but is being mediated through the political culture of Haryana— the push factors of Delhi's restrictive planning process and pull factors of Haryana's liberal regulatory regime (Chatterji 2013b).

The industrial era of Gurgaon began with the establishment of the Maruti-Suzuki automobile plant and its ancillary factories in 1982. Land for the Maruti factory, along the Old-Delhi–Gurgaon Road, was originally allocated during the Emergency (1975–76) period, by the Congress government of Haryana, as it was the pet project of Sanjay Gandhi (son of Indira Gandhi) (Interview: PL-D-59, 4 January 2012). Later on several other factories in diverse fields like auto components, telecommunication equipment, and fashion garments started in Gurgaon. In 1981–82, the DLF Group and Ansal Properties, two big Delhi-based property developers, received licences from the Haryana government to build large private sector residential townships. This led to the development of two pioneering projects: DLF's Qutab Enclave and Ansal's Palam Vihar, bordering Delhi, which began to be occupied from 1991 onwards. Gurgaon's land market, however, hugely benefitted from a concurrent shrinkage of real estate opportunities in Delhi.

Supply and control of urban land within Delhi is closely managed by the Delhi Development Authority, a public sector agency, through a restrictive planning regime. Inspired by the Ford Foundations in the 1960s, the master plans of Delhi contain detailed zoning, land use control and urban design guidelines, with particularly strong restrictions over industrial and commercial usage (Sundaram 2009). But, this rigid land use control mechanism ran into a major crisis during the 1990s, with the proliferation of illegal construction, leading to court cases over environmental degradations and master plan violations. The lengthy legal controversy virtually stopped building activities in Delhi from the mid-1990s, until a revised plan was notified in 2007 (Chatterji 2000, 2003). Supply constraints in Delhi during a vital phase of economic growth stirred the property markets of the suburban towns in the neighbouring states (Chatterji 2007). At this stage, Gurgaon's nearness to Delhi airport and availability of high-quality real estate turned it into a sought-after destination for the business process outsourcing industry. Taking advantage of Haryana's liberal land regime, and cheaper property prices in Gurgaon, big developers who had been amassing land banks in the region started quickly churning out up-scale projects. The absence of a local regulatory regime (in the form of a municipality) further fast-tracked the permits and clearances from friendly parastatal agencies (Debroy & Bhandari 2009).

GE Capital's decision to locate its call-centre facility in 1997 in a DLF business park set the trend for other MNCs to establish branch-platforms in Gurgaon. Almost as a rule, the MNCs operate from leased space in business parks promoted by the property developers, which provide high-quality infrastructure, matching the specifications of the global corporate sector. As already discussed in Section 5.7, leasing of space, rather than direct property ownership, provides them with operational flexibilities in scaling up and down their establishment sizes with the ebbs and flows of the global economy, but also shelters them from the messy dealings of land and property markets. The corporate real estate sector, in this situation, has come to represent global capital as the point of interface between the MNCs and the local state.

However, this private-developer-led model has produced a patchwork quilt development pattern. Unplanned growth at a rapid pace has put severe pressure on Gurgaon's civic infrastructure. Seven to eight hours of power outage is almost a daily occurrence. Up-scale residential enclaves and corporate business parks all provide power back-up through diesel generators, along with good quality internal infrastructure. But the villages abutting the boundary walls of these enclaves are in an abysmal condition due to inadequacies in water supply, sewage and drainage facilities. While the newly extended metro rail has improved connectivity from the commercial core of Gurgaon to Delhi, there is no public transport for inner city commuting within Gurgaon. Corporate firms in Gurgaon regularly operate chartered bus and taxi fleets to transport their employees. For those without a personal vehicle, the only commuting option is to hitch a ride in crowded three-wheeler auto rickshaws. Cycle tracks and pedestrian walkways are practically non-existent.

7.4.2   Institutional structure of urban governance

Planning and developmental responsibilities of Gurgaon are handled by a number of state- and local-level agencies, often with overlapping or conflicting jurisdiction. Management of Gurgaon's urban transformation has suffered due to such multiplicity of agencies and institutional deficiencies. Unlike cities like Bangalore or Kolkata, Gurgaon does not have a metropolitan development authority. Although Gurgaon had been growing extremely rapidly since the early 1990s, it did not have any elected municipal body until 2008. Before 2008, the urban limits of Gurgaon were restricted to an area of only about 37 sq km, which mainly covered the old town area around the railway station. Thus, almost the entire new development, IT business parks, SEZ, posh apartment complexes, shopping malls and hotels that have come up in the post-1990s construction boom, have happened in areas which were classified as 'rural' and under the jurisdictions of local panchayets (rural council). A new Municipal Corporation was constituted in 2008 and held its first election in May 2011. However, like most other elected urban local governments in India, the Municipal Corporation of Gurgaon (MCG) has extremely restricted operational power and technical capacity.

Planning responsibilities for Gurgaon are handled by the Haryana government's Department of Town and Country Planning (DTP) which is based in Chandigarh, the state capital. In 2008, DTP launched the Gurgaon–Manesar Master Plan 2021. This is primarily a land use control guideline and discusses making land available for globalisation-driven economic growth through public–private partnership. The plan's vision statement reads as follows:

> The Haryana Urban Development Authority in public sector and licensed colonizers in private sector through Town and Country Planning have played a prime role in achieving planned development in Gurgaon–Manesar Urban Complex. The Haryana Urban Development Authority and the licensed colonizers collectively have developed about 8000 hectares of land for residential, commercial, institutional and industrial purposes to meet the demand of the public. The areas of Gurgaon–Manesar Urban Complex which have so far been developed in public and private sector including existing town and village *abadis* would accommodate 22 lacs (2.2 million) population. In order to cater the future demand of Gurgaon–Manesar Urban Complex an additional 21,733 hectares has been added in the form of urbanisable area for the said complex to accommodate 15 lacs (1.5 million) additional population. Thus the total urbanisable area of Gurgaon–Manesar Urban Complex would accommodate 37 lacs (3.7 million) population by 2021 AD. (Department of Town and Country Planning 2007, p.3)

Neither environmental sustainability nor social equity finds any mention in this planning document focused on bringing economic growth through public–private partnership. Yet this joint mode of city building suffered considerable handicaps due to lack of coordination—in phasing of development by different public and private agencies; and delivering basic infrastructure services, like water supply, power and sewage disposal. Several prominent local architects stated during a seminar on 6 January 2011, that the DTP was entrusted with responsibility for ensuring coordinated development. But land configurations and project phasing by the private developers tended to follow the logic of land assembling through negotiations with local farmers, rather than the phases prescribed by the DTP's Master Plan. This in turn has created difficulties for routing of trunk utilities (Biswas 2006). The absence of a strong locally based planning agency had further compounded the problems of development coordination. A number of state and local agencies are involved in plan implementation, each with piecemeal jurisdiction. Haryana Urban Development Authority (HUDA), a state-level agency, having a local office, is responsible for developing roads and provision of water supply, sewerage and drainage in the newer parts of the city, which includes master planned sectors directly developed by HUDA and the gated enclaves, developed by the private builders (colonisers).

For private enclaves, the developers provide internal services and pay External Development Charges to HUDA, for trunk services linkage. The industrial estates, like Udyog Vihar, are under the Haryana State Industrial Infrastructure Development Corporation (HSIIDC). The older part of the town is directly under the control of the municipality, while state government's Public Works Department (PWD) is in charge of providing roads and services. The village areas have traditionally been under the jurisdiction of the local panchayets.

In this context, formation of the Municipal Corporation of Gurgaon (MCG) in 2008, covering an extended area of 207 sq km, generated much hope amongst a large section of the urban and rural population alike (Chatterji 2013b). The first election of the MCG was held in May 2011. It was anticipated that the MCG would become the overarching body for coordination of the developmental activities and become a platform for negotiation between the diverse stakeholders. But inadequate devolution of power by the state government has come in the way of effective functioning of the nascent municipal body. While the councillors of the MCG have been elected from an extended jurisdiction covering 207 sq km, their real authority is extremely limited. Only old Gurgaon (about 37 sq km), which was earlier under the Municipal Committee, and 37 village pockets which were earlier under panchayets, are now under the direct control of the MCG, informed PL-D-60, the Chief Engineer of MCG (Interview: 5 January 2012). Vast new developments—all HUDA sectors, HSIDC industrial estates, privately developed residential enclaves, and business parks—are effectively out of bounds for the MCG (Chatterji 2013b). CS-D-56, one of the newly elected councillors, expressed her difficulties, with the fractured jurisdiction.

> With election of the MCG, we expected that the HUDA areas and the private enclaves will come under the MCG's control, so that we can integrate the services. But forget about the private housing colonies and the SEZs, not even the HUDA sectors are given to us. People in these areas have elected us, when they come to us with complaints, how do we respond? (Interview: 24 December 2011)

Till now, there has been neither any time frame, nor any agreement between the two bodies on how to account for the civil works undertaken so far, and the extent of pending tasks. Thus, even after assuming office, the elected councillors are unable to deliver and are getting discredited. The local agencies, the municipal committee and village panchayets have been the weakest entities in Gurgaon's transitional journey, lacking financial, technical and legal capacity for urban management (Chatterji 2013b). Parastatal agencies like HUDA and HSIIDC, which have technical or financial capabilities, tended to act more like private entrepreneurs, in parcelling out new land developments, rather than enforcing overarching development controls or coordinating delivery of public services.

7.5   Illustrated case study: DLF IT SEZ Silokhera

The DLF IT SEZ Silokhera, as the name suggests, is developed by the DLF Group, the premier real estate company, which has developed much of Gurgaon. The architect for the project is Design Plus, a well-known Delhi-based practice. Figure 7.4 shows a view of the project.

Spread over 14.97 hectares of land, the DLF IT SEZ Silokhera is located in Sector 30 of Gurgaon. It is just off NH-8, the main connecting road between Delhi and Gurgaon and about 10 minutes drive from the Delhi–Haryana border. It is also about 5 km away from the international terminal and about 10 km from the domestic terminal of Delhi's IGI airport. On the northern edge of the project is an office block entirely occupied by IBM. On the southern edge is DLF Star Mall, one of the largest air-conditioned shopping malls of Gurgaon, built by the same developer. To the rear of the project site is the Silokhera Village. Figure 7.3 shows the location map for the project.

The Silokhera SEZ includes 481,000 sq m of office space in five buildings. Construction work for the project began in 2007 and was scheduled for completion by 2009. However, the economic slowdown due to the GFC from 2008 onwards has impacted the schedule. The construction pace has been reduced. Thus by 2011 only two blocks were fully completed while the third building was in a partial stage of completion. Construction of two other blocks had been deferred due to a GFC-related slump in demand. The site plan indicates that all the buildings are arranged around a landscaped open court. The original plan was to build a two-level underground parking structure below the open court. However, slackening of demand has ruled this out for the time being. Now there are parking provisions for 1200 cars in the basements of the constructed buildings. Additionally, there is a health club with a gymnasium.

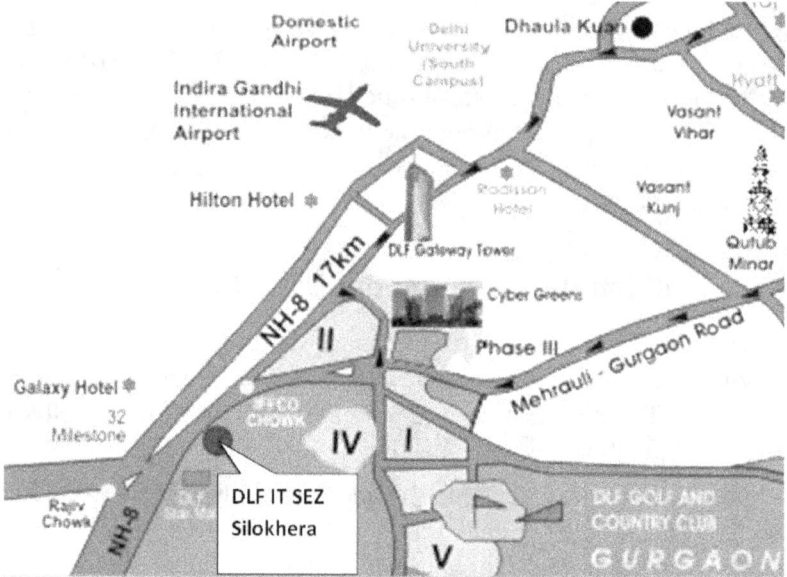

Figure 7.3 Location map of DLF IT SEZ Silokhera [*Source*: DLF Group]

About fifteen thousand people work in this IT-SEZ. Table 7.2 provides a synopsis of the business activities of the companies operating from here.

Table 7.2 Occupants' list: DLF IT SEZ Silokhera [*Source*: Project Manager, DLF Group, Personal Communication 17 January 2011]

Company	Functions and activities
IBM Daksh (now renamed as IBM Global Process Services)	BPO services in the areas of Customer Relationship Management, Human Resource Management, Supply Chain Management, Finance and Administration. Works mainly for Banking, Insurance, Retail and Telecom industries
Genpact (earlier GE Capital)	Business process and technology management, in areas of Banking, Insurance, Capital Market, Retail and Healthcare
Accenture	Part of the company's global delivery chain, focused on software customisation for banking and financial services
Max New York Life	Operations and technological support for shared administrative services, payroll management, etc.

The project provides a high level of security infrastructure. The whole complex is surrounded by a high perimeter wall. Access is restricted through a manned security gate. According to RE-D-17, who is the chief architect of the DLF Group, "All buildings in Silokhera SEZ are designed to comply with USA's NFPA (National Fire Prevention Authority) requirements in addition to Indian building code provisions. Buildings also comply with Gold Standard for Green Building classification" (Interview: 12 January 2011). The complex provides full power back-up for all electrical supply, including central air-conditioning. Ambulances and fire tenders are stationed in the complex for 24 hours a day, as it has become the common practice in all high-end buildings.

Figure 7.4 Inside DLF IT SEZ Silokhera [*Source*: Author]

The SEZ project and the nearby shopping malls and office building have been built on land which was part of Silokhera village till 1987 and was used for cultivation of wheat, millet, red lentils, peas and tomatoes. Now only the *abadi* (residential part) of the village is in existence. All other land has been converted to urban usage between 1987and 1990, informed LC-D-50, former Sarpanch (Chairperson) of the Silokhera Panchayet, when interviewed on 27 February 2011. He advised that the village has a population of 7000 to 8000 and is inhabited by Pundits (Brahmin caste), Yadavs / Ahirs and lower caste Dalits. Village inhabitants, both upper caste and lower caste are now fully engaged in urban occupations. LC-D-50 further stated,

> Working age males of the Dalit households are generally working as security guards, cleaners, drivers or electricians. Upper castes are engaged in property trading, owning small businesses or house renting. Better educated younger generation are engaged in more diverse activities. (Interview: LC-D-50, 27 February 2011)

The houses in the upper caste areas of the village were mostly well built. But the lower castes live in slum-like conditions as shown in Figure 7.5. Conditions of the roads and drainage are extremely poor in the entire village (see Figure 7.6). Pointing out the difference between the poor quality civic infrastructure in the village areas and the glittering new office buildings and shopping malls, the former Sarpanch of Silokhera complained,

> Just look at our condition. How could all these *Sheesh Mahals* (Glass palace, meaning the new buildings which use lot of mirror glass in facade to give a modern look) have come up here, if we had not given land? What did we get back in return? (Interview: LC-D-50, 27 February 2011)

While residents of Silokhera village have adjusted to the urban way of life, they still feel bitter about losing their land and have been fighting a court case against the IT SEZ. The change of land ownership in Silokhera happened mostly due to acquisition by the state government, while real estate developers have purchased the remaining part. The state government acquired 85.1 hectares in January 1989 and another 68.3 hectares in January 1990, for residential and commercial usage (Business Standard 2011a). Out of this, 12.1 hectares of land was later given to

East India Hotel Ltd. (one of India's leading hotel chains), to develop a hospital, a hotel management institute and executive apartments.

Figure 7.5 Slums of Dalit villagers outside the SEZ boundary [*Source*: Author]

Figure 7.6 Access road to Silokhera village [*Source*: Author]

But later on, East India Hotels transferred this land to the DLF after obtaining a 'no-objection certificate' from the government. These 12.1 hectares of land make up the major part of the 14.97-hectare DLF IT SEZ Silokhera. When asked about the compensation payment, several other members of the former panchayet board, who had assembled in LC-D-50's sprawling living room during the interview, interjected, and protested,

> What compensation? How much did we get? We got absolutely peanuts. We had 3 to 4 hectares of land. Those days land price was only about USD 4700 to 6700 per hectare. So how much we got? Prices of everything had gone up so much. We had to educate our children, marry the daughters. So what is left? Now we've no money no land. (Interview: LC-D-50B, 27 February 2011)

The local discontents are to a large extent linked to the huge increase in property prices in the area, and feeling left out of the gains. As LC-D-50C, one of the original inhabitants of Silokhera and a well-to-do property dealer now, explained,

> Between 1987 and 1990, when land was acquired here property prices moved up from eighty thousand per acre (USD 3,675 per hectare) to two and half lakh rupees per acre (USD 11,485 per hectare). The circle rate (compensation rate under the Land Acquisition Act) was fixed accordingly. But now it is between fourteen and fifteen crores (USD 6,431,880 to 6,891,300 per hectare). So only those who invested the money back into land or property had made money, but most had blown away. (Interview: LC-D-30C, 27 February 2011)

After a long drawn legal battle, the Punjab and Haryana High Court gave a ruling on 5 February 2011 which termed this transaction as illegal and ordered partial demolition of the SEZ. The DLF group has now challenged the High Court judgement in the Supreme Court of India (Business Standard 2011a).

7.6 Stakeholders in transformation of the urban fringe

7.6.1 Role of state and local government

Haryana government's liberal, business-friendly policies, particularly on the issue of land supply have played a major facilitative role in the IT outsourcing-driven growth story of Gurgaon. Pro-market land legislations such as the HUD Act of 1977 and HUDRA Act of 1975–76, enacted at a time when socialistic distributive models were being followed by the national government and almost every other state government were much ahead of their times. It was also the first state government to ratify the SEZ Act of 2005, while Haryana's IT Policy simplified the conversion of agricultural and industrial land to develop IT business parks. These enabling legislations allowed corporate real estate firms and parastatal agencies (e.g. HUDA, HSIDC) to acquire large land parcels in the NCR belt, when land prices were low. As the Indian economy started opening up from the late 1980s, the existing land bank allowed the developers to quickly churn out high-quality production and consumption spaces matching Western quality standards, in strategic locations near Delhi airport, scripting the transformation of Gurgaon.

Market-led land purchase mechanisms in which real estate developers directly negotiate prices with the farmers have allowed this transformation process to be far less conflictual than in Kolkata or elsewhere in India, where land is usually acquired by the state agencies by invoking the power of eminent domain. At a time when land conflicts gripped almost every state in India, Haryana was seen as remarkably trouble free. Haryana's land policy which supposedly provides a 'win-win' situation, by paying 'market price' to the farmers and allowing land to be easily made available to meet the needs of urban and industrial projects, has drawn the attention of the national government and the other state governments.

However, fieldwork investigation revealed that the mechanism is not entirely conflict free as is commonly made out to be. Parastatal agencies often do play a significant role to facilitate the interest of the real estate developers, directly or indirectly. The direct method was employed in the case of Silokhera IT SEZ as discussed in Section 7.5. The land was originally acquired by the state government agencies, and was subsequently transferred to private companies. In the process, the original purpose of acquisition, from developing hotel management institute and apartment buildings, also changed to developing an IT SEZ. The indirect method of manipulating valuation of land was discussed in Section 7.4. In Shahpur Turk village, acquisition notices were issued and then withdrawn after the private developers purchased substantial chunks. These fieldwork examples along with Kennedy's (2012) research about the Reliance SEZ project discussed in Section 7.4, taken together, suggest very strong linkages between the state government and the real estate lobby. There is a strong likelihood that this connection was spurred by many influential politicians owning large land parcels in the Gurgaon area, as hinted by Debroy and Bhandari (2009).

Despite these aberrations, economic growth of the region enabled a large number of farmers in Gurgaon not just to switch over from a rural to an urban economy, but to become active stakeholders in the process. Comparatively larger land holding sizes, along with continuously rising prices in the Gurgaon area since the 1990s have induced several farming households to voluntarily move away from agriculture and explore new opportunities in property trading, building construction, retail or transport sectors. Rapid economic growth of the region has not only created livelihood opportunities for the local poor, but has also attracted huge migration from other north Indian states. As can be seen from the Silokhera IT SEZ example, Dalit villagers work as security guards or as skilled workers in the locality. The explosive population growth of Gurgaon, as indicated in Table 7.1, supports the argument. This happened because successive governments of the state, whether headed by Congress, INLD or HVP, followed similar pro-growth economic policies. However, Haryana government's role in Gurgaon's IT cluster development is facilitative and indirect, centring on land supply, in areas within the extended metropolitan belt of Delhi. It does not depict any strategic vision, apart from ensuring land supply through market mechanisms.

However this indirect approach has contributed to a chaotic urban development pattern in Gurgaon, with acute infrastructure deficiencies, and sharp polarisation between planned and unplanned developments. Management of Gurgaon's transition from a rural town to global business hub has severely suffered due to a multiplicity of institutions and the lack of a strong coordinating agency. From the mid-1990s onwards, as Gurgaon started to expand rapidly, powered by the new economy-driven property boom, the political leadership of the state, nurtured in the rural-centric socio-political environment, was taken aback by the rate of change. As PL-D-59, a former chief secretary of Haryana, observed, "In those days, nobody in Chandigarh had any clue that things would move so fast. Gurgaon needs its own development authority. Planners sitting in Chandigarh cannot coordinate such a fast-growing area on a daily basis" (Interview: 4 January 2012).

Not only did the Chandigarh-based political leadership fail to act, by not putting in place a strong institutional structure to coordinate the growth of Gurgaon, but some of them even further compounded the problem. For instance, the INLD-led coalition (1999–2004) approved such a large number of shopping malls over a short strip of Mehrauli–Gurgaon Road that the area came to be popularly known as 'mall mile', with acute traffic congestion. LC-D-61, a local municipal councillor, stated: "The Chief Minister, on a visit to Singapore, was very impressed by the Orchard Road, and wanted to recreate that in Gurgaon (Interview: 5 January 2012)".

While the Chandigarh-based political leadership showed alacrity in approving real estate projects to meet the demands of the growing economy, the formation of a representative Municipal Corporation and formal expansion of the urban limits of the city were inordinately delayed. Thus, all these townships, shopping malls, IT SEZ, expensive apartment blocks or posh hotels, were built on areas which were, till then, officially 'rural'. The urban limits covered only a small patch adjoining the railway station and the Civil Lines area. The ambiguous governing regime of Gurgaon, during a vital part of its growth and in the absence of a strong local institutional setup, worked further to the advantage of the real-estate–politician nexus. This quickened land acquisition from the weak village panchayets and, secondly, expedited regulatory approvals from the friendly parastatal agencies. (Debroy & Bhandari 2009) allege that this benefitted several influential politicians in Delhi and Chandigarh, who owned large land parcels in Gurgaon. LC-D-61 complained, "For all these years, Gurgaon has been treated as Haryana's cash cow. Gurgaon generates half of Haryana's revenue. But what does it get back in return?" (Interview: 5 January 2012). Similar resentments against the way the Chandigarh-based state leadership had handled the state of urban affairs of Gurgaon, were expressed by almost every politician and civil society activist interviewed, indicating a rare degree of unanimity amongst the local elites in an otherwise fractious environment.

7.6.2   Role of corporate sector

The IT-outsourcing industry is responsible for the present prosperity of Gurgaon and for bringing it into the global corporate map. In terms of engagement in the governance process, it plays a rather low-key role. This is in sharp contrast to the other global economic hot-spot of India, Bangalore. Gurgaon, like Bangalore, has several regional head offices, where top ranking executives work and live. Yet their role in local governance is extremely restricted. The difference stems from two main factors: Firstly, the relative newness of the Gurgaon story, compared to the longer and slower process of Bangalore's development, and secondly, the virtual absence of any direct contact between the government machinery and the IT-ITES community. When asked why the IT industry does not take up the bad-infrastructure issue with the government agencies more vigorously, IT-D-63, Vice President, Cognizant Technologies, attributed this to the transient nature of the professional population.

> There was nothing here originally. People have come here from all different parts of India. Initially, they considered staying in Gurgaon only as a temporary step in their career ladder. However with the passage of time, they started growing roots, purchased property and taking more interest in civic affairs" (Interview: IT-D-63, 3 January 2012).

IT-D-19, who started the GE Capital's Bangalore operations and now, is the CEO of Simon Carves (a British engineering company) in Gurgaon, had also, similar views when interviewed and said,

> See IT guys basically don't want to deal with the government, unless it is absolutely unavoidable. Most people who moved in to Gurgaon were initially busy in establishing themselves, in new job, in new environment, setting up their families, kids school, etc. Initially things were not so bad. There was less traffic, more open space. Water was also not a problem. Yes power was a problem. But we had generators. Work did not suffer. We did not realise things would deteriorate so quickly. (Interview: IT-D-19, 12 January 2011)

IT-D-57, a senior manager at IBM's Silokhera SEZ office, who had lived for over 8 years in the USA, when asked about the quality of civic infrastructure in Gurgaon, observed,

> Quality of life in Gurgaon is pretty good. Frankly we don't feel much of power and water problems, which get written about in newspapers. My office is in this business park, where I spend average 60 hours a week. I live in DLF Royal Gardens in Sector

90, which is a gated complex, with very good security, so I don't need worry about my family. We've clubs and shopping malls all inside. It is only when we need to travel, from home to work, we face the problem. Main problem of Gurgaon is traffic. It is too chaotic. My wife can't drive here, though she used to in America. So we've employed a driver, I would say, solve traffic problem and life in Gurgaon will be better than in America. (Interview: IT-D-57, 17 January 2011)

The point is: the IT-ITES sector enjoys an extremely sheltered life in Gurgaon. During weekdays, they work very long hours from business parks and SEZs, like the DLF IT SEZ Silokhera. On weekends the middle and young crowd go to shopping malls like DLF Star Mall to watch movies and eat out, while the top bosses go to golf clubs. Most of them stay in gated apartment complexes while others commute from Delhi by chartered shuttles provided by the companies. Their entire life revolves within the sanitised private spaces developed by the big builders. They have only marginal contact with the outside vernacular world of Gurgaon, and that is mostly through their drivers, maids or security guards, although occasionally they go to the neighbourhood markets to shop for green groceries. The main problem the IT sector people encounter is about traffic and this has created the first major engagement between the IT sector and the local government in Gurgaon.

A new organisation called Cyber City Welfare Society (CCWS) has recently come into being. It is affiliated to NASSCOM and is supported by leading companies like, American Express, Deloitte, Oracle, IBM, etc. CCWS has started traffic management and pedestrian safety measures by deploying traffic marshals and improving signage in major intersections. It has also begun environmental improvement initiatives in local parks, in cooperation with the MCG, after it came into being in 2008. However, on the whole, the IT-ITES sector's role is extremely limited in Gurgaon's governance system, even though it is the main globalising force. For the most part, it remains spatially confined to the gated fortresses built by the real estate companies. There are gated enclaves in Bangalore and Kolkata, but they are not as pervasive as they are in Gurgaon. It is the real estate sector which has become the main arbitrator between the local and global in Gurgaon.

The real estate sector overwhelmingly dominates the developmental landscape of Gurgaon and vastly overshadows the roles of the state government and the IT corporate sector. While the business-friendly policies of the Haryana government have undoubtedly created the facilitative environment, it is the entrepreneurial dynamism of the real estate sector which has transformed Gurgaon from a small rural town to northern India's preeminent corporate and lifestyle destination. The visionary leaders of the real estate companies realised that the rapid growth of Delhi and the rigid land use control system of Delhi would eventually lead to spill-over into Haryana. They extensively lobbied with the Haryana government to liberalise the land regime.

The real estate 'czars' also had the foresight to realise Gurgaon's developmental potential. Before this, until the 1980s, it was the most neglected suburban town of Delhi. Taking advantage of its location near Delhi and the global demand for IT outsourcing, they virtually created the new Gurgaon from scratch. The overwhelming dominance of the real estate sector may be gauged from the fact that all 33 IT SEZ's in Gurgaon have been developed by the realty companies (Government of India 2012). Most BPO firms, multinational management and engineering off-shore developmental centres, IT software companies, even the big name Indian outfits, operate from leased spaces produced by developers, as in the case of Silokhera SEZ. This is in sharp contrast to Bangalore and even Kolkata, where Indian IT majors like Infosys, TCS and Wipro have their own SEZs and office buildings.

But an even more striking contrast is the absence of an IT promotion organisation within the Haryana government. Karnataka government actively promotes IT investments through KEONICS and KBITS as was discussed in Chapter 6. Similarly, WBEIDC plays a major role in soliciting IT investments in West Bengal, as was discussed in Chapter 8. However, there is no parallel organisational set-up in the Haryana government. Officially, the task of promoting IT investments in the state rests with the HSIDC, the general purpose industrial promotion agency. HSIDC has a separate department for IT and biotechnology sectors. Yet their roles are not substantial. As PL-D-59 pointed out,

> Haryana government did not make any conscious effort to encourage IT investments. We had been lucky. From 1997–98 onwards, BPO firms and call-centres started moving into Gurgaon. Then there was a realisation that Gurgaon and Haryana, as such has a potential in this sector. Quickly, an IT policy was drafted in 2000. (Interview: PL-D-59, 4 January 2012)

Similarly, when asked about the absence of any special IT department, the General Manager of HSIDC's IT cell replied,

> We've framed our IT policy, which matches the tax rates etc. But our government never felt the need to aggressively market the state, compared to, say, states like West Bengal, which are struggling for investments. We don't need to. A large number of multinational companies, not so much in the software field, but mostly in the ITES field, BPOs and others, have moved into Gurgaon, as it is close to Delhi. Real estate companies like DLF or Unitech do their own marketing. Our role is to facilitate growth by providing tax breaks and other policy incentives. (Interview: PL-D-32, 2 February 2012)

While the government departments have confined themselves to creating the enabling environment, the real estate sector of Gurgaon has become the arbitrator between the global economic processes and local development. The entrepreneurial dynamism shown by the real estate sector has been largely responsible for Gurgaon's rapid urban makeover from a small rural town to a centre of the global outsourcing industry. Three big companies, DLF, Ansals and Unitech, played a particularly strong role in this, with DLF being the leader.

DLF (originally known as Delhi Lease Finance) and Ansals initially began their business in Delhi. However, as the land market in Delhi came under increasing restrictions during the 1960s, they moved into Haryana. Taking advantage of the liberal land policies of the state government, these companies developed huge land banks during the 1970s and 1980s in the areas near Delhi, particularly in Gurgaon. In Gurgaon, their initial focus was on developing large scale gated residential townships, to attract the growing middle-class population from Delhi. But later on, from the mid-1990s onwards, they started building higher-end business parks for the IT-BPO companies. As the Chief Architect of the DLF Group put it,

> Our first venture in Gurgaon was DLF Qutab Enclave, what is called DLF City now. In those days we primarily targeted the middle and upper middle-class homebuyers from South Delhi. Although we developed office buildings and shopping centres, but those were not popular. People were used to commuting to Delhi. In fact we used to run shuttle bus service, to Connaught Place, for the Qutab Enclave residents. Otherwise it would have

been very difficult to get buyers. The office boom began as our chairman Mr K.P. Singh managed to convince Jack Welch of General Electric, to set up their call centre here in Gurgaon. Mr Singh knew Mr Welch, for a long time, and this helped. (Interview: IT-D-17, 12 January 2011)

GE's call centre not only sparked the corporate real estate market of Gurgaon, but also opened up the entire business process outsourcing market in India, which was till then restricted to the software development and customisation segment in Bangalore. The resultant BPO-led construction boom completely transformed Gurgaon and indeed brought agricultural Haryana to the country's IT export map. The DLF group owns over 12 sq km of contiguous land in Gurgaon and is currently building a private LRT line connecting the DLF Cyber City to Delhi Metro's Sikanderpur Station on the Mehrauli–Gurgaon Road in Gurgaon.

The shaping of Gurgaon has also hugely benefitted the companies associated with its growth story. DLF, Ansals and Unitech, which were until the 1990s only local companies, used to operating around the Delhi region, have now become major national players developing SEZ and other real estate projects in all major Indian cities. Development of Gurgaon was the springboard which catapulted them to national prominence.

7.6.3   Role of civil society and community organisations

Civil society and local community activism in Gurgaon remains at a very low level and thus has only marginal influence over governance issues. This in turn had allowed the real estate lobby-led growth machine almost unhindered political space in Gurgaon. As social scientist Madhu Kishwar expressed her opinion, "There are no Medha Patkars[2] in Gurgaon. There are no *lal-jhandas* (red flags). People are here to make money" (Interview: 14 January 2011). In terms of scale, activities of the NGOs and other voluntary groups for the most part remain confined to immediate everyday problems pertaining to infrastructure deficiencies at the residential neighbourhood level and rarely go on to address pan-

---

[2] Ms. Medha Patkar is India's best known social activist, who led the anti-dam movement Narmada Bachao Andolan and was also at the forefront of anti-land acquisition agitations in West Bengal.

urban issues. Here too, residents of the rural and urban areas of Gurgaon follow separate ways to engage with the state, reflecting acute social schism.

Residents of the urbanised villages like Silokhera tend to follow the party-based political system, by seeking help from the political leaders— who generally have deep local ties. But the middle-class professionals engaged in ITES-BPO and other services, who reside in the planned HUDA sectors and private colonies, prefer the 'apolitical' route. In recent times, neighbourhood associations of the formal, planned areas, called Resident Welfare Associations (RWA) have emerged as the main vehicle articulating the voice of the middle class. All HUDA sectors and builder enclaves have their own RWAs, elected by local residents. However, these RWAs are only consultative bodies. Management control rests with the original developers: HUDA for planned HUDA sectors and private real estate companies for the privately developed apartment complexes and townships, even decades after people have moved in. LC-D-56, an elected councillor of the MCG stated,

> The private developers don't want to transfer ownership of the projects to the residents. They avoid obtaining Completion Certificates, by keeping a small part of their project incomplete, to retain control of the areas developed. The Town Planning department in Chandigarh keeps on extending the project time frames, in lieu of only token penalties (Interview: 24 December 2011).

To press their claims, the RWAs and NGOs of Gurgaon have taken up the role of petitioning HUDA about the infrastructure deficiencies of the city and about non-compliance with the master plan guidelines by the private developers (Chatterji 2013b). But they are yet to score any major success. During a meeting with several RWA committee members on 3 January 2012, it was frequently alleged that the private developers had not delivered community facilities as promised. A member of the Sushant Lok RWA alleged, "The land which was marked for the Community Centre has been converted into a membership-only club. Now there is no space to organise festivals like Bhagwati-jagarans or Ram-leelas". During the same meeting, other RWA executives complained that in several apartment complexes, builders had converted areas originally marked for local convenience stores into air-conditioned shopping malls, encroached roads and children's parks and frequently hiked monthly maintenance charges. CS-D-58, a prominent community activist, expressed his helplessness about complaining to HUDA about private builders:

> We keep going round and round. We visit HUDA office and submit petitions. The officers sympathetically listen to us. Treat us nicely and offer tea and coffee. But that's the end of it. Nothing further happens. The files don't move. Nobody dares to take any action against the builders. (Interview: CS-D-58, 3 January 2012)

Initially content with playing second fiddle to the big developers and HUDA, the RWAs of Gurgaon have becoming increasingly active politically. In 2005, more than one hundred RWAs of Gurgaon came together to form an apex body, called Joint Action Forum for Resident Associations (JAFRA), to more effectively lobby the local administration. Representatives of a few village areas were also accommodated, to give it a more inclusive character. Since then JAFRA has been at the forefront of demanding formation of a more responsive local government with overarching power over various public agencies for integrated urban development. However, being essentially a body of middle-class professionals, JAFRA had shunned any direct confrontation with the state agencies, and had been content with intensified lobbying activity.

But JAFRA's effectiveness as a lobbying body is to a large extent compromised due to its internal contradictions. The day-to-day problems faced by the HUDA sectors and the private enclaves tend to differ, except on bigger issues like mass transport or public parking spaces. There is also a huge trust deficit between the village areas and the planned enclaves. It is a common feeling amongst the educated elites of Gurgaon that local rural people, many of whom had become rich overnight by selling land, lack 'education, culture and social manners'.

There are strong symbiotic economic relationships between the formal and informal settlements. Shopping malls and markets within the planned residential enclaves accommodate only a few high-end shops. Thus, most residents of the gated complexes depend on the informal village bazaars for their daily needs. The villages also accommodate the entire service population of the formal economy. The security guards, electricians, and maids, who work in the business parks and the apartment buildings, reside in the nearby village pockets. Yet the middle-class areas detest the presence of the rural enclaves. A former Sarpanch (Chairperson) of the Chakkarpur Village and now a prominent BJP leader of Gurgaon put it:

> The educated and sophisticated city-bred people living in these apartment enclaves want all the services of the villages of Gurgaon, but do not want to recognise them or see them. They want their maids, cooks and drivers to come, do their daily duties, and then just disappear at the end of the day. Is this Arabian Nights? Where would these people go? (Interview: LC-D- 61, 6 January 2012)

Similarly, LC-D-50, the former head of the Silokhera village panchayet, pointed towards the multi-storeyed apartment complex adjoining the DLF IT SEZ and said,

> People in these big multi-storeyed buildings and working in these glass palaces [meaning IT business parks—most of which sport glass facades] think they are from heaven. They are superior breed, because of their education. But education should teach them humility. They should be respectful towards our local culture and local people. After all, these are our land. We want new people, educated people to come in. It is good for our future also. But they should try to mix with us, not keep us away, as if we are outcasts and untouchables. (Interview: 27 February 2011)

LC-D-62, another young political activist and a MCG councillor, also observed, "Highflying people living in these high-rise towers look down upon us, as rustic, uneducated blokes. They don't give us any respect. We live in two worlds even though we live, side by side" (Interview: 6 January 2012).

Engagement between the civil society activists and the local government received a major boost in 2008, with the formation of the municipal corporation (Chatterji 2013b). Like other municipalities of India, the MCG has two wings: a legislative wing consisting of the mayor and the elected councillors of each ward, and an administrative wing directly under the Municipal Commissioner. During 2008–11 the commissioner took several steps towards forging a partnership with the civil society and particularly emphasised the use of e-governance tools.

Since the urban middle class in India typically consider urban local bodies to be 'corrupt' and 'inefficient' he attempted to create a template for a 'transparent and efficient civic body' before the start of politicking, with the arrival of the elected councillors. PL-D-33, Commissioner of the MCG explained,

> I'm trying to harness the power of the IT to break the barrier between the in-groups and the out-groups. The main point is about information sharing. If you do not share information, then people immediately start thinking that there is something to hide. Unfortunately, most government departments in India, and MCG is no exception, there is a tendency to keep things under the wraps. Here in Gurgaon, we've lot of highly qualified technical people, particularly in IT companies. But they don't engage with us. I'm trying to change this culture, by roping in good NGOs to partner us. (Interview PL-D-33, 2 February 2011)

With the objective of achieving greater transparency, the MCG started to upload information about contracts and tendering for municipal projects on its website, apart from regular items such as property taxation, birth, death and marriage registration, and a section for lodging of complaints. The MCG also initiated monitoring and evaluation of tenders by Citizen Supervisory Committees for each ward. Payments for small civic works, such as road repairs, were linked to getting a satisfactory report from the citizen committees of the concerned ward. Additionally, the MCG partnered NGOs like 'I'm Gurgaon' to launch environmental improvement programmes like creating shelters for stray cows, turning rubbish dumps into parks and cleaning of local markets (Interview CS-D-34, 3 February 2011).

However, participation of the civil society groups in urban governance took a downward turn after the municipal elections, due to the social gulf that exists between the urban-elite-dominated 'apolitical' NGOs and the 'rustic' political leadership which came into control of the MCG following the election (Chatterji 2013b). As the Convenor of 'I'm Gurgaon' mentioned a couple of months after the election, "Oh no, the MCG councillors are the typical rustic, uncultured, rural types, here to make money and gain influence. There are not the right class. They don't know how to talk respectfully to ladies. We can't work with these guys". (2nd Interview: CS-D-34, 24 December 2011)

Similarly, CS-D-31, head of the CCWS, expressed his difficulties in working with the elected political leadership of Gurgaon, who are "more interested in caste politics than development" (2nd Interview, 3 January 2012). This cultural barrier between the IT-elite-led civil society groups and the rural-centric political leadership of Gurgaon (and Haryana) not only robbed the nascent MCG of much technical and managerial capacity gap at a crucial stage, but also further diminished the possibilities of greater engagement in urban governance, leaving the field open for the real estate lobby.

7.6.4   Characteristics of the governing regime

Based on the role of the different stakeholders in the transformation of the peri-urban landscape of Gurgaon discussed above, the following section identifies the main characteristics of the local governance regime, using DiGaetano and Strom's (2003) framework.

- *Governing logic* – In case of Gurgaon the governing logic is based on particularistic exchanges. The rich farmer-led top echelons of Haryana politics have aligned with big property developers for transformation of the urban space of Gurgaon, through induction of global investments. 'Land' has played a key role in Haryana's economic policy from the mid-1970s onwards. Emergence of the ITES-BPO economy and the construction boom have enriched the big farmers, particularly the Jat caste lobby, who wield considerable power in the state. Irrespective of change in government at the state level, the basic contours of the liberal land policy have remained intact, as the key beneficiaries remained unaltered.

- *Governing relations* – Governing relations are based on reciprocity. Over four decades of liberal land policy and minimal regulatory control enabled the developers to amass large land parcels from the peri-urban farmers, to create production and consumption spaces for the IT-BPO-led new globalised economy. Rural Haryana, particularly in the NCR belt, has become one of the top destinations for FDI in real estate. While the big farmers have become richer and continue to the wield main political power in the state, the middle farmers have also gained, due to astronomical jumps in land value. Rapid growth of the region also created downstream opportunities for the rural poor and the landless, in the urban informal sector. These new economic opportunities have prevented land conflicts from emerging in this region on a big scale.

• *Key decision makers* – The key decision makers in Haryana are the real estate sector and their patrons, the Chandigarh-based top echelons of Haryana politics. Neither the IT-ITES sector, nor the local municipal level elected politicians wield much decision-making power in the governance structure. Unlike Bangalore and Kolkata, the IT-ITES companies almost exclusively operate from leased spaces developed by the realty companies, which minimises their interface with the local state. Similarly, the RWAs and the civil society groups are rather marginal in influence, particularly, when dealing with the powerful real estate developers.

• *Political objectives* – The politics of Haryana are polarised along caste lines, in which the landed Jat farmer lobby retains its dominance. Political objectives here are shaped by direct material gains. Alliance with the real estate sector has provided direct economic gain for the big and middle farmers and politicians. Deep social cleavage along caste lines is also a factor here. Mobilisation of the landed rural interests by Jats and Yadavs left out the landless lower caste Dalits. Pushed out of the rural economy due to land use change, these disadvantaged people had moved into the bottom strata of the informal urban economy. However, fast expansion of the economy has absorbed them into the urban sector and prevented social conflicts.

Overall, the characteristics of the local governing regime may be termed as 'clientelistic'. This clientelistic nature of the governing regime has resulted in a highly fragmented urban landscape in Gurgaon, marked by deep social inequalities and huge infrastructure deficiencies. Yet it makes no major dent in the electoral prospects of the local governing regime.

Table 7.3 below contains a synopsis of Gurgaon's urban governance characteristics discussed above, following DiGaetano and Strom's framework.

Table 7.3 Characteristics of Gurgaon's urban governance regime [Source: Compiled by author based on DiGaetano and Strom's framework]

Parameters	Characteristics of the governing regime
Governing logic	• Dominated by 'particularistic personalised exchange'. • Gurgaon's locational proximity to Delhi and growth in the IT services has opened up new opportunities for economic development through large-scale real estate development and reduced dependence on agriculture. • The spin-off benefits of large-scale land development for the IT sector are directly benefitting rich-farmer-led top political leadership.
Governing relations	• Governing relations are based on reciprocity. • Close association between the real estate sector and the politicians are promoting crony capitalism.
Key decision makers	• The key decision makers are the property developers and their patrons in state politics. • The IT sector is not directly represented in the policy matrix. Their interests are indirectly represented by the real estate sector. • Civil society activism is at a nascent stage. Much of the educated middle class are not local and not represented in the political system. • Politicians with close rural (and caste) ties control power at the municipal government level.
Political objectives	• Direct material gain through large-scale land development. • Opportunity through conversion of land use from agriculture to production and consumption spaces for the IT and knowledge economy services have created close links between the big politicians and big builders.

7.7   Summary of case study findings

This chapter analysed the development of the IT cluster in the fringe areas of the extended metropolitan belt of Delhi–National Capital Region. The development pattern of Gurgaon, the pre-eminent IT cluster in the NCR area has clearly followed a very different trajectory from that of Bangalore. The real estate sector has been at the forefront of Gurgaon's dramatic transformation from a small rural town at the outskirts of Delhi to a global IT-BPO outsourcing hub. While the state government has provided a facilitative environment, it plays a much more indirect role compared to Bangalore and Kolkata.

The characteristic of the governing regime is clientelistic. The rich farmer-led top echelons of Haryana politics have aligned with big property developers for transformation of the urban space of Gurgaon, through induction of global investments. The liberal land policy and minimal regulatory control enabled the developers to amass large land parcels from the peri-urban farmers, to create production and consumption spaces for the ITES-BPO-led new globalised economy. By churning out high-quality built spaces matching the specifications of the industry, the real estate sector has become the interface between the global investors and the local state, from the very inception.

The outcome is a highly unsustainable urban landscape, marked by environmental degradation and stark disparities between planned and unplanned areas. The development pattern has followed the ease of land assembly, rather than a coordinated plan. Haryana's administrative and legislative leadership, inexperienced in managing big cities and steeped in a rural-centric political milieu, displayed a rentier-like attitude towards Gurgaon—prospering from its economic growth, but neglecting to strengthen the capacities of the local institutions for development coordination. The parastatal agencies, in the name of facilitating the private enterprise-led growth machine, had relegated their planning responsibilities.

Difficulties in physical planning notwithstanding, the impressive economic growth of the region enabled a large number of farmers to move away from agriculture and become stakeholders in the new urban economy. Peri-urban farmers have sold off their land holdings and invested the surplus capital in the residential and commercial property market in the urbanised villages, or in running transport shuttles for the IT-BPO workers. But the politics of this urban transformation is marked by a high degree of social stratification. Rural–urban dichotomies, caste rivalries and power struggles between local- and state-level politicians, which had marked the everyday politics of Gurgaon from the 1990s, surfaced in a big way with the formation of the Municipal Corporation and its subsequent election.

In Gurgaon, the approach towards public participation in governance is marked by duality, conforming to the pan-Indian pattern. The urban middle class prefer the route of civil society activism, while people of the rural areas follow the route of direct electoral politics. The social gulf between the urban middle class and the rural rich-dominated political system has reduced the influence of the civil society groups over the local governance of Gurgaon, compared to Bangalore. The local rural elites have captured power in the newly formed MCG, but its power to implement developmental works is extremely restricted due to a complex interplay of institutional deficiencies, horizontal and vertical power relationships between the parastatal agencies and caste-centric politics. Incomplete devolution of administrative power from the state government has made the elected representatives of the local government ineffective. Political interests of the top leaders had taken precedence over meeting the developmental expectations of the people.

8

Case study III: Kolkata IT cluster

8.1   Introduction

This chapter, through a case study of the IT clusters in the Kolkata (formerly known as Calcutta) metropolitan region, presents a contrasting development pattern compared to Bangalore and the Gurgaon (NCR), discussed previously. Despite strong efforts by the West Bengal state government, Kolkata's IT cluster remains the smallest amongst the top seven cities in India. While the business press frequently writes about the 'huge growth potential' of the region, local educated youth continue to move out to Bangalore, Gurgaon and other faster growing IT-ITES hubs. In this light, it provides a contrasting development path to the other two cases.

It is hard to imagine now, as Kolkata has not only fallen off the list of high profile global cities, but urban blight, poverty and hyper crowding have come to dominate the city's image to outsiders, yet till the early 1950s it was not only India's leading city, but the preeminent urban centre of a vast trading area stretching from Aden to Hong Kong (Lubell 1974; Myint-U 2011; Tan 2007). Calcutta was founded in 1690 by the East India Company as a trading port and was the capital of the British Indian Empire until 1912. As the seat of the government, commercial hub and entrepôt to a region rich in natural resources (e.g. coal, iron, jute and tea), the city grew in economic and political importance with the expansion of British colonial power from Bengal to the rest of the Indian sub-continent in the 18th and 19th centuries (Tan 2007).

However, the economy of the Bengal region sharply declined between the 1940s and 1970s due to continuing socio-political turbulence, such as—partition (1947), wars (1965, 1971) and radical leftist insurgency, that reached a peak between 1967–69 (Raychaudhuri & Basu 2007). The industrial economy of the Kolkata metropolitan area, which weathered the early shocks, was badly hit by the upsurge of trade union militancy from the mid-1960s and thereafter went into a long spell of stagnation (Goswami 1989). There is a general agreement in the scholarly literature (Chatterjee 1990; Goswami 1989; Sinha 2005) that socio-political turbulence in the Bengal region, the refugee influx following partition and wars, the loss of its economic hinterland due to partition, militant trade unionism and radical leftist insurgency have fundamentally altered the socio-political characteristics of West Bengal and its principal city Kolkata. But, as India's third largest urban economy, and the main city of eastern India, Kolkata still includes a very large educated middle-class population base. Since the early 1990s, the West Bengal government has been making significant efforts towards the resurgence and revival of Kolkata's industrial economy, meeting with partial success and large obstacles. Impressive growth of the IT-ITES sector is the most remarkable success story in this turnaround battle.

The remaining part of the chapter is organised as follows. Section 8.2 provides an overview of the growth of the IT-ITES industry in Kolkata. Section 8.3 then discusses the state-level political-economic culture of West Bengal, which stands in the way of Kolkata's IT services sector realising its 'full potential'. Section 8.4 then takes up the spatial implications of the IT-services industry on the urban development pattern of Kolkata. Section 8.5 includes an illustrative example of one IT business park in Kolkata. Section 8.6 analyses the roles of various stakeholders associated with the growth of Kolkata's IT cluster and its urban transformation using DiGaetano and Strom's (2003) framework. Section 8.7 concludes the chapter through a summary and provides pointers to the differential shaping of local impacts of global forces by place-specific factors.

8.2   Development of IT services sector

Kolkata, the capital of West Bengal state, has the largest IT-ITES cluster in eastern India, though in all-India terms it ranks seventh in terms of export earnings and also employment generation (STPI 2010). There are about 500 IT-ITES companies in Kolkata's extended metropolitan region, employing about 100,000 people (Chatterjee 2012). But the number of persons employed in Kolkata's IT services sector is just one-fifth of Bangalore's, even though in population terms Kolkata, is more than one-and-a-half times larger than Bangalore and has a longer history as an educational and economic magnet. Moreover, educated urban youth from Kolkata (and the rest of Bengal) now constitute a significant portion of the IT-ITES workforce in Bangalore and other Indian cities. For example, a sample survey of the call-centre workers in the Delhi NCR found that Bengali ranks as the most common first language, after the local language Hindi (James & Vira 2012). A similar study in Bangalore also observed a high proportion of Bengali speakers, only exceeded by speakers of the South Indian languages (Upadhya, C. & Vasavi 2006). Locational attractiveness and risk analysis by corporate bodies for IT sector investments, point out Kolkata's cheaper real-estate, lower attrition rates, and availability of a large human resource talent pool as key attractions compared to Bangalore, Delhi-NCR and other Indian IT hubs (for example NASSCOM & A.T.Kearney 2009). Frequent political agitations and strikes are commonly attributed as roadblocks.

As the political and economic centre of India during the colonial times, Kolkata developed a large educated service-class population base in the city. The head office of the colonial mercantile companies which owned tea gardens, collieries and jute mills in distant parts of eastern India, were all located in Kolkata (Goswami 1989). Similarly the regional head offices of the corporate firms which ran the engineering and equipment-manufacturing industries in the Kolkata industrial belt (or elsewhere in eastern India) were all centralised in the city (ibid.). In its heyday, Kolkata also had a large financial services industry, next only to Mumbai in transaction volume.

Running this urban economy required a large army of educated workers, and a number of tertiary educational institutions began to be established in Kolkata from the early nineteenth century onwards, such as Presidency College (1817), Bengal Engineering College (1856) and Calcutta University (1857). The spread of the English language and modern education turned Kolkata into India's pre-eminent educational hub and provided a head-start to the local Bengali middle class in knowledge services. However, Kolkata's entry into IT-ITES services was considerably delayed due to the ideological positions of the Communist Party of India (Marxist) [CPI(M)] led Left Front coalition, which came to power in West Bengal in 1977, and remained so until 2011.

The Left Front government was opposed to the introduction of computers in offices, fearing that this would lead to retrenchment of workers. Thus, during the 1980s, when computerisation of banks and offices started growing in India due to liberalisation of import regulations by the national government, the Left Front government in West Bengal not only opposed the move but also tacitly supported the labour unions in organising protests (Sen, R 2009). The most notable incident in this regard was the strike involving the Hong Kong Bank, when it wanted to introduce computers in its Kolkata branches in 1981–82. A former trade union leader associated with the CPI(M), who took part in organising the strike, recapitulated his memory,

> We believed that computerisation was a conspiracy of the capitalist class. We were taught that way by the party and we honestly believed that. So we were utterly determined to prevent the computerisation of the Hong Kong Bank. We wanted to make it an example, so that no other office in Calcutta dare bring computers. The government officially said nothing, but provided tacit support to us (Interview: CS-K-67, 17 January 2012).

The hostile political environment and declining work culture discouraged corporate offices and banks in Kolkata from carrying out modernisation. Not only did Kolkata stop receiving new economic investments, but the prevailing situation compelled several corporate houses (e.g. ICI, Phillips, and Shaw Wallace) with long association in the city to relocate.

The Left Front's education policies—abolition of English in 1982 from state-funded primary schools; refusal to allow private engineering and medical colleges; and steady politicisation of educational institutions—further accelerated Kolkata's decline by eroding its long-held advantage as a centre for higher learning and started a process of youth exodus (Malik 2011; The Telegraph 2011a). By the 1990s, this exodus of the middle-class youth to Bangalore (and other southern cities) to study engineering reached such a magnitude that Indian Railways started running special trains during entrance test times.

However, the Left Front changed direction in the mid-1990s in response to changing national circumstances. A new economic policy encouraging private investments was announced in 1994. The IT sector was identified as a priority area, based on a report prepared by the local business chambers and global management consultants McKinsey (Shaw & Satish 2007). To boost investor confidence, the IT sector was designated as a critical infrastructure—a safeguard against industrial strikes. Owing to urban middle-class pressure, English was reintroduced from 2000 and restrictions against private engineering colleges were removed.

Starting late, Kolkata however registered quick progress in securing IT investments. By 2006, MNCs like IBM, Siemens and Price Waterhouse Coopers and big Indian companies like Wipro and Tata Consultancy Services (TCS) opened offices in the city. A top executive of TCS's Kolkata operations observed,

> Bengali middle-class families had always prioritised education. Despite the problems, Kolkata's academic standards are still high. So it is obvious that Kolkata will be a great location for the software industry. Employee salaries are here about 15 to 20 percent lower. Attrition rates are low. People here don't change jobs quickly as in Bangalore. Options here are far limited. (Interview: IT-K-52, 16 March 2011)

Office rental values in Kolkata are also cheaper than Bangalore and Gurgaon. According the RE-K-06 (Interview: 21 December 2010), a general manager of the corporate realty firm DLF, monthly rent for 1000 square metres of Grade-A office space in Salt Lake Sector V (Kolkata's first IT hub) is between USD 69 and 86 and in Rajarhat (second IT hub) about USD 55 to 60. Whereas, for the same type of office space in Bangalore rent varies between USD 77 and 112 and in Gurgaon from USD 82 to 155. Opening of the IBM office provided a major boost to Kolkata's IT software industry, much the same way as opening of Texas Instrument's R&D centre sent a message about Bangalore's potential as a research hub to the global market. According to IT-K-68, the head of the Eastern Zone office of NASSCOM,

> Entry of IBM was very crucial step in several ways. IBM left India in 1977 on political grounds. But now they are back and that too in Communist Calcutta. It sent a big positive signal to the international community that Calcutta is back in business. Attitude of the leftist government has changed; they are ready to do business, even with the Americans. (Interviewed: 18 January 2012)

IBM has a big setup in Kolkata employing about 6000 people, working in the areas of business analytics, software product development and customisation (Guha-Thakurta 2012). The office was initially established purely as a back office to serve the US market, but increasingly its role as a business hub for eastern India and the neighbouring countries like Nepal, Bhutan, Bangladesh and Myanmar, is expanding. But on the whole, Kolkata's economic resurgence is yet to take off fully. Far from achieving the ambitious target set in the IT policy of 2003 (Government of West Bengal 2003), which projected that by 2010 West Bengal will climb up to the third slot nationally by capturing 15–20 percent of India's IT export market, Kolkata (where the state's IT economy is almost exclusively concentrated) still languishes at seventh position.

The Trinamool Congress (TMC) government, which came to power in 2011, has also identified the IT-ITES as a priority sector, framed a new policy and has reiterated the state's goal of capturing 15 percent of the country's revenue by 2020 (Government of West Bengal 2012). As discussed in Section 5.5.2, the policy emphasises the gaming and animation sectors to build synergy with the state's existing strength in cultural and creative industries; provides a focus on small IT companies and start-ups; and, taking a leaf out of Karnataka government's approach towards a hub-and-spoke model, it also provides special incentives for setting up IT clusters in smaller towns. Yet despite the stated aims, West Bengal faces severe difficulties in implementing the policies due to its adversarial political culture, as discussed below.

8.3   State and local socio-political culture

West Bengal is a small, poor and predominantly rural state having an extremely high population concentration. The state's urban population percentage is 31.89, which is comparable to the national percentage of 31.16; but the population density of 1029 persons per sq km is 2.7 times greater than the national average of 382 persons per sq km (Census 2011), putting high pressure on land. West Bengal's GDP per person of USD 1181 is less than the national per capita GDP of USD 1239 (The Economist 2012c); and West Bengals's average annual real state GDP growth rate at 7.20 percent from 2004–05 to 2011–12 is also lower than the national growth rate of 8.28 percent (Planning Commission of India 2012).

The state of West Bengal was formed at the time of Indian independence in 1947, and involved the partition of Bengal along communal lines. The eastern two-thirds of the state first became East Pakistan and then subsequently became Bangladesh in 1971. Long periods of socio-economic upheavals and stagnation, particularly unemployment amongst the educated youth, have contributed to a charged and antagonistic political landscape in West Bengal, characterised by a rural–urban dichotomy, and sharp polarisation along party lines (Banerjee, PS & Roy 2005; Mayers 2001). There are two major political formations in Bengal. The 'leftist' forces revolve around CPI(M). Traditionally, the Congress party used to be the main home for the 'centrist' forces. However, since 1998, the breakaway faction Trinamool (grassroots) Congress (TMC) has occupied that space. But such ideological labels are difficult to apply strictly. Irrespective of the party affiliation, educated Bhadralok communities (usually but not necessarily belonging to upper castes) dominate the top tiers of the political space in Bengal (Sinha 2005). The upper castes, who are about 10 percent of the population, have consistently accounted for 40–50 percent of the seats in the state assemblies (Lama-Rewal, Stephene Tawa 2009).

Early access to modern education provided a head-start to the upper caste Bengalis in white collar vocations in the administrative and economic settings during the colonial times. The very identity of the Bhadralok community got intimately entangled with earning a livelihood through intellectual means or rather not being involved in vocations which require manual labour (Bhattacharya, T 2007; Sinha 2005). Diffusion of Western philosophies and ideas from the early days sparked an intellectual awakening and a socio-cultural movement amongst the Bengali Bhadralok, which subsequently played a key role in the political, cultural and social spheres of Bengal and beyond. But from the early twentieth century, the ideational discourse of the Bhadralok started taking a radical turn towards leftist politics (Chatterjee 1990; Sinha 2005).

The leftist parties led by the educated middle class, began in urban areas by mobilising the refugees, unemployed educated youth and factory workers during the 1940s. But subsequent expansion into the rural areas, by providing leadership to the agrarian land reform movements during the 1960s and 1970s, enabled the leftist parties to consolidate the support base amongst lower castes, and laid the foundation of the Left Front's long rule, from 1977 to 2011. After coming to power, the Left Front regime devoted major attention towards rural affairs. Land reforms were institutionalised as a governmental program and implemented through democratically elected local panchayets (Banerjee, PS & Roy 2005). Strengthening of the panchayet system and the fact that many of these small local instructions became focal points for the delivery of governmental services, received much international attention (Fuerstenberg 2010; Mayers 2001; Nielsen 2010). Devolution of power also helped the leftist parties to build a social coalition by accommodating people from lower and disadvantaged castes into the local power matrices. As CS-K-02 explained,

> By controlling the Panchayet system they controlled the rural power structure and the patronage network. It provided a political platform to the lower party functionaries, mostly from lower or middle castes. They also got co-opted in the governance machinery (CS-K-02: Interview: 17 December 2010).

This co-option of different caste and community groups into the local governance framework enabled leftist parties to spread their organisation deep into the rural areas and urban neighbourhoods. This was accomplished through a vast cadre network (Banerjee, PS & Roy 2005). But in the course of time, this also blurred the distinctions between the party machinery and formal state institutions and facilitated the development of extortion rackets. Writing about the pervasive control exercised by the CPI(M) over everyday life in Bengal, Bardhan puts it,

> If you want a public hospital bed for your seriously ill family member, you have to be a supplicant with the local party boss; if you want to start a small business or be a street vendor you have to pay protection money to the party dada; if you want to ply a taxi or an auto-rickshaw you have to pay a tribute to the local party union; if you want a schoolteacher's job you have to be approved by the "local committee" and pay them an appropriate amount ... (Bardhan 2011 p.10)

The pervasive party control was not restricted to the rural or urban poor, but also included the topmost levels of the state. 'The CPI(M) headquarters in Alimuddin Street became the *de facto* government while the Writers' Building that housed the government remained a cipher' (Chakrabarty 2011, p.158). The extra-constitutional authority of the party encouraged its district- and village-level committees to usurp the institutional powers of the state over everyday life.

While concerted attention towards rural issues yielded rich electoral dividends to the Left Front year after year, from the early 1990s it became necessary for the Left Front to change track and encourage industrialisation. The leadership realised that due to gradual decline in land–man ratios with rising population density, the scope for land reforms was limited and agricultural productivity suffered as plot sizes become unviable. However, in India's national economic context in the 1990s, with the neoliberal turn by the national government, new growth opportunities could only come through private investments. The Left Front government's New Economic Policy of 1994 acknowledged these realities and began to court domestic and foreign investments. But, by the 1990s West Bengal had already slid into the backwaters of India's industrial map and the state found it very difficult to attract big investments in industrial manufacturing. (Raychaudhuri & Basu 2007)

Nevertheless, adoption of pro-market policies brought in fresh service sector investments in IT-ITES, speciality healthcare, etc., and between 1992–93 and 2002–03, West Bengal recorded a high 8.5 percent average annual state GDP growth rate compared to the national average of 6.87 percent (Guruswamy, Sharma & Mohanty 2005). However, from 2006 onwards, a series of protests erupted in West Bengal over acquisition of agricultural land for urban and industrial projects, which in certain cases was done through coercive methods (Banerjee, PS 2006; Nielsen 2010). These rural protests not only stalled a chemical industries hub at Nandigram and an automobile factory at Singur, but are widely acknowledged to have been the principal cause behind the Left Front's defeat in 2011 (Bhattacharya, D 2011; Ray, S & Ray 2011; Sen, S 2011).

The Left Front leadership's dreams of rapid industrialisation and mass employment generation were repulsed by the livelihood vulnerabilities of the rural electorate. The Bhadralok leadership ignored the advice of their own rural cadre network in their zeal to speed-up industrialisation (Banerjee, PS 2006). Rather than seeing the land issue as insiders, (as perhaps the rural rich dominated political class of Karnataka and Haryana would have done), the urban middle-class leadership of West Bengal looked at the problem in abstract theoretical terms—that of a shift from agriculture to industry as a natural progression as in a classic development model. However, implementation of the policy proved problematic, as the Left Front, which had earlier given land titles to the small and marginal farmers, could not convince them to part with land. The state's history of industrial strife and the inability of the Left Front government to reopen hundreds of closed factories despite decades of attempts did not set an encouraging picture of future prosperity in front of the peasants.

Direct and sustained involvement of the state's main opposition party, TMC, turned the localised land conflicts into national and even international news events. Since its formation in 1998 by splitting from Congress, TMC acquired a street fighter image by vigorously opposing the Left Front, while its base largely remained confined to Kolkata and its depressed industrial periphery. The party largely revolves around a charismatic leader Mamata Banerjee (Bhattacharya, D 2004). Strong identification with the anti-land acquisition movement enabled it to expand its rural base and the party's electoral campaign was built around the themes 'Ma-Mati-Manush' (Mother, Land and People) and 'Poriborton' (Change) (Ray, S & Ray 2011).

The Mamata Banerjee-led TMC has been in power since May 2011, but the party shows difficulties in the transition from populist agitational platform to administrative responsibilities. There are regular tensions in policy framing due to vastly different expectations from its newly acquired rural and core urban support bases. TMC's electoral manifesto promised an industrial resurgence of Bengal by reviving the manufacturing sector and bringing new investments in IT and tourism (AITC 2011). But it has not been able to make much headway due to the vexed land issue. The TMC government has declared that it will not acquire land for private sector projects but will allow direct purchase, which the investors feel is not feasible in Bengal (BBC 2012). Land reforms had made plot sizes fragmented so that it is almost impossible to assemble large land parcels without state intervention.

The land question is holding up investments in the IT sector as well, fuelling discontents amongst TMC's core urban middle-class Bhadralok constituency. Immediately after taking office, Mamata Banerjee announced a carte-blanche offer to the IT sector at a business meet; "From our side, we can say whatever support is needed, it is an open option. I give it to you. You just tell me, I will do it." (The Telegraph 2011d). Also, as discussed in Section 8.1, the TMC government framed a new IT policy under the guidance of Sam Pitroda (who fashioned the STPI and Telecom policies in the early 1990s) and Narayana Murthi (Infosys founder). But its implementation is proving more problematic.

The TMC government is keen to attract investments from Infosys and Wipro and has expedited an offer made by the previous government to provide each company with 20 hectares of land at Rajarhat at a highly subsidised rate of USD 689,130 per hectare along with a host of other incentives under the state IT policy (The Telegraph 2012a). Each project is expected to generate fifteen thousand jobs. But at the same time, conscious of its newly acquired rural vote, Chief Minister has categorically ruled out confirming the 'SEZ' tag, which has become notionally associated with rural land grabs. Yet, without this designation (which was offered by the previous government) the IT companies are unwilling to invest. Both the projects have been stalled over a year on this issue, despite the state's IT minister holding several rounds of meetings.

Yet, unlike the Left front, which ruled West Bengal for several decades on the strength of its rural-poor support base, ignoring Kolkata's vocal middle-class, TMC is essentially an urban party, and most of its leaders hail from Kolkata. Being aware of this, it has announced a number of steps for Kolkata's economic and physical renewal, including a fanciful wish to reclaim the city's old glory as a world class metropolis emulating London (The Telegraph 2011e). The next section explores Kolkata's urban transformation and its connections to globalisation and the IT industry.

8.4   Urban development pattern

8.4.1   Location

Kolkata is located along the River Hooghly about 200 km upstream from the Bay of Bengal and is a huge urban conurbation having a 16.6 million population (Census 2011). The most significant factor of Kolkata's location, unlike Bangalore or even Delhi NCR, is its regional dominance. There are no other major urban centres in India within hundreds of kilometres of Kolkata. It is *the* predominant city of the whole of eastern and northeastern India and also the neighbouring countries like Nepal and Bhutan (Dhungel, Pun & Thapa 2009; Lubell 1974). Figure 8.1 shows the location of Kolkata.

Figure 8.1 Location map of Kolkata [*Source*: http://www.mapsofworld.com Accessed 9 January 2013]

8.4.2   Growth pattern

The extended metropolitan region of Kolkata is oriented along a north-south longitudinal axis with the River Hooghly running through the middle. The Kolkata Municipal Corporation (KMC) area (as shown in Figure 8.2), hemmed in by the presence of wetlands and salt marshes to the east and the river to the west, and with a staggering population density of 78,355 persons per square kilometre, forms the core (Urban Age 2007).

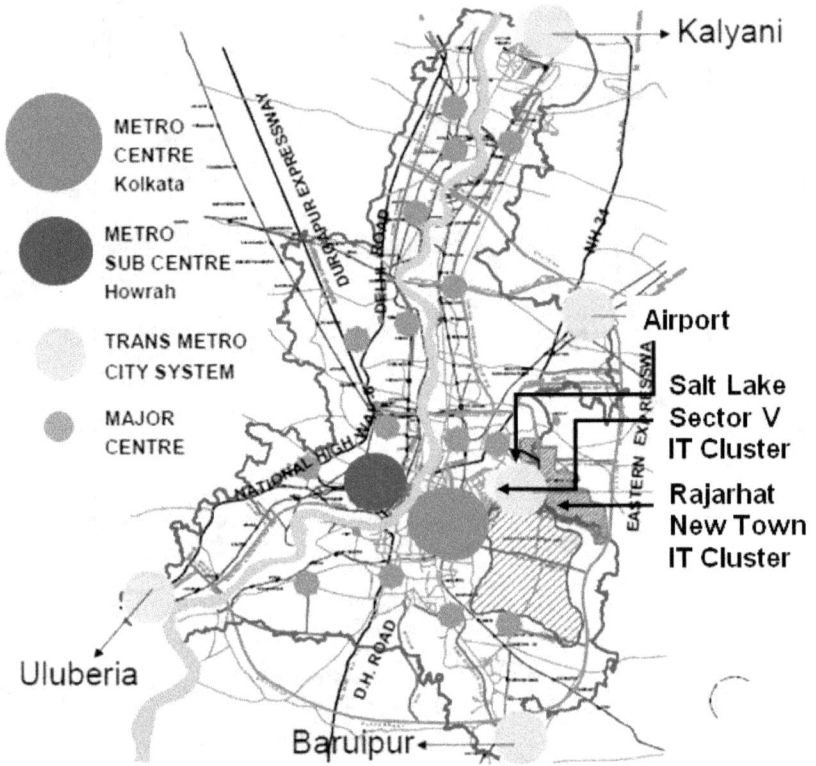

Figure 8.2 Location of IT clusters in Kolkata Metropolitan Region [*Source*: Kolkata Metropolitan Development Authority]

Kolkata's regional spatial structure was originally shaped by the physical features, history and the demands of colonial economic production. But in recent years, the growth of the IT outsourcing economy at the eastern fringe is reconfiguring this linear structure to an east-west multi-polar arrangement.

With the port as the nucleus, an industrial complex formed around Kolkata from the 1850s. Tracks running along the river connected the suburban mill towns to two big rail nodes at the western and eastern edge of the CBD. The two major railheads, at either end, were linked through an elaborate tramways network to the metropolitan core by the early 1920s. During the 1980s, a north-south metro rail line was built—which was India's first metro rail. A new east-west metro line is now under construction.

However, beyond the regional transportation structure, the city had mostly grown haphazardly. The population of the urban agglomeration doubled from 3.62 million in 1941 to 7.42 million in 1971, due to refugee influx and migration, which severely strained the civic services (Lubell 1974). Slums and squatter settlements developed all over the city. However from 1981 onwards, migration has slowed down, and Kolkata has recorded a slower growth rate compared to other Indian metro cities—to a large extent this may be attributed to the city's economic decline.

A major effort towards arresting Kolkata's decay was initiated in the early 1960s through the launching of the Basic Development Plan (BDP), with assistance from the Ford Foundation (Bagchi 1987; Banerjee, T & Chakravorty 1994). Taking into consideration Kolkata's role as the primate city of eastern India, the BDP (1965-85) adopted a two-stage framework. At a macro-regional level, it proposed establishment of alternative urban-industrial growth poles within West Bengal (Bagchi 1987). At a metropolitan regional scale, the BDP advocated a bipolar spatial structure to decongest Kolkata, by developing a satellite township about 45 km upstream along the river and suggested a comprehensive urban renewal plan for Kolkata's decaying industrial belt. But political uncertainties in the late 1960s came in the way of implementing many of the suggestions (Bagchi 1987; Banerjee, T & Chakravorty 1994).

Departing from the rail-transit-oriented linear urban structure, Kolkata Metropolitan Development Authority's (KMDA) Perspective Plan (1976) and the subsequent Traffic and Transportation Plan (2001–25), adopted a poly-centric urban form, envisioning suburban growth centres around the metropolitan core (Dasgupta 2007). Although, in reality, much of the growth since the 1960s has been at the eastern fringe, directly abutting the urban core, through large scale land filling of fisheries, salt marshes and low-lying paddy fields, jeopardising vulnerable ecosystems of the wetlands.

From the 1990s, the locus of Kolkata's urban economy started shifting towards the fringe, with the emergence of IT clusters, SEZs and gated townships—production and consumption spaces for the new economy. Kolkata's eastward surge began with the launching of the Salt Lake township in the 1960s, which after two decades turned into a prime up-scale suburb (Dasgupta 2007). West Bengal government's Secretary,

Urban Development, informed that Sector V of Salt Lake was originally earmarked for non-polluting industries, but remained under-utilised for three decades. But between 2001–08, the area became saturated due to demands generated by IT firms as the state liberalised land use norms (Interview: PL-K-04, 20 December 2010). The impressive growth of Salt Lake Township encouraged the West Bengal government to take up development of the adjoining Rajarhat area from the late 1990s. The Rajarhat New Town covers 35 sq km in area and has a target population of 1 million. Salt Lake and Rajarhat are both in close proximity to Kolkata airport and have together become eastern India's prime IT hub. Land constraints, which prevented development of big IT parks in Salt Lake, have started to come up in Rajarhat New Town.

8.4.3   Institutional structure of urban governance

The extended metropolitan region of Kolkata includes 3 municipal corporations, 38 municipal councils,[1] and 22 panchayet samitis (rural councils) in an area of 1851 sq km and 16.6 million population (KMDA 2007). While day-to-day civic functions are handled by elected municipal governments, the urban planning responsibilities for the extended region are handled by the KMDA, which functions directly under the Urban Development Department of the West Bengal government. By convention, the Urban Development Minister of the state heads the KMDA.

KMDA (formerly known as CMDA) was established in 1970 following the recommendations of the Basic Development Plan (1966–86) (Bagchi 1987; Banerjee, T & Chakravorty 1994). It was the first such development authority to be established in India and was subsequently replicated in all Indian big cities. As discussed in the previous section, the BDP adopted a broad regional outlook in addressing Kolkata's urban issues. In line with this argument, the BDP recommended formation of an overarching planning agency which could coordinate planning and infrastructure development spanning across several administrative jurisdictions. Moreover, there was a felt need to insulate long range planning from narrow everyday politicking at the municipal level.

---

[1] Urban local bodies for small towns with population less than one million are called Municipal Councils, bigger cities have Municipal Corporations.

Immediately after its formation the KMDA addressed a number of critical urban infrastructure issues, related to water supply, sanitation, drainage and transportation, through generous assistance from the World Bank and the national government (Bagchi 1987; Banerjee, T & Chakravorty 1994; Shivaramakrishnan 2011). The slum improvement programme, in particular, received much international attention. Formation of the KMDA was undergirded by the political realisation that Kolkata's rapid physical decay and unsanitary conditions, with the proliferation of the slums and squatter settlements, were not only causing health and environmental problems, but also breeding social discontent and anti-establishment feelings. However the political support behind the KMDA declined in the 1980s, with the advent of the Left Front government in 1977, as in the initial period the leftist regime was suspicious of the agency because of its American links (Banerjee, T & Chakravorty 1994).

The general approach of the Left Front government to urban governance was towards strengthening the elected bodies. In this regard West Bengal is considered as the leading state in adopting the recommendations of the 74th Constitutional Amendment Act, passed by the national parliament. But even the Left Front government has retained the urban planning functions under its own wing, through its control over the KMDA. However, the mechanism for development of the new townships, such as Rajarhat or Salt Lake's Sector V, has run outside the planning framework of the KMDA. In both cases, the townships have been established under the Industrial Township Act, directly by the administrative order of the state government (Interview: PL-K-04, 20 December 2010). In 2005, administration of Sector V was separated from the elected municipality of Sal Lake to create a nominated body called 'Nabadiganta Industrial Township'.

Similarly, planning and development of the Rajarhat is directly handled by the state government. Initially, the project was handled by KMDA, but in 1998 it was taken out from KMDA and was given to another agency, HIDCO (Housing and Infrastructure Development Company) which reports to the Housing Department, as Gautam Deb, the Housing Minister in the Left Front government took the leadership role in shepherding the project. The Chief Planner of the Rajarhat informed when interviewed on 18 December 2010, that, consequent to the transfer of the project from the Urban Development Department to the Housing Department, the 24 mouzas (land subdivisions) which constitute Rajarhat were taken out of the Kolkata Metropolitan Area and turned into a separate planning area, with HIDCO as the planning and development authority.

For the development of Rajarhat, HIDCO acquired the land, built the roads and laid basic infrastructure. However for the development of residential and commercial projects, a public–private partnership approach was adopted. But the mechanism for involving the private sector was vastly different in Kolkata compared to Bangalore or Gurgaon. Conscious of its 'pro-poor' image, the Left Front government wanted the development in the area to be more 'inclusive', and attempted to keep speculative investors away. Thus, to develop the housing projects, the state government formed eight joint venture housing companies, with reputable private companies. All these ventures have 'Bengal' tied into the name like Bengal DCL, Bengal Ambuja, and Bengal Peerless. In these companies, PL-K-03 stated,

> Government holds 49 percent shares, the rest 51 percent are with the private partner. But the boards have 50:50 representations. Chairman is from Government, Managing Director is from private developer side. 50 percent of the apartments are for high income group people. Prices for which are decided by the private partner. 25 percent units are for middle income and 25 percent for low income group. Prices and unit sizes for the middle and lower income categories are set by the government. (Interview: PL-K-03, 18 December 2010)

However the commercial projects are developed by private companies. The new township was showcased as a major achievement of the Left Front government during the 2011 assembly election. However, it has also become controversial over land acquisition issues. The government helped those who lost land to form cooperatives or 'syndicates' to supply building materials to the area's booming construction industry. But the area is witnessing intensification of protests by the local population, over inadequacies of compensation payment and loss of livelihood. Protests have delayed development of roads and civic infrastructure. The next section, through the case study of the DLF-IT SEZ, concentrates on the development of Rajarhat.

8.5   Illustrated case study: DLF IT SEZ Rajarhat

The DLF IT SEZ Rajarhat, as the name suggests, is developed by the DLF Group of Delhi, the premiere real estate company, which has developed much of Gurgaon. The architect for the project is Design Plus, the same Delhi-based architectural firm which designed the IT SEZ at Gurgaon, as discussed in the previous chapter. However, unlike Gurgaon, where the DLF group is directly engaged in land purchase, here, the land was directly acquired by the government agency HIDCO. Subsequently it was handed over to DLF on a long-term lease.

Spread over 10.4 hectares of land, the DLF IT SEZ is located in Action Area I of Rajarhat. This project is also commonly known as DLF IT Park-II, as the DLF group had earlier developed another IT Park in Rajarhat, which operates under the old STPI scheme. The project is conveniently located as part of the IT corridor stretching from Salt Lake Sector V to Rajarhat New Town. It is also about 15 minutes' drive away from the international airport. Several other business parks and SEZs, such as Unitech IT SEZ, Bengal Ambuja IT Park and SP Info City are located close by. The Rajarhat's main arterial road runs along the north-western edge of the project and provides the main access (see Figure 8.3).

Figure 8.3 Location map of DLF IT SEZ Rajarhat [*Source*: DLF Group]

Another expressway is planned to run along the north-eastern boundary, but construction of this road has not started yet. A drainage canal runs along the south-western boundary. The plot adjoining the south-eastern boundary was vacant at the time of the site visit. Beyond this plot, another IT Park has been established. Shanties and squatter settlements have come-up along the drainage canal and also across the land demarcated for construction of the expressway.

About five thousand seven hundred people work in this IT-SEZ. Table 8.1 provides an outline of the business functions of the companies operating here.

Table 8.1 Occupants' list: DLF IT SEZ Rajarhat [*Source*: Project Manager DLF Group, personal communication on 5 March 2013]

Company	Functions and activities
IBM	Implementation and maintenance for software like SAP, Oracle, etc., research in Linux products, business analysis for banking, insurance, retail and telecom industries
Tech-Mahindra	Business process and technology management, in areas of banking, insurance, capital market, retail and healthcare
Ericson	Global operation support services for mobile network, core network, microwave transport, mobile broadband network, system integration and customer support
CMC	System engineering, integration, application design, testing, and ITES services for international clients

As is common for the IT business parks discussed in previous chapters, the IT SEZ has provisions for a gym, health club and business centre. One retail-cum-entertainment area has been planned adjoining the business park, but it cannot be accessed from inside the complex, as the project operates under the SEZ guidelines. Thus all incoming and outgoing items within the SEZ boundary area are required to be certified through the SEZ Commissioner. The project also provides a high level of security infrastructure. The whole complex is surrounded by a high perimeter wall. Access is restricted through manned security gates. However unlike the Gurgaon project, which is designed to conform with US norms for fire fighting, this project only conforms to Indian standards. RE-K-51, the project manager, stated when interviewed on 11 March 2011 that IT office space market in Kolkata is more budget conscious compared to Bangalore or Gurgaon. There are no takers for ultra-high quality spaces. The complex provides 100 percent power back-up for all electrical supply, including central air-conditioning. Ambulances and fire tenders are stationed in the complex for 24 hours a day, as has become the common practice in all high-end buildings. Figure 8.4 shows the external view of the project.

IT-K-66, a young executive working in one of the companies in SEZ, who had earlier worked at Bangalore and also had a short stint in London, commented that,

> This IT Park in Rajarhat is just like any other IT office building. Functional, efficient, but nothing really great. There are hundreds of such buildings in Bangalore, but in Kolkata, there are hardly a few. The choice here is very limited. (Interview: 11 January 2012)

IT-K-55, head of the Kolkata branch of a prominent Indian software company, had also expressed similar views when interviewed on 23 March 2011 and said, "We need many such projects, to bring Kolkata up to the level of Gurgaon or Bangalore". But it is also a complex game of demand and supply. The IT companies in Kolkata are suffering from lack of experienced professionals. Even senior Bengali executives who once left the city for greener pastures are unwilling to return. The Managing Director of WBEIDC observed,

> IT companies in Kolkata are suffering from man-power shortfall, particularly at the middle management level. There are good supplies in fresh graduates. But there are no managers. People who are 35 plus, married and settled are not willing to return. Not even the Bengali professionals. There is less number of firms here. So less chance of job hops. Quality of life is also an issue. There are too few good schools, hotels or apartments. (Interview: IT-K-59, 22 March 2011)

The point was further reinforced by IT-K-68, eastern zone head of NASSCOM (the industry chamber), "It is becoming a catch-22 situation. You can't build if there is no demand. But demand cannot increase unless the people are willing to come here. Kolkata, at least for the outsiders, does not provide exciting lifestyle opportunities" (Interview: 18 Jan 2012). The SEZ project has been established on low-lying farm land which was part of Lashkarhati village until 1998 and was used for the cultivation of rice, jute and potatoes. A large number of people were also engaged (many still are) in fisheries, as there are several large ponds and shallow water bodies, as may be seen in Figure 8.5.

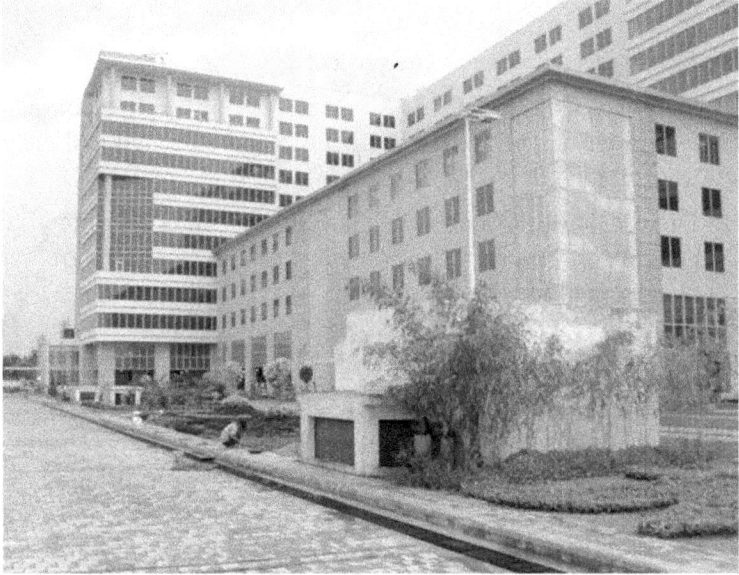

Figure 8.4 Inside DLF IT SEZ Rajarhat [*Source*: Author]

Figure 8.5 Laskarhati village ponds and agricultural lands [*Source*: Author]

LC-K-70, a member of the local panchayet, said that the village has a population of about 2000 and is inhabited by Muslim peasants. The area is undergoing rapid change now and the livelihood of the village households span across urban and rural vocations, as in a typical peri-urban area. The older villagers are still engaged in agricultural activities in the residual areas. But the younger generation are attempting to enter urban life. Those villages which received compensation payments from HIDCO for land acquisition have built permanent brick houses, though in terms of construction quality and finishing, these are far inferior to those in Gurgaon or Bangalore discussed in previous chapters.

There is a huge discontent amongst the villagers about the land acquisition process and a feeling that they were cheated out of their 'just' compensations. People in this area were mostly small and marginal farmers having less than 10 decimals (407 sq m). LC-K-70(A), a panchayet leader, belonging to TMC, advised that,

> Land in this area was acquired between 1995 and 1998 at the rate of INR 7000 to 8000 per *cottah* (Approximately USD 2.09 to 2.39 per sq m). Then they are selling for INR 40–45 *lakh* per *cottah* (USD 247 per sq m). This is not land acquisition. This is land loot. That's why they (Left Front) got punished. (Interview: 19 Jan 2012)

Another middle-aged ex-peasant, LC-K-70(B), turned small-time shop keeper complained,

> "We did not want to give our land. But we were pressured to. Irrigation water supply was cut off. We were told that the pumps are not working. We complained. But nothing happened. The money I got also evaporated quickly. Elder son wanted to set up a provision shop. Another son forced me to buy him a motor-cycle. Now I've neither money nor land. I'm completely finished".

HIDCO's stated aim of keeping the building promoters and speculative investors away from Rajarhat has not been successful. Governmental land development has also triggered a parallel rush by private builders. Investments by the IT companies, and building of high quality projects like DLF IT SEZ, Unitech IT SEZ, etc., has turned Rajarhat into a fashionable up-market neighbourhood. Consequently, land prices in the area have escalated. But 'officially' conversion of rural land to non-agricultural usage is problematic. So small-time promoters, with the 'right' local-level political connections, rule the land market. Rural pockets around Rajarhat and the extended eastern fringe of Kolkata are the prime targets of this land-grabbing racket. The local press regularly features stories of such illegal land conversion, as well as the filling of ponds and wetlands (Times of India 2009). LC-K-71, a member of the Rajarhat Jomi Bachao Committee (Rajarhat Save Land Committee), complained that CPI(M) cadres and property dealers having political connections pressurised people to surrender land.

> In those days the panchayet was ruled by CPI(M). This was the area of Haridas Mondol (name changed) a notorious local thug. His goon squad used to come and dump construction debris in the agricultural farms at night. They also used direct threats. In the name of HIDCO, local building promoters and party cronies also grabbed hundreds of acres. (Interview: 21 Jan 2012)

In the completely polarised political milieu of Kolkata, it was not possible to verify these allegations. CS-K-72, a journalist who writes on the land issue in the local press, observed when interviewed on 21 January 2012, that some coercion did take place, as the rural area of Rajarhat, just like elsewhere in Bengal, was a fiefdom of CPI(M)'s local leadership. The local party bosses ran their extortion rackets and patronage networks, with the connivance of the government machinery.

However, compared to the land conflicts of Nandigram or Singur, land acquisition in Rajarhat had happened in a much quieter manner, although in terms of scale, Rajarhat is far larger than either of the other two industrial projects. The tensions in Rajarhat surfaced from 2008 onwards after the Nandigram and Singur movements became household news, whereas land acquisition in this area was mostly done between 1995 and 1998. CS-K-02, (2nd Interview: 27 December 2011) an erstwhile political activist turned analyst who intimately studied the Nandigram and Singur incidents, attributes the deft handling of the issue to HIDCO, who involved local leaders from TMC, BJP, etc., from the inception stage. When asked about the role of the opposition parties in the Rajarhat land issue, LC-K-70 also noted, "We had been asking them for support but they were not forthcoming". (Interview: 19 Jan 2012)

Apart from involving the opposition party leaders in the planning stage, HIDCO also attempted to rehabilitate the land losers by organising them into 'cooperatives' or 'syndicates' to supply building materials.

Several such 'syndicates' have emerged in the Rajarhat area. They supply bricks, sand, cement and stone chips to the area's booming construction industry. However, the 'syndicates' have turned into local mafia. Several local architects and even HIDCO officials stated under conditions of strict anonymity, that it is the 'unwritten law of Rajarhat' that these items are to be sourced through the syndicates—paying an 'exorbitant' price. Even a big company like DLF has to follow the local rules of the game. RE-K-51, project manager for the DLF IT SEZ at Rajarhat admitted that bricks, cement, etc., are sourced from the syndicate only (Interview: 11 March 2011).

The syndicates enjoy political patronage and have parcelled out territories within the township. Recent years have also seen an eruption of turf wars between the rival syndicate gangs, leading to violence, including murder. Earlier, most of them were aligned to the Left Front. However, over the past couple of years, they shifted allegiance to TMC, the rising power in Bengal politics. In keeping with the times, the syndicates have named themselves after the TMC electoral slogans, such as Ma-Mati-Manush (Mother-Land-People) Syndicate or Poribartan (Change) Syndicate (The Telegraph 2011b, 2012c).

In the Rajarhat area, the flow of new investment opportunities and the creation of new employment opportunities for the educated middle-class Bhadralok youth in the globalised IT sector have in turn yielded parallel opportunities for the rural youth in the form of the building material syndicates and extortion rackets. But in the charged and intensely politicised atmosphere of Bengal, these have taken on political colours. The spatial transformation of Kolkata's fringe areas is deeply embedded in this political context. The next section looks at how different stakeholders are negotiating this political space.

8.6   Stakeholders in transformation of the urban fringe

8.6.1   Role of state and local governments

The West Bengal government has played a strong and supportive role in Kolkata's insertion in the orbit of the IT outsourcing-driven new Indian economy. However, the local political culture has substantially influenced how the state has responded to meet the demands of the new economic order. Compared to the non-ideological nature of the

Karnataka and Haryana polities, West Bengal is far more politicised along party lines, due to a long history of class struggle and the influence of leftist political thought. In the intensely politicised environment of West Bengal, the elected political leadership is opposed to a model of a developmental state like that of Karnataka, where the 'bureaucratic elites' command a stronger position in the policy space (Kadekodi, Kanbur & Rao 2007; Leftwich 2010). This supremacy of the party-oriented political leadership was strongly entrenched during the three-and-a-half decade long rule of the Left Front.

During the 1980s, powerful trade unions aligned to the ruling parties actively opposed computerisation of offices, fearing job losses. The educational policies of the Left Front also opposed setting up of private sector engineering colleges. These ideological positions not only delayed Kolkata's entry in the economic geography of India's IT services map, but spread a negative image amongst the business communities. Even after its gradual policy reorientation from the mid-1990s, the Left Front leadership's initial focus was on the big manufacturing sector, not IT services.

However, once the Left Front regime realised the potential of generating jobs for the middle-class youth of the state through the growth of the IT services, the state government played a proactive role. West Bengal's IT policy not only matched the other states in offering investment packages, but went a step further, by designating the IT services as essential infrastructure and thus legally sheltering the sector from the culture of frequent industrial strikes and work disruptions (Government of West Bengal 2003). It also designated WBEIDC as a single window agency to facilitate new investments. This proactive engagement of the state in facilitating IT investments has continued even after the change in government from Left Front to TMC in 2011. West Bengal government also sought to directly provide production and consumption space for the IT services sector—initially in Salt Lake and subsequently at Rajarhat New Town. Both of these areas are conveniently located—near the airport and not far from Kolkata's urban core, thus ensuring a steady supply of skilled technical labour. Developmental processes of both these townships also depict the strong hand of the state—from planning to project implementation and from land acquisition to landscaping. The differences between two prominent examples of post-1990s urban space of India, Gurgaon and Rajarhat, are stark and contrasting. The big real estate developers, which own thousands of hectares of land in Gurgaon, take leases of a paltry 10 hectares from the parastatal agencies to develop IT SEZs in Rajarhat.

In shaping the Rajarhat New Town, the Left Front government sought to create a more 'just' urban space compared to the utterly fragmented Gurgaon. Development of the township, spearheaded by the Housing department, through its subsidiary HIDCO, was, from the inception, underpinned on the notion of equity. As PL-K-03, the chief planner of HIDCO put it, "Being a state project, the objective was to provide accommodation for all classes of people, not just the rich" (Interview: 17 December 2010). So the state government not only did the planning, but also entered into formal partnerships with reputable private companies, and formed joint venture companies. Likewise, commercial development was also done through well-established companies with proven track records.

Moreover, the Left Front government, which had gained a reputation across India for facilitating participatory urban and rural local governance, sought to separate out the development of the IT-dominated urban spaces from elected municipal governments. Thus Salt Lake's Sector V is administered by 'Nabadiganta Industrial Township Authority' and Rajarhat is under HIDCO under the Industrial Township Act and administered by bureaucrats, rather than elected politicians. The state's Urban Development Secretary sought to justify this, "These are prime economic locations. MNCs and high-tech companies are located here. We need to provide professional services and safeguard from politicisation" (Interview: PL-K-04, 20 December, 2010).

However in the partisan political culture of West Bengal, the scope for this kind of bureaucratic–technocratic planning is far more limited compared to Karnataka. From land acquisition to resettlement of the affected rural population, wherever the administrative institutions of the state had come in contact with local communities, these issues have been mediated through the organised networks of the political parties. In the days of CPI(M)'s stranglehold over power, this mediation was systematically managed by the party apparatus or the 'local committee'. This in turn allowed the party's Bhadralok-dominated upper echelon to accommodate people from various lower social strata in the power matrix and strengthen its social coalition (Banerjee, PS & Roy 2005).

But this also blurred the distinctions between the party and the state institutions (Bardhan 2011; Chakrabarty 2011).

The close link between the party and the state snapped with the resounding defeat of the Left Front in 2011. But the new incumbent in power, the TMC, which is essentially a breakaway faction of the Congress party, is a charismatic leader-driven (in the form of Ms. Mamata Banerjee) set up. It neither has CPI(M)'s grass root level organisational strength nor the support of an entrenched social coalition (Bhattacharya, D 2004). The spectacular electoral victory of TMC was made possible through a strange alliance between the urban middle class and rural peasants. As CS-K-02 explained,

> It was a vote for change. Land conflicts were the spark which ignited the desire. Kolkata's middle-class Bhadralok intellectuals to rural peasants fearful of losing land had all combined to vote out the Left Front. But they have very different expectations. (Interview: 27 December 2011)

TMC's policies towards development of Rajarhat reflect the tensions and conflicts arising out of these 'very different expectations'. It is keen to develop the IT outsourcing and other white collar services in the financial services economy of Rajarhat. It is offering land at a throw-away price to Infosys and Wipro—which can create job opportunities for the Bhadralok youth. By developing museums and art galleries, it is keen to be seen as a promoter of art and culture—which again has a strong resonance with the Bhadralok communities. But at the same time it is extremely conscious of its new found popularity as protector of rural livelihoods. Fearful of rural backlash, it has categorically ruled out extending the 'SEZ' tag to the Infosys and Wipro projects. PL-K-73, a top official in West Bengal's IT department, expressed his strong disapproval and mentioned under strict anonymity that, "if such populist issues continue dominate decision making, then we can never compete with other states". (Interview: 22 February 2012)

8.6.2   Role of corporate sector

The role of the corporate sector in the development of Kolkata's IT services economy lies somewhere between the two contrasting patterns seen in Bangalore and Gurgaon. In Kolkata, the role of the IT-ITES corporate sector in the policy realm is far less conspicuous than in

Bangalore, where the high profile IT elites have become part of the urban governance framework. But it is not as small as in Gurgaon either, where the real estate sector acts as intermediaries between the IT corporate sector and the local state.

Kolkata had for long been one of India's leading commercial cities, and until the late 1960s, hosted several corporate headquarters and business chambers (Goswami 1989). But on the other hand, Kolkata's political elite, the Bengali Bhadralok class, had an ambiguous relationship with the city's corporate economy. It is interesting to note here that while the educated middle-class Bhadralok-dominated Kolkata's political, social and cultural landscape, they never had a strong presence in the city's economic space (Goswami 1989; McLean 2001; Sinha 2005). During the colonial times, this space was occupied by European entrepreneurs. It was then was taken over by the north Indian Marwari trading communities. There were hardly any Bengali capitalists. The Bengali Bhadralok occupied from managerial to clerical white collar desk jobs, but seldom controlled the capital.

Capital flights started taking place from Bengal during the economic recession and political turbulence of the 1960s. Even in those companies which retained their head offices in Kolkata, new investments were channelised to other, more business-friendly states. These factors further widened the schism between the political and the economic elites of Kolkata. Bengalis accused the Marwaris of asset stripping of old British era industries, not investing in technological modernisation and indulging in speculative investments, while the industrialists blamed lack of work culture and political hostility as the cause for capital flight (McLean 2001).

This hostile relationship began to change from the mid-1990s with the Left Front government initiating economic reforms and courting investments. The West Bengal government set up a high profile policy advisory team, under the leadership of R.P. Goenka, an eminent industrialist of Marwari descent (McLean 2001). Whilst the majority of the members of this committee were drawn from the old established corporate concerns, its core focus remained on heavy engineering industries. But the inclusion of a few technocrat–entrepreneurs drawn from Kolkata's consulting engineering circle opened up the possibility of IT services outsourcing as a new priority area.

A few large multidisciplinary engineering consulting firms, such as M.N. Dastur and DCL (Development Consultants Ltd.), had long been operating from Kolkata. From the early 1990s, they slowly started providing drafting, digitisation and other engineering drawing related services to US-based engineering firms. According to PL-K-53, Managing Director of WBEIDC,

> Presence of Dr S.C. Dutt (Chairman of DCL) in Jyoti *babu*'s (Jyoti Basu, Chief Minister, 1977–2000) inner circle made a key difference. DCL's impressive growth, providing employment to over one thousand engineers and its track record of handling complex projects abroad made a big impression in the Chief Minister's mind. (Interview: 22 March 2011)

The impression was further strengthened by the McKinsey report, which articulated Kolkata's advantage in the IT-ITES outsourcing sector and the Left Front officially started welcoming the IT sector, putting aside the ideological objections of the early 1980s. After the defeat of the Left Front, the TMC government continued a similar strategy of industry consultation. West Bengal's new IT policy was informed through the advice of Infosys founder Narayana Murthy, management guru Sam Pitroda and the IT industry body NASSCOM. According to IT-K-68, the head of NASSCOM's eastern zone, "The industry consultation helped shape the new IT policy. It has a strong focus on animation, games and graphics. The effort is to build links with Kolkata's strong art and film communities" (Interview: 18 January 2012). But the role of the IT-ITES corporate sector remained confined to this policy framing stage only. The more arduous task of policy implementation has remained stuck in the conflicting political pulls of the rural–urban dichotomy within the governing parties.

8.6.3   Role of civil society and community organisations

For a city with a high degree of political awareness and a large middle-class population, it is reasonable to expect that Kolkata will have strong civil society groups involved in the area of urban development. This however is not the case. A sharp divide along political lines and the long period of single-party dominance have stifled the scope for NGOs or non-partisan civil society groups to have an involvement in urban planning and governance issues (Bardhan 2011). Consequently, the roles of civil society groups in shaping Kolkata's urban transformation are not only smaller than Bangalore, but even less than Gurgaon. The anti-land acquisition movement in the Singur and Nandigram movements saw large-scale mobilisation of Kolkata's civil society—writers, poets, painters, film makers, actors and celebrities associated with Kolkata's vast cultural industry (Chakrabarty 2011). But these were well-known individuals; the organisation of the movements was largely carried out by the TMC and a few other small leftist parties (Nielsen 2010).

On urban issues, the voices and demands of organised NGOs and community organisations continue to be somewhat mute in Kolkata. It is the local units of the political parties, which act as the point of interface between the state and the people. Close involvement of the political activists, rather than NGOs and community organisations, on all civic issues, lead to frequent partisan conflicts on everyday issues. And these conflicts erupt into street protests and other disruptive activities with far more intensity or regularity compared to Bangalore and Gurgaon.

Urban planning in Kolkata, like elsewhere in India, had traditionally been handled in a top–down fashion by bureaucratic and technocratic institutions like local area development authorities. As discussed in Section 8.4.2, the first comprehensive, city wide urban planning activity was undertaken under the guidance of Ford Foundation experts during the 1960s (Bagchi 1987; Banerjee, T & Chakravorty 1994). Following that, the Calcutta Metropolitan Development Authority (CMDA, now renamed as KMDA) was established at the behest of the World Bank, as a centralised and technocratic planning agency to insulate planning from the vagaries of everyday politics and provide a long-term vision. After coming to power, the Left Front government attempted to curtail the powers of KMDA. At the same time, the Left Front sought to expand the scope for participatory planning through devolution of financial and administrative powers to the village panchayets and urban municipalities. These reforms drew wide attention, and at a later date informed the framing of the 73rd and 74th Amendment Acts in the Indian Constitution (Fuerstenberg 2010; Shivaramakrishnan 2011). But the scope for public participation under this model is closely mediated through the political party channels. This meant in the case of Bengal, hierarchical controls were imposed through CPI(M)'s party machinery. Pal (2006) attributes the decline of civil society activism to percolation of party-based politics in every sphere of life during the long reign of Left Front, which left no scope for any alternative approaches. He observed,

> Extreme politicization of public decision making along party lines prevented access to the political space needed in order for nonpartisan, non-state civic associations to participate effectively in the planning process in Kolkata. That is, excessive politicisation of local decision making is in fact detrimental to the cause of decentralized metropolitan planning. (Pal 2006, p.504)

Pal's view was supported by several planning officials, when discussed in the context of planning for Rajarhat. Planning for the township was handled exclusively by HIDCO, a public sector company, under the Housing Department and in the words of a local news report, considered to be the "fiefdom of Gautam Deb", the Housing Minister in the Left Front government. As PL-K-03, the Chief Planner of the township noted, public participation was done through "consultation with the local leaders of various political parties, including TMC". (Interview: 18 Dec 2010)

While 'excessive politicisation' in Bengal did not yield any space for independent NGOs and middle-class-dominated civil society activism as in Bangalore, on the other hand, it increased bottom-level political awareness. In almost all cases the spate of land acquisition-related protests was started by local organisations. Subsequently, involvement of the mainstream political parties added greater momentum. In Rajarhat also, a section of the evicted rural population formed an organisation called "Rajarhat Krishi Jami Adhigrahan o Rastriya Santras Birodhi Committee" (Rajarhat Anti Farmland Acquisition and State Terrorism Protest Committee), which spearheaded the local protests and petitioned various political parties for support. LC-K-54, a leader of the organisation said, "We went to every political party—TMC, BJP—everybody. They didn't listen to us" (Interview: 18 March 2011). When mainstream parties did not show much enthusiasm, a small radical leftist party came into the scene and helped the local people to organise. But in the process the movement took party colour. This pattern of mobilisation of peri-urban rural population and their protests in Kolkata stands in huge contrast to Gurgaon and Bangalore.

8.6.4   Characteristics of the governing regime

Based on the role of the different stakeholders in the transformation of the peri-urban landscape of Kolkata discussed above, the following section identifies the main characteristics of the local governance regime, using DiGaetano and Strom's (2003) framework.

- *Governing relations* – In recent years, the governing relationship in Kolkata shows efforts towards an inclusionary mode of development, managed through the formal bureaucratic machinery. But this relationship underwent several radical turns. During the colonial period, Kolkata's economic growth was driven by private capital. However in the post-colonial era the gap widened along ethnic lines between the Marwari-dominated capitalist class and the Bengali Bhadralok-dominated political class, with the latter gradually turning towards socialistic ideology. But the relationship between the state and the capital were again reappraised following the economic reforms of the 1990s. In this post-reform phase, the state made strident efforts to reinscribe Kolkata's position as one of India's leading economic hubs, this time in the IT-ITES sector. Growth in this sector has brought about a close synergy between the political and economic elites, as jobs created in this sector largely benefit the middle-class Bhadralok. The state sought to extend support to the IT-ITES sector—developing production and consumption spaces in new townships at Kolkata's urban fringe through a top–down, formal bureaucratic apparatus. The involvement of the private sector in this new urban space is carefully monitored by the state. However, due to prevalence of its strong leftist ideology, the state has made consistent efforts to follow an inclusionary development model, at least in Rajarhat especially—through resettlement of the affected rural poor. In this partisan political environment, such efforts of the state administration have come to be mediated through political parties. This in turn has contributed towards politicisation of the administrative institutions.

- *Governing logic* – Governing logic in Kolkata has been driven by the mobilisation of popular support in the larger political space of West Bengal. Kolkata's urban and industrial infrastructure considerably declined during the 1980s as the focus of the Left Front government was on consolidating its rural support base through agrarian land reforms. Pursuance of populist politics such as objection to computerisation and the abolition of English teaching from primary schools considerably reduced Kolkata's position as an attractive destination for corporate investments. In later years, as the Left Front government sought to step up its industrialisation drive, it was couched in the language of creating mass employment. In order to step up the process of industrialisation, the Left Front government went about large-scale land acquisition through the bureaucratic machinery, without adequate consultation at the local level. But in the process, it ended up creating a conflict over land acquisition. The successor TMC government's politics have been throughout guided by populist rhetoric to placate and reassure its newly acquired rural support base, against fear of governmental land acquisition. However, the government's stand on land acquisition for industrial development or extension of SEZ status to new IT business parks has come in the way of receiving high-value investments.

- *Key decision makers* – A strong imprint of the state is inscribed throughout the development process of Kolkata's IT sector. But unlike Karnataka, where the state also played a very strong role in facilitating economic growth, in the politicised environment of West Bengal, the political elites have been the key decision makers. The long rule of an ideologically oriented leftist coalition allowed it sufficient leeway in the policy space. There were frequent allegations that the party ideologues held greater leverage in framing policy decisions than the elected executives. The same pattern has continued under the TMC rule.

- *Political objectives* – Politics in Bengal is sharply polarised along party lines. Cutting across this partisan divide, there is a strong undercurrent of leftist political ideology. Despite this, Bhadralok upper castes hold the levers of power at the apex. To retain this hold, the political leadership has sought to make the development process more inclusionary and incorporate the rural poor and the lower castes in the support base. While some of the rural development measures have helped in fighting poverty, they have also resulted in much populist posturing which has hurt the state's economic prospects, particularly in areas like knowledge-intensive IT services. In situations of apparent conflict between urban economic growth and protection of rural livelihood, the political leadership has tended to support the latter—at least in espousing political slogans. But its record in delivering development is less strong.

Table 8.2 below contains a synopsis of Kolkata's urban governance characteristics discussed above.

Table 8.2 Characteristics of Kolkata's urban governance regime
[*Source*: Compiled by author based on DiGaetano and Strom's framework]

Parameters	Characteristics of the governing regime
Governing relations	• Efforts towards an inclusionary development model, managed through bureaucratic machinery and closely overseen by the political leadership
	• Attempt to create downstream economic linkages and rehabilitate the rural poor by forming building materials supply syndicate. But the local syndicates are mediated through political channels
Governing logic	• Growth in the IT services has created new opportunities to revive Kolkata's economic growth and create employment opportunities, after long period of stagnation.
Key decision makers	• Political elites are the key decision makers.
	• Disconnection between political and economic elites due to ethnic divides and the prevalence of strong leftist political culture. Growth in the IT services sector has somewhat bridged the gap by creating opportunities for the urban middleclass. But the corporate sector is still very weak in the decision making process.
	• There is high degree of politicisation and partisan divide. This has prevented the non-partisan civil society groups from playing any meaningful role in urban economic governance issues.
Political objectives	• The small urban middle-class-dominated political leadership depends on the rural poor for political survival.
	• In situations of conflict between urban economic growth and protection of rural livelihood, the political leadership has tended to support the latter.

Overall, the characteristics of the local governing regime may be termed as 'populist'. While the pursuance allowed the local regime's long innings in governance, it has retarded the state's progress in the market-driven global economy. Thus despite having the advantage of a large supply of educated work force, the state is unable to leverage its potential in the IT-ITES sector and continues to suffer a flight of the middle class to Bangalore, Gurgaon and elsewhere.

8.7   Summary of case study findings

This chapter analysed the development of the IT-services sector in the fringe areas of Kolkata. The West Bengal government has tried to play a strong and proactive role in bringing new investments in the sector. However, the acrimonious local political culture has substantially come in the way of Kolkata leveraging its full potential as a region with a large educated population, in the skilled labour-intensive IT services sector. Compared to the relatively non-ideological nature of the Karnataka and Haryana polities, West Bengal is far more politicised along party lines, due to long histories of class struggle and influence of leftist political thought. In the intensely politicised environment of West Bengal, the elected political leadership plays a much stronger role in shaping the developmental processes. This increases the possibility of economic policies being held hostage to narrow partisan considerations, uncertainties and delays. The political risk becomes higher for global investors in the IT-services sector, which seek policy stability.

Militant trade-unionism contributed to the decline of Kolkata's industrial and corporate services economy during the 1960s and 1970s. Then in the 1980s, rigid ideological positions of the leftist parties against computerisation in offices, fearing job losses, substantially delayed Kolkata's entry into the IT-services sector, conceding first mover advantage to other cities. From the mid-1990s, the steady flight of middle-class educated youth to other faster growing regions of India and abroad (as well as the inability of the government to attract industries in the manufacturing sector) forced a policy rethink.

Cutting across the political divide along partisan lines, the governance system at the apex is held by the urban middle-class Bhadralok elites, who had been historically associated with white collar professions. The Bhadralok community feel a strong attachment for the IT-services sector, for their own career aspirations, and see the industry as a natural fit. Thus, steady migration of its own youth folk to Bangalore, Gurgaon and other cities places, for IT sector jobs, put pressure on the state political leadership to change. West Bengal government not only declared IT as a priority sector but also provided subsidised land and high-quality infrastructure to the industry in the master-planned township of Rajarhat adjoining Kolkata. However, after a promising start, the growth suffered major hindrances due to conflicts over acquisition of rural lands by the state to meet the demands of the industry.

Market-based land supply mechanisms, which ensured rapid growth of Gurgaon and were subsequently adopted by Bangalore, are yet to mature in Kolkata. An equivalent class to the landed rural elites, who profited from opportunities in the commoditisation of peri-urban land does not exist in Kolkata, due to land reforms carried out in earlier decades. Agrarian land reforms helped the middle class, leftist leadership of the state to create a social coalition with the rural poor. However, this, in the course of time, turned into oppressive control by the ruling party. In Rajarhat, the state government sought to accommodate the livelihood concerns of the local poor by organising them, through party machinery into building material supply syndicates. However, these syndicates have turned into extortion rackets and the local tensions erupted into major conflicts, impacting land supply.

Caught in the vortex, between creating new economic opportunities for the middle-class youth, addressing livelihood concerns of the rural poor, and tackling political corruption at the lower level, the state's higher leadership has resorted to populist rhetoric and sloganeering, but has been unable to create a functioning land market. Thus, despite having an advantage in terms of skilled labour supply, Kolkata is unable to attract proportionate IT investments.

Synthesis and conclusion

9.1   Introduction

This chapter answers the research questions by synthesising discussions about the development of the IT clusters in the fringe areas of Bangalore, Delhi NCR and Kolkata. The rest of the chapter is organised as follows. Section 9.2 sequentially addresses four research questions and then provides a summary of the research findings. Section 9.3 then takes up the broad theoretical implications arising out of the research by interrogating the main analytical framework. Section 9.4 then discusses the policy implications of the research in the context of ongoing urban changes in India. Section 9.5 then suggests onward research possibilities. Section 9.6, the final section, concludes the book through a summary.

9.2   Answering research questions

9.2.1   Globalisation at the urban fringe

The first research question asked: What are the factors leading to the formation of the IT clusters in the fringe areas of the Indian cities?

Clustering of the IT outsourcing industry at the outer peripheries of the big Indian cities is happening due to a complex interplay of forces operating at multiple scales—economic globalisation; advancements in ICT technology; India's national economic restructuring; political decentralisation; ambitions of the regional- and state-level political elites; rising career aspirations of the Indian middle class; and growing linkage between the IT services sector and the real estate sector.

Advancement of information and communication technologies facilitated outsourcing of low value and routine office jobs to cheaper destinations globally from the early 1980s, following a similar trajectory to the shifting of Fordist manufacturing processes from the old industrial centres of the Global North to cheaper destinations worldwide (Dossani & Kenny 2003; Parthasarathy 2004). Starting off at the lowest level of the outsourced services value chain during the mid-1980s, over the next two decades, India has emerged as the leading player in this segment, capitalising on the availability of a large educated workforce and a supportive business environment.

Growth in the IT services industry has become a crucial component of India's impressive growth story in recent years and has run parallel to the process of national economic restructuring. The IT sector now accounts for 7.5 percent of the country's GDP, earns 25 percent of the foreign exchange, and as the largest private sector employer, directly and indirectly employs 11.7 million people (NASSCOM 2012). But these direct and indirect jobs taken together are miniscule compared to India's total labour force, and this has led the critics to doubt its role as an economic engine and to question supportive state policies (Benjamin 2010; D'Costa 2011; Upadhya, C. & Vasavi 2006).

However, to understand the political dynamics behind the support to the IT sector, we need to situate the development within the larger context of structural changes in India's economy and its spatial articulation. The trend of the Indian economy over the past six decades shows that the service sector has been steadily climbing up in proportion to the country's GDP while the proportion of agriculture is going down. The proportion of industrial manufacturing is also increasing, but at a lower rate (Reserve Bank of India 2012). The rate of this change, substantially accelerated from the early 1990s, with the opening up of the economy and the beginning of IT services exports. The post-liberalisation boom has also substantially expanded the size of the urban middle class (McKinsey Global Institute 2007).

Growth led by the IT services has got intimately entangled with the career aspirations of this rapidly expanding new urban middle class and has fuelled the hopes of the policy elites who see, through the success of the industry, a hope to fast-track economic development of the country, after it has languished for several decades. Employment generated by the IT-ITES, although insignificant if viewed at a national scale, does matter at the urban scale, particularly in the biggest cities of India. Seven big urban agglomerations together account for 92 percent of the export trade volume (NASSCOM & A.T.Kearney 2009). The nature of the industry, which requires a labour force with high technical and communication skills, has led to clustering of the firms around these cities, which have large educated middle-class populations (Parthasarathy 2004).

Being associated with the aspirations of the vocal middle class in the largest urban centres of the country along with the nation-building dreams of the political elites, have enabled the IT sector to favourably negotiate the policy environment at national and state levels for a long period. The national government initially provided 20 years of tax holiday under the STPI scheme (1991–2011) and then extended it for another 15 years under the SEZ Act of 2005. A host of other fiscal and regulatory benefits are available from the state governments as well. There is increasing economic competition between the state governments to attract the industry to their own cities. As the incentive packages are designed through industry consultation, this has brought about a high degree of similarity between the facilities offered by different states. In this scenario, ability of the states to organise supply of *land*, in sufficient scale to meet the production needs of the industry near major urban centres with large educated *labour* has become the key differentiator, determining the economic geography of the IT services in India.

The locational trends of the Indian IT industry depict a twin-track approach. It is, at once, a force of concentration as well as dispersal. Thus, when seen at the national scale, the IT companies are showing a clustering tendency in the metropolitan regions to meet their *labour* requirements. Paradoxically however, at the metropolitan region scale, the firms tend to disperse away from the urban core and cluster in fringe areas to meet its *land* requirements. Earlier research had shown that the IT companies—particularly those at the higher end of the market, for whom corporate image and high-quality infrastructure are main concern, prefer suburban business parks against CBD offices (Aranya 2008). This locational paradigm differs from the norm that the producer services companies tend to prefer CBD locations which facilitate face-to-face interactions with their clients (Sassen 2001).

This difference may be explained by the fact that even though the Indian IT sector works for services verticals like banking, insurance, tourism, engineering design, etc., they essentially perform specific assignments outsourced by their Western partners and do not perform producer services work in the truest sense. They are linked with their remote clients through telecommunication networks, and CBD location does not provide any additional advantage. Rather, the big companies, having extensive international clientele, prefer gated business parks which offer high-quality infrastructure matching Western standards. The business parks also offer ready-to-move-in facilities and also customised building solutions to meet the industry needs. The CBD areas of most Indian cities suffer acute congestion and infrastructural deficiencies and are unable to meet the spatial demands of the new economy, neither in quality nor in volume. To accommodate the land and labour requirements of the industry, the parastatal agencies are facilitating development of new townships in the fringe areas of the big cities, bypassing inner-city squalor.

Recent changes in the regulatory environment, and the switch over from the STPI scheme to the SEZ scheme have added a further push to the suburbanisation of the industry and also institutionalised the bonding between the IT and real estate sectors. The two sectors acting in tandem have become the major force, driving spatial expansion of the Indian cities towards the outer periphery. In order to get tax benefits, the IT companies are now required to be physically located within a designated SEZ complex. But, it is almost impossible to find the minimum stipulated area required to meet SEZ norms in the congested inner-city areas.

Most IT-centric SEZs are being promoted by the property developers. Construction activities in the scale to build an IT SEZ are beyond the core strength of most software and BPO companies. The smallest SEZ situated on 10 hectares of land has the potential to generate between 200,000 and 300,000 sq m of built space (Interview: RE-D-19, 18 January 2011). Whereas case studies in three IT business parks (in Sections 6.5, 7.5 and 8.5) showed that even big companies like Microsoft and Yahoo occupy between 25,000 and 40,000 sq m of office space. The projects also accommodate a large number of small tenants who occupy area in the 1500–2500 sq m range. Moreover, multinational companies typically prefer to lease, rather than own space in India, as this allow greater flexibility in scaling up or down in response to the global economic climate.

It is also important to note here that construction and building activities are amongst the messiest sectors in the Indian economy, with cumbersome regulatory mechanisms which further deter the MNC and Indian IT companies from venturing into SEZ or office park developments. On the other hand, these difficulties have created opportunities for the property developers, with appropriate local networks and connections. As soon as the SEZ Act came into vogue in

2005, the Indian real estate sector seized the opportunity in a big way and launched a series of IT-centric projects. As many as 285 out of the 355 approved IT SEZ projects are being promoted by the real estate companies (Government of India 2012). By providing customised built spaces to the IT industry, within secured SEZ enclaves, the real estate sector has become the interface between the global and the local. Until 2005 the relationship between the IT and real estate sectors had been growing as per market demand, but then there was a paradigmatic shift and the bonding became institutionalised.

Almost simultaneous liberalisation of the FDI norms in the construction and building sector provided additional stimulus to the real estate industry, bringing new financing options and expanding the market volume. The combined impact of the SEZ Act and the relaxation of the FDI norms on the land and property market were phenomenal. Within 2 years, investments worth USD 11.3 billion were made in the forms of real estate-linked mutual funds (Jones Lang LaSalle 2010, 2012b). It is important to note here, just as multinational IT companies avoid directly entering the Indian land and property market, likewise global fund houses also prefer the indirect route investing *equity stakes* in high value investment grade projects like IT SEZs, prestigious office parks, and exclusive residential complexes. For the real estate industry, as discussed in Section 5.7, from 2005 onwards, equity became the main route to project finance as the debt option dried up. As the FDI inflow in the Indian land market started increasing, the Reserve Bank of India began to tighten money flows into the real estate market, and stopped bank lending for land acquisitions, to protect the banking sector from overexposure in the volatile land market. As bank lending stopped, the property developers turned to the global fund houses, offering equity stakes in projects, to finance their land acquisition drives.

In spatial terms, the bulk of these investments went into the fringe areas of the big cities, the locus of the new economic growth. Much of these investments are, of course, speculative. The post-2008 meltdown in the global economy has impacted the IT outsourcing industry. Visits to IT SEZ sites during fieldwork revealed that construction schedules have slowed down, due to slackening of demand. Nevertheless, the developers are holding on to the land that they acquired at the peak of FDI inflow, while the property prices in the neighbourhood have substantially appreciated.

The link between the IT sector and the real estate sector has turned into a powerful growth machine, driving spatial expansion of the Indian cities towards the outer fringe. Several civil society activists and even high government officials interviewed during the fieldwork accused the IT sector of turning into a front for real estate activities. The IT-ITES sector directly accounted for 48 percent of office space demand in 2010 (Jones Lang LaSalle 2010) and is *the* foremost stimulant behind premium housing complexes, hotels, shopping malls, educational institutes and specialty hospitals which are appearing in the new cities like the Electronic City (near Bangalore) Gurgaon (near Delhi) and Rajarhat (near Kolkata). These are the spaces of accumulation, which are intimately tied to, and articulate global capital. These are also the spaces of work and leisure of India's new urban middle class, from the software start-up entrepreneurs to the humble call-centre operator. However, the production process of these globalised spaces demonstrates the strong influence of the place-specific political dynamics, which have contributed to a differentiated, regionally articulated developmental landscape, as discussed in the next section.

9.2.2   Local political dynamics and global economic processes

This section answers the second research question, which asked: How do differences in local political dynamics impact on the development of the IT clusters?

Case studies of Bangalore, Gurgaon-NCR and Kolkata demonstrate that even though all three urban regions function under the overarching macroeconomic and regulatory structure of the post-reform Indian national state and are trying to attract the same type of industry, agential factors play a decisively strong role in shaping the growth trajectory of each local IT cluster. These differences may be attributed to place-specific socio-political factors—such as political contestations in terms of rural–urban affiliations; and the interplay between class and caste interests and identities, which ultimately impact the effectiveness of the governing regime in perusing its economic objective.

The outcome of regional variations in political culture, measured in terms of growth generated through the IT services sector, shows stark differences, as shown in Table 9.1. Bangalore, the smallest in population, has generated the maximum economic growth in the sector, followed by the NCR belt, while Kolkata lagged way behind, even though it has a large educated population base and lower property prices. Economic opportunities in both Bangalore and the NCR have drawn large numbers of migrant labour, whereas Kolkata's growth rate is more modest.

Table 9.1 Comparison of three Indian IT clusters [*Source*: Population (Census 2011), Export earnings (STPI 2010), Number of SEZs (Government of India 2012), Number of companies and number of employees – (Chatterjee 2012; Government of Karnataka 2011), Office availability (Jones Lang LaSalle 2010), Monthly rent (Jones Lang LaSalle 2012a)

	Bangalore	National Capital Region	Kolkata
Urban agglomeration population in 2011 (million)	8.73	21.75	14.62
Urban agglomeration population in 2001 (million)	4.13	12.79	13.21
Export earnings in Indian Rupees (million)	625,000	267,180	54,300
Number of IT-ITES-oriented SEZs	34	53 (Gurgaon – 34)	15
Number of IT-ITES companies	2084	1700	500
Number of employees	500,000	375,000 (Gurgaon – 250,000)	100,000
Office space availability in 2010 (million sq m)	4.99	4.04	0.96
Monthly rent for 1000 sq m office space in 2012 (in USD)	77 to 112	77 to 146	55 to 86

While the state governments are providing a range of fiscal and non-fiscal incentives to attract IT investments, the ability of the local governing regimes to ensure a steady supply of *land* in close proximity to the big cities having an educated *labour* pool has become the most crucial determinant of 'success' in attracting the industry. Consequently, the parastatal agencies are facilitating development of greenfield townships adjoining their major urban centres. However, this process of arranging land supply to meet the spatial needs of the new economy, through horizontal expansion of the cities, clashes with the livelihood concerns of the peri-urban agrarian communities—often with serious political implications. At this point of intersection between the local and global forces, the roles of local political leadership become crucial as mediators between competing claims. And political choice of the local leadership sets the direction of the urban economy.

It is important to remember here two crucial attributes of India's urban governance system. First, the locus of power over urban economic policies rests at the state government level, not with the elected municipal governments. Second, in all major states, the rural areas hold considerable power in electoral terms (Shivaramakrishnan 2011). In this situation, pursuance of an economic agenda, particularly one which involves land issues at the urban fringe, depends to a large extent on the processes of accommodation between rural and urban interests; the composition of the governing coalitions; and the power relationships amongst its constituents.

As discussed earlier, political polarisation in both Karnataka and Haryana is essentially along caste lines, whereas in Bengal, which has a leftist political legacy, polarisation is along class and party lines. The non-ideological nature of the political parties, along with regular changes in government, helped to evolve a broad consensus about a pro-globalisation, market-oriented economic policy in both Karnataka and Haryana. However, it is also evident that the rent-seeking objectives of a section of the politicians had a role in shaping this consensus. Increasing interrelationship between the IT and the real estate sectors has 'sweetened' the appeal of the globalised new urban economy to a large number of rural-centric politicians with a direct interest in peri-urban land conversion issues.

Increasing opportunities for accumulation through commoditisation of land explain the political support from the rural-centric leadership of Haryana and Karnataka in favour of the IT-driven real estate growth machine. Dominant communities, the Lingayat and the Vokkaligas of Karnataka and the Jats of Haryana, who hold the leverage of political power in these two states are essentially landed agriculturists, as opposed to middle-class Bhadralok-dominated Bengal (Jodhka & Dhar 2003; Kennedy 2012; Shastri 2009; Sinha 2005). Important political families also own large land holdings near Bangalore and Gurgaon. The rise in agricultural land prices directly benefits them. In recent decades, both Karnataka and Haryana have witnessed a spurt in allegations of political corruption, particularly about illegal land transactions.

Comparatively, the top leadership of Bengal has a higher reputation for probity. But the state's growth rate is lower, the political regime is more fractious, and is torn between urban–rural dichotomies. The leadership's keenness to generate economic growth and middle-class jobs by bringing in IT investments is held back by the fear of antagonising the rural poor. Urban middle-class Bhadralok communities hold the levers of power at the apex in all political parties and government. But unlike their Karnataka and Haryana counterparts, Bengal's political elites have no direct leverage over the land economy.

There is a strong leftist political culture in Bengal, and the political leadership had sought to make the development process more inclusionary by incorporating the rural poor in the governance structure. Governing logic here had been driven by the mobilisation of popular support in the larger political space of rural West Bengal, outside Kolkata. This to a great extent hurt the metropolitan region's urban and industrial economy, the region's main growth driver for over two centuries. Populist decisions like objection to computerisation, opposition to English teaching and militant trade unionism drove away the city's strong financial and corporate services sector (along with industrial manufacturing) and discouraged new investments during the 1980s. Thus, just about the time the globalisation process in Bangalore and Delhi NCR began to take-off, Kolkata was being pulled back by the local political forces.

From the mid-1990s, the Left Front changed direction and began to woo private capital for IT services and other sectors. Thus both Kolkata and the NCR began about the same time to seek IT investments, though both cities were about a decade behind Bangalore. Availability of a large educated labour force and supply of land—though state machinery— attracted many IT-ITES-BPO companies to open office in Kolkata. Later, as the Left Front further stepped up its industrialisation drive, it was unable to 'sell' the idea to its rural support base and ended up creating conflicts in several areas over land acquisition.

It is important to take note of the difference in the land supply mechanism in three metropolitan regions. Under influence of the real estate lobby, Haryana pioneered a market-oriented land policy from the late 1970s, which allowed the developers to directly procure and assemble large land parcels. Later, these areas were turned into high-quality gated enclaves to cater to the demands of the global corporate sector. Gurgaon is a product of this neoliberal city-building process with minimal state intervention. However it is also a highly fragmented urban space, marked by severe infrastructure shortfalls and environmental degradation, which are becoming apparent as the city grows.

Karnataka, which has a strong state tradition, initially sought to encourage investments in the IT sector by arranging land through state machinery, as in the case of Bangalore's Electronic City. As Bangalore's growth momentum picked up, the city faced land scarcity and infrastructure deficiencies—which also threatened capital flight. Taking a cue from Gurgaon, Bangalore liberalised land-supply processes, allowed developers to directly purchase agricultural lands and simplified zoning norms for conversion of agricultural lands for IT projects. The second and third IT clusters of Bangalore had come about through this private route and ensured better returns for the farmers, with a steady escalation in property prices. But unlike Gurgaon's laissez faire approach, Bangalore's expansion is managed through a metropolitan-level planning mechanism—for coordinated infrastructure delivery.

However, Bengal with a leftist political tradition persisted with the state-led approach towards land supply. No doubt, close governmental attention ensured coordinated infrastructure development and good urban environmental quality for the master planned township of Rajarhat, but the area also faced more land conflicts and local discontents than Gurgaon or Bangalore. Bengal's middle-class leadership approached the issue of transition from agriculture to industry and rural to urban, in abstract theoretical terms, as in a classic developmental model. They did not visualise the land supply angle as insiders, as perhaps the more rurally rooted leadership of Karnataka and Haryana would have done.

Table 9.2 Comparison of agricultural land holding sizes [Source: Modified by the author after acquiring basic data from (Rawal 2008)]

	Distribution of land holding sizes in 2003–04 (in percentage)			
	Less than 2 ha	2–5 ha	5–10 ha	More than 10 ha
Haryana	28.20	35.87	23.72	12.21
Karnataka	35.35	37.15	16.13	11.37
West Bengal	84.76	13.05	2.20	0.0
India	42.47	30.53	15.21	11.77

Land-holding size also matters. Farmers in Kolkata's peri-urban belt, whose land holding sizes are much smaller compared to their counterparts in Gurgaon and Bangalore, are less willing to give up the land and move into the uncertainties of the urban economy. While data about city-wise land ownership patterns were not available, a state-level comparison of land ownership as shown in Table 9.2 indicates that in Haryana, 35 percent of the land parcels are bigger than 5 hectares, whereas in Bengal, due to land reforms, 85 percent of the lands are held by small and marginal farmers. Thus, individual farm households near Kolkata get only a meagre amount of money for their land compared to those in Gurgaon and Bangalore, which reduces their incentive to sell.

On the contrary, the legacy of peasant mobilisation on the land issue enabled Bengal's main opposition party, TMC, to channelise livelihood vulnerabilities of the rural poor on the land issue into a desire for change, and unseated the Left Front in 2011. Bangalore also witnessed major land conflicts, which delayed the new international airport and the third IT cluster. Yet these agitations led by Janata Dal (S) petered out after a while, as increasing land values rapidly lured away the peri-urban farmers and rural elites from opposing new developments. Gurgaon, which had been going through such market-driven accumulation processes for over three decades, did not encounter any major political resistance, and the discontent of the local communities remained locally contained.

Opportunities for accumulation through commoditisation of land received a further boost from 2005 as FDI began to flow into India's real estate market. During the boom phase in the global economic cycle between 2006–08, high-value projects like IT SEZs attracted over USD 11 billion in FDI—which the property developers utilised to finance land acquisitions (Jones Lang LaSalle 2012b). Liberal land policies allowed Gurgaon and Bangalore to garner high proportions of this FDI investment. Naturally, land prices in these dynamic but volatile markets increased faster compared to the more controlled environment of Kolkata. And as a consequence, landed rural elites in Gurgaon and Bangalore developed closer ties with the IT-driven real estate growth machine, compared to the small peasants in Kolkata's rural periphery.

Synergy between 'land' availability in areas proximate to 'labour' supply pool in the big cities, has become the crucial equation which determines the economic geography of the Indian IT services sector.

Case studies in Bangalore, Kolkata and Gurgaon (NCR) demonstrate that how these regional IT clusters develop and link with the global opportunities is to a great extent shaped by local agential factors, which play crucial roles on issues like land supply. The IT sector has become the engine of the growth machine behind the spatial expansion of Indian cities. The local political regime plays the crucial role of steering this machine, how it turns and which direction it takes. But to understand how this road map is configured, it is necessary to look at the roles and relationships between the key actors of the local governing regime, as discussed in the following section.

9.2.3   Actors and in transformation of the urban fringe

This section answers the third research question: Who are the key actors and what are their roles in the development of India's regional IT clusters?

Partnerships and coalitions between political and business interests have become the dominant paradigm in contemporary local economic development strategies under neoliberalism in many cities. However, manifestations of such elite coalitions are contextual. Rational choice of the individual actors in the partnerships and thereby the nature of their collective relationship are shaped by place-specific factors including degree of local autonomy, modes of raising revenue and the nature of public participation in governance (Davies 2003; Kantor, Savitch & Haddock 1997).

Case studies about the formation of IT clusters around the metropolitan regions of Bangalore, Gurgaon-NCR and Kolkata demonstrate that variations in local histories, social contexts and contemporary political contestations have led to the formation of contrasting patterns of governance in the three metropolitan regions. The regime in Bangalore is corporatist. The upper bureaucracy, IT corporate sector and civil society elites have formed a compact, to turn the city into a prominent hub in the global knowledge economy. A property development-led, laissez faire regime is in place in Gurgaon-NCR, which turned it into a global BPO hub within a short time frame. And thirdly, a state-led approach is in place in Kolkata to fashion economic regeneration by attracting investments in IT services, and offset the decline of industrial manufacturing.

As discussed in Chapter 6, Karnataka government plays a very strong role in supporting the knowledge economy sector of Bangalore, even though the foundation for the same could be attributed to the decision of the national government to concentrate electronic and aeronautical industries through public sector investments during the 1950s to 1970s. The governmental elites, particularly its strong civilian bureaucracy, have a long tradition of supporting industrial development and higher academic research through the state machinery (Kadekodi, Kanbur & Rao 2007). In recent years, this has turned into extensive patronage for the IT-ITES, biotechnology and aerospace industries. It was the first state to formulate an IT policy, which later inspired other states. Similarly it also pioneered the suburban business park as a spatial model for the IT outsourcing industry, by facilitating the development of Electronic City in Bangalore's southern periphery, through provision of land and civil infrastructure.

Policy elites of Bangalore are acutely conscious of retaining the city's leadership position as India's pre-eminent knowledge industry hub in the face of regional economic competition. To realise this objective, the administrative and political leadership of Bangalore have broadened the governance network to include the non-state actors in corporate and civil society. Rapid economic growth and population increase began to severely strain Bangalore's civic infrastructure from the mid-1990s onwards, leading to severe criticism from the IT-ITES corporate elites. At the same time, neighbouring Hyderabad began to aggressively woo the sector. Faced with threats of regional economic competition and capital flight, the top leadership of the state formed partnerships (e.g. BATF) with the IT-ITES corporate sector and civil society elites to restructure the governance arrangements of Bangalore, improve infrastructure and also to generate new growth spaces.

However, the evolution of this new policy mechanism was made possible due to the political leadership provided by Chief Minister S.M. Krishna, an urbane and sophisticated politician, who wished to cultivate a modern image (Scoones 2003). Currently the incumbent BJP government has also adopted a similar strategy of including the IT and biotech corporate elites as well as civil society leaders in the ABIDe task force. The close cooperation between a growth-oriented upper bureaucracy, senior political leaders, top corporate leadership and a pliant civil society in fashioning the urban growth story, in many ways depicts the 'model' developmental state as characterised by Leftwich (2010).

Like Bangalore, the state institutions also play a key role in the development of Kolkata's IT-ITES sector. But unlike Bangalore, where the governance processes have incorporated the corporate sector and the civil society, here the approach is more top-down state-centric. Also unlike Bangalore, where civil service bureaucrats hold huge leverage in economic governance—in the sharply politicised environment of Kolkata, the political elites have been the key decision makers. Moreover, the roles of the corporate sector and civil society are purely secondary in Kolkata.

Development of Rajarhat's IT hub clearly demonstrates these points. The state sought to extend support to the IT-ITES sector by developing production and consumption spaces in the new townships through a top-down, formal bureaucratic apparatus. HIDCO, the state agency, exclusively acquired land, master planned the area, laid the infrastructure and then invited 'select' IT companies and IT SEZ developers by allocating land to them, through exclusionary negotiation. Due to deep rooted socio-political factors, there is no space for the corporate sector or the civil society in this state-led process. The long rule of an ideologically oriented leftist coalition allowed it sufficient leeway in the policy space. The political leadership—in the form of Gautam Deb, the Housing Minister of the Left Front government—took the key leadership role. The same pattern continued under the TMC rule. Under a mass leader like Mamata Banerjee, the party's populist electoral manifesto has become the guiding template for key economic policy decisions.

The Bhadralok middle class which dominates Bengal's political landscape never developed close ties with the economic elites of the city, which was earlier dominated by the Europeans and then taken over by Marwari trading communities (Goswami 1989; Sinha 2005). Thus, there is a social distance between the political and economic elites of the city. But this gap is obviously far less in the context of the IT outsourcing industry, when compared to the manufacturing sector. The Bengali middle class had traditionally identified itself with white collar service jobs, and this affinity is evident in the way the leadership is trying to lure in IT companies like Infosys and Wipro, through lucrative land deals. But at the same time, in a politician-dominated governance system, each decision is also seen through the lens of electoral risk. In situations where economic decisions are likely to cause adverse political fallout, the political leadership quickly backtracks. Whereas, in Bangalore, economic policies are more bureaucratised and thus comparatively shielded from electoral politics. Also unlike Bangalore, scope for civil society activism in Kolkata's urban policy regime is extremely limited. The injection of partisan political ethos in every sphere of life during the long years of the Left Front rule eroded space for non-partisan NGOs (Pal 2006). Rather, it is the imprint of the state which is strongly inscribed in the development process of Kolkata's IT cluster and its resultant urban transformation.

In comparison, Gurgaon's growth is more laissez-faire. The strong middle class which is guiding Bangalore's planning machinery is only at a very nascent stage of development in Gurgaon and does not have any real power. Here the corporate real estate sector dominates the stage with the state government agencies providing tacit, background support. The Haryana government pioneered a very liberal land policy in the late 1970s much before the advent of economic reforms at the national scale. The liberal regulatory regime enabled the real estate developers to leverage Gurgaon's locational proximity to Delhi, to bring in a large volume of IT sector investments. State agencies played a supporting role.

The entrepreneurial leadership by the real estate sector is evident throughout Gurgaon's developmental journey. Strategic choices made by the big property developers, whether in buying land near the airport, and/or developing high-quality properties matching global corporate specifications and attracting the IT-ITES sector to invest in the region— have shaped the evolution of Gurgaon. In this market-led mechanism, the role of the state agencies is secondary. Prior to the 1990s, Haryana was a predominantly rural agricultural state, without any big cities. The top political and bureaucratic leadership sitting in distant Chandigarh, inexperienced in large scale urban management and steeped in a rural-centric political milieu, 'outsourced' Gurgaon's urban development to the real estate developers. The characteristic of the regime is clientelistic.

Neither the IT-ITES sector nor the civil society wield much decision-making power in this governance structure. Unlike Bangalore and Kolkata, the IT-ITES companies almost exclusively operate from leased spaces developed by the realty companies, which minimises their interface with the local state. Civil society groups are rather marginal in influence, particularly when dealing with the powerful real estate lobbies. The crony capitalism promoted by the regime resulted in a highly fragmented urban landscape in Gurgaon, marked by deep social inequalities and huge infrastructure deficiencies. Yet it makes no major dent in the electoral prospects of the local governing regime, which thrives on support drawn through caste mobilisation and earnings from the property market speculations.

Analysis about the roles of the key actors behind the development of India's three big regional IT clusters demonstrates the importance of the local actors and the social contexts which influence their decision-making process. Similarity of the macro-economic environment or the regulatory constraints does not automatically lead to similarity in the response of the local governing regimes. The agency of the local leadership plays a crucial role in determining its own alliance partners based on specific local political dynamics, and this in turn guides their rational choice about economic direction. Global actors such as the IT-ITES corporate sector demonstrate a high degree of flexibility in negotiating within the local context. Thus for instance, in Bangalore the IT sector has become an important part of the corporatist urban governance network. But in Gurgaon, they operate under the shadow of the powerful real estate sector, which operates as an intermediary between the global corporate sector and the state. In Kolkata, the situation is somewhat in between. The IT sector is directly wooed for investments by the state government, but does not share much influence in the governance mechanism.

However, just as the linkages between the local political and global business interests are shaped by the place-specific context, similarly these linkages impact the local communities. These impacts become hugely important and often turn conflictual when the political and business interests start reconfiguring the peri-urban landscape to make space for the globalised economic enclaves at the fringe areas of the big Indian cities. The next section looks at how the planning systems of the Indian cities are trying to balance the conflicts between the global corporate sector and the local communities.

9.2.4   Balancing the local and the global

This section answers the fourth research question: How the governing regimes of the Indian cities are trying to deal with the tensions between the technology clusters and the local communities.

Urban planning in India has traditionally been a top-down exercise, conceptualised by a technocratic elite, and implemented by bureaucratic administrative machinery, with little scope for either meaningful public participation or rehabilitation of people displaced by new developments, beyond a one-time monetary compensation. The decision-making powers are concentrated in the hands of the urban development authorities functioning directly under the provincial state governments with minimal involvement of the municipal state. In the post-globalisation era, emergence of the IT-ITES sector as the driver of a real estate growth machine leading to rapid horizontal expansion of the Indian cities into the peri-urban fringe, has brought in several additional complexities in the planning process, as people of two vastly different socio-economic backgrounds have come to coexist side by side (Dupont 2007). As she puts it, "arbitration and management of these coveted spaces are rendered problematic (as) they are situated beyond the administrative limits of the city in zones that are generally not identified as specific entities of planning" (Dupont 2007, p.90).

IT clusters in India are being developed in these peri-urban areas, which are located beyond the municipal administrative domains of the core city and lie in the panchayet or rural council areas, such as Gurgaon, Rajarhat and Electronic City. Globalised IT-ITES executives and the rustic rural population now coexist in these new urban spaces, leading to new claims and contestations.

However, it is vitally important for the local governing regimes to accommodate these conflicting or diverse stakeholders in the planning process. With the proportion of urban population still constituting less than one-third, the balance of power at state level is still heavily loaded in favour of the rural electorate, and any major political step which can impinge on rural livelihood or cause distress can backfire politically. Several state-level election results, such as TDP's debacle in Andhra Pradesh in 2004, Congress government's loss in Karnataka 2004 and most recently, the Left Front government's complete rout in West Bengal have been attributed to pursuance of economic policies which sought to fast track economic growth through urbanisation and industrialisation— neglecting rural concerns (Malik 2011; Sainath 2005). In this context, it is essential for the local governance coalition to politically accommodate the concerns of the rural population in the peri-urban areas. This process of accommodation, however, takes multiple trajectories depending upon the contours of the local political terrain.

Bangalore's urban expansion and development processes are managed through the Comprehensive Development Plans (CDP) prepared by BDA. CDP (2005–15), the one currently in vogue, covers the entire extended metropolitan region of 1306 sq km. Unlike earlier generations of master plans in India, the CDP has attempted to go beyond mere physical planning and integrate economic and social equity issues. Even the familiar three overlapping circles diagram is also included in the document to show its commitment to sustainable development. But, symbolism notwithstanding, the core thrust is on deriving economic growth through globalisation. The vision document outlines its key objective, "to retain its pre-eminent position as a City of the Future through its cosmopolitan character and global presence, and to enable and empower its citizens with growth opportunities to promote innovation and economic prosperity..." (Bangalore Development Authority 2007, p.24)

On the social equity front, there are detailed discussions about slum rehabilitation and urban informal trading, but there is no indication about how it will ensure the livelihood of the rural population at the urban fringe, which gets engulfed in the urban expansion process. The only indication that these people are being considered is the note in the CDP about paying market rates for governmental land acquisitions. From 1999 onwards, Bangalore's land acquisition policy has undergone a major shift and has come to increasingly rest on market principles. The Karnataka government simplified procedures for conversion of agricultural land to IT business parks and other commercial uses and reduced direct acquisition to aid private sector projects.

This change is evident through the growth process of its three IT clusters. Electronic City, the first cluster, was built entirely on land acquired by the state agencies. But for the second cluster, at Whitefield, the state agencies acquired land only for the ITPL business park, in which the state government directly holds equity stakes. Anchoring the city's eastern edge, it helped to spur the land market over a large area, stretching from Koramangla to Whitefields. Similarly, building of the new airports spurred the land market at the northern fringe, the newest IT hub.

This market-driven land policy of Bangalore was clearly inspired by the Haryana government's neoliberal model, which fuelled the real estate growth engine of Gurgaon. However, Bangalore's development continues to be more closely regulated through planning instruments. Gurgaon's growth process is almost entirely laissez faire. Planning responsibilities for Gurgaon are handled by Haryana government's Department of Town and Country Planning (DTP) located in Chandigarh, the state capital. The DTP launched the Gurgaon–Manesar Master Plan 2021 in 2007 (Department of Town and Country Planning 2007). Neither social equity nor environmental sustainability feature amongst the key objectives of this document, whose main priority is to ensure land supply for globalisation-driven economic growth through public–private partnership. The private developers are in the driving seat of this 'public–private partnership', with very limited roles for the state agencies. Momentum of spatial expansion is driven by market demand and ease of land purchase, rather than the set course of a master plan. Rapid growth over a short time span has engulfed more than 40 village areas, which have turned into urban slums. Gurgaon is an archetypical example of 'splintering urbanism' (Graham & Marvin 2001), where urban space is marked by sharp discontinuities between planned and unplanned areas, shortfalls in basic infrastructure like water, power and sewerage and drainage and an overall environmental degradation.

In comparison, Rajarhat New Town on the outskirts of Kolkata demonstrates a much more pleasant ambience. Being a fully master planned settlement, planned and executed by the state agency HIDCO, the area has good roads, regular electric power, and other basic services. Planning of Rajarhat also demonstrates the strongest commitment towards achieving social equity, no doubt informed by Kolkata's deeply rooted leftist political culture. Initiated and led by the state's housing minister, Gautam Deb—an elected politician, rather than a bureaucrat, social housing is Rajarhat's primary objective. Housing projects are developed by joint venture companies in which the state government holds equity stakes and each project has 50 percent of its units earmarked for low- and middle-income groups. But most notably, the plan sought to bridge the rural–urban gap by accommodating the livelihood needs of the people, not just the land losers, but also the sharecroppers and agricultural labours. HIDCO helped them to form building materials syndicates, which supply cement, sand and stone chips, to the construction industry in Rajarhat. But, in the sharply politicised environment, these syndicates have turned into extortion rackets in close connivance with the small time local politicians. The area also suffers from petty crimes on a daily basis.

Current political dispensation in Kolkata, just as in Bangalore earlier, favours a market mechanism along the 'Gurgaon model' which allows the realty firms to purchase land directly from the farmers paying 'fair' or 'market price' for development of private enclaves like IT business parks and gated townships, as a solution to the discontent about land acquisition through the state mechanism. Yet the 'Gurgaon model', which is an archetypical example of 'splintering urbanism' (Graham & Marvin 2001), could hardly be touted as a possible role model for Kolkata, Bangalore or any other Indian city for that matter. In this model, parastatal agencies are becoming subservient to the real estate lobby, in the guise of facilitating economic growth. Urban planning is receding into the background, rather than becoming an effective tool for development coordination. Tensions over urban space and infrastructure mark the everyday lives of the new middle-class residents and the original village people alike. Even the market-based pricing of land, which is at the heart of this concept, could hardly be deemed equitable.

It is important to note here that a purely land value-centric approach to accommodating the needs of the rural poor in the peri-urban areas benefits only those with surplus disposable land. But a large portion (Haryana: 25.96 percent, Karnataka: 30.76 percent and West Bengal: 34.69 percent) of the rural households do not own any land apart from the homestead (Rawal 2008). Increasing commoditisation of land drives out these people—what is being termed as 'secondary dispossession' (Harvey 2003). In the Indian social context, these are the people who also happen to be from the lowest and most vulnerable caste brackets. They are increasingly moving into the urban informal sector or what is called the 'bazaar economy' in India. All new urban spaces in India, be it in Gurgaon, Rajarhat or Whitefields, have attracted large numbers of urban poor, whose livelihoods frequently transcend the 'local' and the 'global'. They work in the high-tech business parks, designer apartment complexes, and swanky shopping malls as guards, drivers, cleaners, sweepers, maids and mechanics, but live in the peripheral villages or the new urban slums. They lack the economic clout of the IT corporate sector, or the political power of the local agrarian communities, and form the shadow economy of globalisation at the urban fringe. A planning mechanism that holistically addresses the diverse needs of the people, the IT corporate sector, the local communities and the new migrant labour, who inhabit the fringe areas of the globalising urban regions of India, is yet to emerge. Rather, gradual withdrawal of the state in the era of neoliberal globalisation is leading to an utterly fragmented landscape at the peri-urban areas, marked by socio-spatial tensions at multiple scales between its diverse stakeholders.

9.2.5   Conclusion: Local mediation of global forces

This section concludes the key points discussed in answering the research questions, to redirect our focus back to the broader issue of local mediation of global economic forces in shaping the urban transformation process in emerging economies of the Global South.

Following case studies of IT clusters in three metropolitan regions using DiGaetano and Strom's framework, this research addressed four inter-related research questions. The first research question analysed how a complex interplay of structural forces involving operation at multiple scales, economic globalisation, advancements in communication technology, state restructuring, regional economic competition, middle-class career aspirations and the growing linkage between IT services and the real estate sector is rapidly altering the peri-urban dynamics in the metropolitan regions of India. The second question then discussed how differences in local political dynamics lead to unevenness in the developmental outcomes of the IT clusters, even under a similar structural context. The third question then examined the roles of the key actors in shaping of the regional IT clusters, and showed how variations in local histories, social contexts and contemporary political contestations led to the formation of contrasting patterns of governance arrangements at a sub-national level. The roles of the local governing regime in balancing the contrasting aspirations between the globalised IT clusters and the local rural communities were analysed through the discussion of the fourth research question.

The broad picture that emerges out of this analysis is the importance of local contextual factors in shaping developmental trajectories, even in the context of globalisation. Growth in the IT services economy in India is a direct corollary of contemporary economic globalisation, which made possible relocation of tasks from higher wage destinations in the Global North to cheaper places in the Global South. Leveraging its advantage in supply of a high-quality skilled labour force, India made a favourable entry into a particular niche of this global economic environment. The national government played its part, (to take advantage of the competitive global market) by rolling out a uniform and enabling regulatory environment across the country. However, beyond this overarching global and national structural context, economic outcomes at sub-national state and urban scale were overwhelmingly shaped by the mediation of the local agential factors—particularly on the crucial issue of supplying land near big urban centres that have a large concentration of skilled labour.

Therefore, place-specific political dynamics are contributing towards the emergence of a differentiated, regionally articulated landscape at the fringe areas of the globalising urban regions of India, even though these places are being produced by similar forces linked to global capital, and all operate under the same political context of the post-liberalisation Indian national state. Analysis of the characteristics of the local governing regimes, using the four parameters suggested by DiGaetano and Strom's framework (governing logics, governing relationships, key decision makers and political objectives) showed that the new economic spaces in Indian cities are being produced by distinct localised modes of governance.

Thus, a 'corporatist' regime comprising the bureaucratic–political–IT-corporate–civil-society-elites as the key decision makers are driving Bangalore's urban-economic aspirations. But in Kolkata and Gurgaon, the presence of the IT sector and civil society are almost negligible in the decision-making hierarchy. The real estate lobby with their patrons in Haryana politics, in a 'clientelistic' relationship, are the key change makers in Gurgaon; while in the 'statist' regime of Kolkata, power is overwhelmingly concentrated in the hands of the political leadership.

A governing logic based on 'particularistic exchanges' and governing relations based on 'reciprocity' made possible Gurgaon's dramatic make over from a non-descript rural town to a corporate hub. The rich farmer-led top echelons of Haryana politics have aligned with big property developers in transforming the urban space of Gurgaon, through the introduction of global capital. Prior to the 1990s, Haryana was essentially a rural state with no big cities. Inexperienced in large scale urban management, the top leadership adopted a liberal land policy, which in effect 'outsourced' Gurgaon's development to the real estate lobby but produced a sharply polarised city, lacking overall planning and with huge infrastructure deficiencies.

In contrast, the state plays much stronger roles in managing urban change in Kolkata and Bangalore, which are both well-established urban centres. But in Kolkata the governing logic is 'authoritative', while in Bangalore it is a combination based on 'exclusionary negotiations' and 'particularistic personalised exchange'. Bangalore has a long 'developmental state' tradition and the elites are acutely conscious of retaining the city's leading position in the IT sector. Faced with threats of regional competition, the state elites accommodated non-state elites in the corporate and civil society in the urban governance through institutionalised partnerships. The relationships in this elitist coalition are based on consensus and reciprocity, which seeks to improve Bangalore's civic infrastructure, but also creates new opportunities for commoditisation of land.

Compared to Bangalore's, the governing relationship in Kolkata is more authoritarian, led by politicians, and managed through the bureaucratic machinery. Growth in the 'knowledge intensive' IT sector, with which the dominant political class 'has a natural affinity' opened new opportunities for economic growth after a long period of stagnation. But with an embedded leftist tradition, the state took upon itself the task of creating space for the IT industry through top-down master planning. The political objective of the regime was to generate employment for the urban middle class while protecting the livelihood concerns of the rural poor, its main electoral support base. The state machinery, acting in tandem with the local political party network, sought to create livelihood alternatives for the rural land-losers in the new economic space.

However, despite the direct role of the state in making urban expansion 'equitable', land supply continues to be problematic in Kolkata, and has impacted new investment flows. In Bangalore and Gurgaon, greater opportunities for commoditisation have ensured faster supply. In both of these regions leverage of political power is held by the rural elites who have directly benefitted from speculative investments and spiralling land price appreciation. Accommodation of these influential political actors helped Bangalore and Gurgaon to 'manage' the land conflicts locally. Whereas near Kolkata, the middle-class-led political elites are dissociated from the rural land economy, and face greater difficulty in ensuring synergy between land and IT-labour supply.

9.3   Interrogating the framework

9.3.1   Application of the framework in book

This book applied DiGaetano and Strom's framework, an analytical tool designed to compare urban governance characteristics of the advanced capitalist democracies of the Global North, to test the governance of three cities in India—a large and populous developing country in the Global South. Based on that experiment, this section interrogates in detail, DiGaetano and Strom's framework, so as to comment on its applicability in developing cities.

DiGaetano and Strom's framework provides an integrated platform, combining structuralist, agential and cultural standpoints in comparing urban governance. As discussed in Section 2.5, three basic premises undergird this framework. First, in the contemporary era, globalisation and decentralisation of the nation-state provide the overarching structural environment, within which institutions of urban governance are inscribed. As the market-driven global economy proceeds unevenly, it has created an environment of competition amongst the cities. Second, the place-specific political-cultural context mediates or filters the impact of the global economy at the urban scale. Third, political actors at the urban stage may either facilitate or resist changes in institutions of urban economic governance, based on their own rational choice and informed by local cultural context.

DiGaetano and Strom suggested 'institutional milieu' as the point of integration of the above premises and defined it as "complexes of formal and informal political and governmental arrangements that mediate interactions among the structural context, political culture and political actors" (DiGaetano & Strom 2003, p.363). To analyse the above relationships, the framework proposed four parameters: governing relations, governing logic, key decision makers and political objectives.

This book applied all these four parameters to test the economic governance modes of three Indian cities regarding the development of the IT sector. On the basis of that experiment, it established that it may be possible to extend the scope of the DiGaetano and Strom's framework to wider geographies—to India (and possibly other democracies within the emerging economies of the Global South). This is because the basic features of India's political economic structure are in harmony with the basic premises of the framework. India is a long functioning democratic country, whose constitution and political institutions were modelled on liberal Anglo-Saxon democracies. There are clear divisions in powers and responsibilities between multiple tiers of governance.

Moreover, economic reforms and state restructuring in recent years have more fully integrated the Indian economy with the external world in political-economic terms. There is increasing competition between Indian cities to attract global investments. The democratic structure of India allowed necessary leeway to the regional power elites to pursue economic strategies in line with their political objectives.

However, the socio-economic realities of India are far different from the liberal democracies of the Global North, on which her institutional structures are modelled. And this led to certain difficulties in adopting DiGaetano and Strom's framework in its present form. The following section examines each of the four parameters of the framework in this light.

9.3.2   Key decision makers

Within the overarching structure of economic globalisation and state restructuring, how a city's urban policy is shaped is to a large extent decided by agential factors, including who constitutes the decision-making metric. According to DiGaetano and Strom in this age of globalisation, cities of the Global North, commonly display 'corporatist' modes of governance. One of the primary characteristics of this corporatist mode of governance is that the key economic decisions are taken by an exclusionary alliance between the high-level governmental, corporate and community leaders.

This research showed that amongst the three case-study cities, only Bangalore depicts this kind of a close-knit network between the governmental, IT-corporate and civil-society elites. But the influences of the civil society on urban issues are practically non-existent at Kolkata and Gurgaon. More importantly the IT-corporate sector, the main economic actor, also does not have any direct influence on shaping the urban affairs—neither in Kolkata, nor in Gurgaon. In Gurgaon, the interests of the IT sector are indirectly channelised through the powerful real estate lobby which also have close ties with the state's rural-centric leadership. Whereas in Kolkata (where the city's economic recovery and the job prospects of its vast urban middle class are directly linked with the IT sector) the government is unable to resolve the land supply issue, for the fear of antagonising the rural electorate.

These above anomalies cannot be easily explained through DiGaetano and Strom's framework and require additional exploratory tools. The crucial point here is that unlike the cities of the Global North, the key decision makers on urban economic issues in India are not located at the level of city government, but rather at the state government level. The political constituency of these key governmental actors are spread out over the entire state. And the politics of rural–urban affiliations have a crucial influence in shaping urban developmental outcomes.

9.3.3   Political objective

According to DiGaetano and Strom, political objectives in corporatist regimes are driven by the purpose of achieving high levels of economic growth and securing the city's position in a competitive global setting. In contrast, the objective of direct material gain drives the leadership of the clientelistic regimes. For the populist regimes, the objectives are more symbolic.

This book, however, showed the importance of additional factors, such as caste-oriented political mobilisation in influencing the political objectives of the governing coalition and shaping economic outcomes. For example, in both Bangalore and Gurgaon, close ties between the interests of the dominant caste groups and the rural-centric political establishment facilitated land supply for the IT sector, by creating greater opportunities through commoditisation of peri-urban land. On the other hand, disconnection between the urban elites and the rural land economy constrained the land supply process in Kolkata's IT cluster.

Another crucial issue here is the socio-economic characteristics of the constituents, which have a major bearing in channelising the political objectives of the governing elites in a democratic environment. This research showed that the farmers in Bengal, extremely poor and having tiny land parcels, are resistant to give up land and move into the urban economy; whereas, the more prosperous farmers of Haryana are more willing to commoditise land and move into Gurgaon's thriving urban economy. Thus the livelihood vulnerability of the rural poor guided the actions of Kolkata's political elites towards the land supply issue, just as opportunities for further growth propel Gurgaon's urban expansion.

The issues discussed above, politics of caste affiliations, rural–urban dichotomy, socio-economic make-up and conflicts between multiple scales of governance require widening of the analytical focus beyond DiGaetano and Strom's framework.

9.3.4   Governance relations

According to DiGaetano and Strom, 'corporatist' regimes characterise exclusionary negotiations between the elite state and economic actors, which privilege high-growth-oriented sectors, and promote pro-globalisation policies. In contrast, inclusionary processes characterise more 'populist' regimes. For 'clientelistic' regimes, governance relations are marked by personalised exchanges.

While agreeing with the above basic tenets, this book however demonstrates that governance relations are influenced by the political objectives of the key decision makers. Thus, even the corporatist regime in Bangalore derives its political strength due to its ability to co-opt the rural political lobby in the urban growth machine.

Moreover, the issue of governance relations, between the state, market and community are not purely horizontal, as envisaged in DiGaetano and Strom's framework. The vertical relationships in multiple tiers of governance also influence governance relationships and there are frequent possibilities of conflict. For example, both Bangalore and Kolkata showed the strong role of parastatal organisations (directly controlled by the state governments) in facilitating development of urban infrastructure for IT enclaves. In both these cities, the roles of local municipal leadership are minimal. But in Gurgaon, where a new elected city council has come up, it has generated conflict with the state leadership over the scope of infrastructure delivery.

Thus, the issue of scale is important and governance relationships need to be viewed in association with the political objectives of the key actors at multiple levels.

9.3.5   Governing logic

According to DiGaetano and Strom's framework, governing logic in 'corporatist' regimes are characterised by consensus building amongst the key actors in state, market and community sectors. On the other hand, clientelistic regimes demonstrate direct reciprocity. Mobilisation of popular support is the governing logic for 'populist' regimes.

Research in this book shows that while 'governing logic' as defined by the framework was a useful criterion for understanding governance modes of the Indian cities, the governing logics of the Indian cities were shaped by wider factors, including the political objectives of the key decision makers. For example, the political objective of gaining support from the poor rural peasants shaped the governing logic of Kolkata's ruling alliance towards the land requirements of the IT sector. Similarly, the political objective of sustaining Bangalore's leadership role in the knowledge economy spurred the state actors to build consensus with the business and civil society elites. Objectives of direct material gain through land transactions, underpinned the real-estate-driven growth strategies of Gurgaon.

Thus, the issue of governing logic, although vital, cannot be seen in isolation from the more important parameter—the political objective.

9.3.6   Towards an amended framework

Analysis of DiGaetano and Strom's framework in Sections 9.3.2 to 9.3.5 demonstrate that while the basic premises of the framework remain valid, the change in setting from the Global North to the Global South, from advanced capitalist economies to a transitional economy and from overwhelmingly urbanised countries to the world's largest rural country, requires major change in emphasis—and additional lenses to identify new influences. On that basis, the following modifications are suggested.

First, this book established the need for understanding the scale at which the leadership of urban governance operates. The fact that in India the locus of power about urban policies, including economic development and its spatial implications, is not located at the level of elected municipal governments, but with the state governments, made major differences in how developmental trajectories shape up. As the rural population makes up a majority in all Indian states, city scale policies are in effect tied to the rural–urban power equations at this higher plane. This calls for an additional parameter—scalar location of power in urban governance.

Second, this book showed the necessity of understanding micro-level socio-economic dynamics. Specific local factors such as caste networks, land-holding patterns and the existing level of opportunities in the urban economy, to a large extent influenced the policy orientation of the political leadership. Thus, political leaders with ties to the caste networks of the rural elites were able to channelise land supply for the emerging urban economy. Therefore, it is necessary to include socio-economic characteristics of the region as a specific parameter.

Third, this research showed the roles of political leadership, elites and the governance coalition are far more crucial in the arena of developmental policy in India. The local political leaders, as negotiators between competing interests, steer the direction of the developmental outcome. They can accommodate the rural (and caste) elites in a 'mutually beneficial' coalition, which fuels the globalised IT-services-driven real estate growth machine as in Bangalore and Gurgaon. Otherwise, they can also get stuck with internecine land conflicts as in Kolkata. This inference is in line with earlier research on other Asian countries by Leftwich (2010) and Shatkin (2007). Both of them noted a similar high degree of intervention by local political elites on developmental issues to suit their own economic and political agendas, compared to countries of the Global North, with stronger and more deeply rooted institutional structures. Thus the political objective of the key decision makers in India (and other emerging economies in the Global South) assume a degree of importance not envisaged in DiGaetano and Strom's framework. Considering all these aspects, this research would suggest a prioritisation of the two parameters, 'key decision maker' and 'political objective' over the other two. Thus, two other criteria, governing relations and governing logic, although crucial, are secondary, and dependent on the primary ones.

Therefore, this research would like suggest an amended framework for comparative analysis of the urban governance modes for India and other emerging economies of the Global South, consisting of six parameters: key decision makers; political objectives of the key decision makers; scalar location of power in urban governance; existing socio-economic situation; governing relations and governing logic. In this expanded framework, the last two parameters may be considered as secondary to the first four.

9.4   Implications for urban planning and development in India

Insertion of India in the global business process outsourcing network has accelerated the process of transformation of the peri-urban landscape of the big cities. Production and consumption spaces of the new economy are fast taking over farmlands and engulfing rural habitats. However this has also generated tensions and contradictions at multiple scales— between the career aspirations of a new globalising urban middle class and livelihood vulnerabilities of the existing rural communities tied to the agrarian economy. DiGaetano and Strom's framework enabled us to understand the essentially negotiated nature of this transformation process, where the political objectives of the key decision makers play a crucial mediating role. But at the same time, certain uncomfortable questions also cropped up about the urban planning process in India: How the growth is managed and differences are reconciled.

A major lacuna in the urban planning system in India is the lack of an institutional mechanism, which can bring together the diverse range of stakeholders involved in the peri-urban transformation process in a common platform. As discussed earlier, urban planning tasks in India are handled by development authorities—and function directly under the state governments. But planning decisions at this scale are dominated by bureaucrats, with perfunctory consultation with the community. Secondly, staff at these agencies consist of engineers and a handful of urban planners, who again are trained in physical planning, with very inadequate grounding in social or economic planning (Chatterji 2003).

The 74th Constitutional Amendment Act of India proposed creation of Metropolitan Planning Committees (MPC) to coordinate planning in large urban agglomerations (Shivaramakrishnan 2011). It was envisaged that the MPC would consist of elected representatives of urban municipalities and rural Panchayets, for a more informed and participatory planning process over the metropolitan regional scale. But these are yet to take shape along the desired lines. In Karnataka and Haryana, the state governments have not constituted an MPC at all. In West Bengal, an MPC has been constituted for the Kolkata area. But the IT townships like Rajarhat are administered directly by the state under the Industrial Township Act (like Bangalore's Electronic City), and do not come under the MPC. State-level political elites wish to prolong their hold over the most lucrative land market.

The planning system in its present form is leading to a fragmented landscape at the urban fringe. While constitution of a sufficiently empowered MPC can make a major difference to the existing planning scenario by widening the scope for participation by local, municipal scale political representatives, this book however shows that to accommodate the diverse needs of the people who inhabit the changing peri-urban space, it is necessary to broaden the scope of this overarching planning institution beyond the political actors, by including scope for participation by the corporate sector and civil society.

This book showed that the absence of non-state actors in the planning mechanism has turned Kolkata's statist planning model into an arena for partisan political conflict, while Gurgaon is dominated by crony capitalism. On the other hand, active participation by the corporate sector and the civil society has made Bangalore's planning system relatively more vibrant. Therefore, for holistic planning of the city at the urban-regional scale, it is necessary to have a sufficiently strong planning organisation which would institutionalise scope for participation by state as well as non-state actors.

9.5   Way forward

This book has tried to provide a nuanced understanding about the governing regimes of India's globalising urban regions, in the context of the IT-services-outsourcing-driven economic transformation. The governance modes of these three regions were characterised through a qualitative analysis, with the help of DiGaetano and Strom's (2003) integrated framework, comprising structural, cultural and agential parameters. The overarching picture that emerges out of this analysis is the importance of local contextual factors in shaping developmental trajectories, even in the context of globalisation. It is the political objectives of the local governing elites, their strategic calculations based on place-specific socio-political dynamics, which determine the course a particular urban region's economy will take—not just the global processes alone. This process of local mediation has a filtering effect. It can either swing open the gate or raise entry barriers to global economic processes.

Based on the explorations and findings of this research, there are a number of potential avenues for further future research, including:

- *Comprehensive research on regional IT clusters of India*: This book explored the urban governance regimes of three, out of the seven major IT clusters of India. It would be very useful therefore to utilise the expanded conceptual framework developed in the book to investigate the processes in the other four major Indian IT clusters. This could both further test the framework and potentially lead to its wider application.

- *Indian urban planning mechanisms*: The book also identified specific problems in the way the planning mechanisms in the three case studies tried to deal with the tensions between IT clusters, local communities and urban planning policies. This area was not the main focus of the current research but further research in this area would provide an important basis for improving Indian urban planning mechanisms and approaches.

- *The national spatial form of the IT sector*: It would also be possible to expand the research to investigate the hub and spoke relationship between the metropolitan cities and second tier IT clusters, which are emerging due to rising real estate costs and salaries in the metropolitan cities. Research in this area would help us understand if and how the objectives and governing logic vary between the metropolitan cities and the secondary cities, how the new growth opportunities are the governing relationships in new places and whether we see the emergence of any new set of actors.

- *Micro-level study about local–global interface*: The peri-urban dynamics of the Indian cities are rapidly changing with the emergence of high-end commercial and residential spaces. It would be fruitful to better understand the grass-root-level impact of these new enclaves, to discover how these are contributing towards livelihood and social practices in the adjoining rural areas. Research like this, over a longish period and involving household surveys, can help us understand: What are the new jobs being created? Are these jobs taken by the local residents or usurped by the new migrants? What are their economic impacts on the local community? How are the income structure and consumption patterns changing? How are local communities adjusting to the change? How can we create greater synergy between the new urban middle class and the existing peri-urban communities? How can the corporate social responsibility programmes be reoriented to provide greater physical focus, so that the new economic enclaves help to improve the technical skills of the local population or improve local health and sanitary conditions?

• *The call-centre industry and urban space in India and the Philippines*: In recent years the Philippines has become a major site for the call centre industry, particularly due to rising real estate costs and a shortage of skilled human resources in India. It is necessary to compare and contrast the development of the industry in Manila with Delhi NCR, to better understand the space relations and the roles of the local agents. Here again it is possible to test the amended version of the framework in an international context. How are the local political institutions responding to the spatial demands of the industry? Are there new land conflicts? If so how are these being mediated? As both India and the Philippines are vibrant democracies, research of this kind would enable us to further fine tune DiGaetano and Strom's framework and expand scope for inter-Asian comparative study.

9.6   Summary

This chapter sought to bring together the findings of the book by answering the research questions. Subsequently, implications of this research on relevant theories of urban governance were discussed and further research possibilities were explored.

The dominant strand of literature on urban transformation has sought to emphasise the converging nature of the contemporary global processes. For example, many studies on globalising cities of the South have focused on how mega-urban renewal projects, built to showcase the city to a global audience, have contributed to marginalisation of the urban poor, through evictions and loss of livelihood.

Acknowledging the importance of the above issues, this book however provided a counterpoint to this broad brush understanding, by demonstrating how differences in local political dynamics contribute towards differential outcomes in globalising cities. Case-study research in a sub-national setting allowed for an in-depth and calibrated understanding of the governance modes under a similar national structural condition—in this case, the macroeconomic environment of the IT outsourcing industry and the political arrangements of the Indian national state. It was possible to see the interplay between local and global forces in shaping local economic development, as the overarching structural environment remained constant throughout. The big picture that came out of this analysis is the importance of local contextual factors in shaping developmental trajectories, even in the context of globalisation.

Thus, by demonstrating how the composition of the local governing coalitions, their networks of inclusion and exclusion, and the nature of their relationship with global actors, influence developmental outcome at the urban scale, this book addressed an issue which has not yet received adequate attention in the scholarly literature. Moreover, by testing DiGaetano and Strom's framework, which was originally designed for cities in the Global North, as the analytical tool, this book demonstrated how and in what way, the parameters of the framework require to be recalibrated, so as to expand its applicability to the wider geographies of the Global South.

List of references

A.T.Kearney 2009, *Global Services Location Index*, A.T. Kearney, Inc., viewed 10 December 2009, <http://www.atkearney.com/index.php/Publications/global-services-location-index-gsli-2009-report.html#>.

ABIDe 2010, *Plan Bengaluru 2020*, Agenda for Bengaluru Infrastructure and Development Task Force, Bangalore.

AITC 2011, *Vision Document: West Bengal - A Change for Better and Brighter Tomrrow*, All IndiaTrinamool Congress,, viewed 21 May 2011, <http://aitmc.org/>.

Allen, A, Davila, JD & Hofmann, P 2006, 'The peri-urban water poor: citizens or consumers?', *Environment and Urbanization*, vol. 18, no. 2, pp. 333–51.

Amin, A & Thrift, N 1992, 'Neo Marshallian nodes in the global networks', *International Journal of Urban and Regional Research*, vol. 16, no. 4, pp. 571–87.

Aranya, R 2008, 'Location Theory in Reverse? Location for global production in the IT industry of Bangalore', *Environment and Planning A*, vol. 40, pp. 446–63.

Assadi, M 2004, 'Shifts, New Trends and the Congress Defeat', *Economic and Political Weekly*, vol. 39, no. 38, pp. 4221–28.

Ataöv, A & Eraydin, A 2011, 'Different Forms of Governance: Responses of Two Metropolitan Regions in Turkey to State Restructuring', *Urban Affairs Review*, vol. 47, no. 1, pp. 84–128.

Bagchi, A 1987, 'Planning for Metropolitan Development: Calcutta's Basic Development Plan, 1966–86: A Post Mortem', *Economic and Political Weekly*, vol. 22, no. 14, pp. 597–601.

Banerjee-Guha, S 2007, 'Post-Fordist urban space of Mumbai: The saga of contemporary restructuration', in A Shaw (ed.), *Indian Cities in Transition*, Orient Longman Publishers Pvt. Ltd., Chennai.

Banerjee-Guha, S 2008, 'Space Relations of Capital and Significance of New Economic Enclaves: SEZs in India', *Economic and Political Weekly*, pp. 51–9.

Banerjee-Guha, S 2010, 'Introduction: Transformative Cities in the New Global Order', in S Banerjee-Guha (ed.), *Accumulation by Disposession*, Sage, New Delhi.

Banerjee, PS 2006, 'Land acquisition and peasant resistance in Singur', *Economic and Political Weekly*, vol. 44, no. 46.

Banerjee, PS 2008, *Politics and conflicts behind SEZs in West Bengal*, viewed 8 December 2010, <http://www.indiasezpolitics.org/atricle.php?id=16>.

Banerjee, PS & Roy, D 2005, *Grambanglar Rajniti - A micro-study of Contemporary Socio-political history of Rural Bengal (in Bengali)*, Peoples Book Society, Kolkata.

Banerjee, T & Chakravorty, S 1994, 'Transfer of Planning Technology and Local Political Economy - A Retrospective Analysis of Calcutta's Planning', *Journal of the American Planning Assosiation*, vol. 60, no. 1, pp. 71–82.

Bangalore Aerospace Park 2012, *About Bengaluru Aerospace Special Economic Zone*, Bangalore Aerospace Park, viewed 1 September 2012, <http://bangaloreaerospacepark.com/sez/about-aerospace-sez.html>.

Bangalore Development Authority 2005, *Master Plan 2015*, Government of Karnataka, Bangalore.

Bangalore Development Authority 2007, *Vision Document (Master Plan 2015)*, vol. 1, Government of Karnataka, Bangalore.

Bardhan, P 2011, 'The Avoidable Tragedy of the Left in India - II', *Economic and Political Weekly*, vol. 46, no. 24, pp. 10–3.

Basu, K & Maertens, A 2007, 'The pattern and causes of economic growth in India', *Oxford Review of Economic Policy*, vol. 23, no. 2, pp. 143–67.

BBC 2012, *Business bleak in Calcutta despite political change*, BBC, viewed 21 May 2012, <http://www.bbc.co.uk/news/business-18117337?print=true>.

Benjamin, S 2008, 'Occupancy Urbanism: Radicalizing Politics and Economy beyond Policy and Programs', *International Journal of Urban and Regional Research*, vol. 32, no. 3, pp. 719–29.

Benjamin, S 2010, 'Manufacturing Neoliberalism: Lifestyling Indian Urbanity', in S Banerjee-Guha (ed.), *Accumulation by Disposession*, Sage, New Delhi.

Bhattacharya, D 2004, 'Making and Unmaking of Trinamul Congress', *Economic and Political Weekly*, vol. 39, no. 14/15, pp. 1529–37.

Bhattacharya, D 2011, 'For a Left Resurgence', *Economic and Political Weekly*, vol. 46, no. 47, pp. 71–3.

Bhattacharya, R & Sanyal, K 2011, 'Bypassing the Squalor: New Towns, Immaterial Labour and Exclusion in Post-colonial Urbanisation', *Economic and Political Weekly*, vol. 46, no. 33, pp. 40–8.

Bhattacharya, T 2007, *The Sentinels of Culture: Class, Education and the Colonial Intellectual in Bengal*, Oxford University Press, New York.

Biau, D 2007, 'Chinese Cities, Indian Cities', *Economic and Political Weekly*, vol. 42, no. 33, pp. 3369–72.

Biswas, SP 2006, 'Gurgaon: an Isolated Urbanism', paper presented to Dialogues: A Symposium on the Shaping of Gurgaon, Gurgaon, India.

Booz Allen Hamilton - Fuqua School of Business 2006, *Globalisation of White-Collar Work*, Booz Allen Hamilton and Duke University, Chicago.

Bosworth, B, Collins, SM & Virmani, A 2007, *Sources of Growth in the Indian Economy*, National Bureau of Economic Research, Cambridge, USA.

Breeding, ME 2011, 'The Micro-politics of Vote Banks Karnataka', *Economic and Political Weekly*, vol. 46, no. 14, pp. 71–8.

Brenner, N 2004, *New state spaces : urban governance and the rescaling of statehood*, Oxford University Press, Oxford.

Brenner, N & Theodore, N 2002a, 'Cities and the Geographies of "Actually Existing Neoliberalism"', *Antipode*, vol. 34, no. 3, pp. 349–79.

Brenner, N & Theodore, N 2002b, 'Preface: From the "New Localism" to the Spaces of Neoliberalism', *Antipode*, vol. 34, no. 3, pp. 344–7.

Bunnell, T, Barter, PA & Morshidi, S 2002, 'Kuala Lumpur metropolitan area: A globalizing city-region', *Cities*, vol. 19, no. 5, pp. 357–70.

Business-Standard 2011a, *DLF to approach apex court against order to demolish Gurgaon SEZ*, Business Standard, viewed 11 February 2011, <http://www.business-standard.com/india/news/dlf-to-approach-apex-court-against-order-to-demolish-gurgaon-sez/424655/>.

Business-Standard 2011b, *Industry rues death of STPI scheme*, viewed 6 March 2011, <http://www.business-standard.com/india/news/industry-rues-deathstpi-scheme/426850/>.

Business Today 2007, 'The Telecom Lesson', *Business Today*, vol. January 28, no. January 28.

Castells, M 1996, *The Rise of the Network Society*, Blackwell, Oxford.

Castells, M 1998, *The End of the Millenium*, Blackwells, Oxford.

Castells, M 2005, 'Space of Flows, Space of Places: Materials for a Theory of Urbanism in the Information Age', in B Sanyal (ed.), *Comparative Planning Cultures*, Routledge, New York.

Caulfield, J & Wanna, J 1995, 'Power and Community: Theoritical Approaches', in J Caulfield & J Wanna (eds), *Power and Politics in the City*, Centre for Australian Public Sector Management, Nathan, Queensland.

Census 2011, *Population Census 2001-11*, Registrar General and Census Commissioner, Govt. of India, Delhi.

Chacko, E 2007, 'From brain drain to brain gain: reverse migration to Bangalore and Hyderabad, India's globalizing high tech cities', *Geo Journal*, vol. 68, pp. 131–40.

Chakrabarty, B 2011, 'The 2011 State Assembly Election in West Bengal', *Journal of South Asian Development*, vol. 6, no. 2, pp. 143–67.

Chatterjee, P 1990, 'The Political Culture of Calcutta', in S Chaudhuri (ed.), *Calcutta - The Living City, Vol - II*, Oxford University Press, New Delhi.

Chatterjee, P 2004, *The Politics of the Governed*, Columbia University Press, New York.

Chatterjee, P 2012, *Budget speech of the Minister for Information Technology*, Government of West Bengal, viewed 12 September 2012, <http://www.itwb.org/Budget%20Speech%20English%20&%20Bengali/Budget%20Speech_2012-13%20_English_.pdf>.

Chatterji, T 2000, 'City Blights - The Irrelevance of Master Plans', *Times of India*, 16 December 2000.

Chatterji, T 2003, 'City Blights - Master Plans as Masterly Failures', *Times of India*, 8 September 2003.

Chatterji, T 2007, 'Peri-urban Interface in the Context of Globalisation- A Review of the Planning Process of Delhi', paper presented to IFHP 51st World Congress, Copenhagen, September 2007.

Chatterji, T 2013a, 'Chapter 14: Localising Production of the Globalised Knowledge Enclaves: Role of Sub-national States in Development of IT-ITES Clusters in India', in P Cooke, G Searle & K O'Connor (eds), *The IT Industry in the Asia-Pacific Region*, Routledge, London.

Chatterji, T 2013b, 'The Micro-Politics of Urban Transformation in the Context of Globalisation: A Case Study of Gurgaon, India', *South Asia: Journal of South Asian Studies*, vol. 36, no. 2, pp. 273–87.

Cheema, GS & Rondinelli, DA (eds) 2007, *Decentralizing Governance*, Brookings Institution Press, Washington D.C.

Chen, X, Wang, L & Kundu, R 2009, 'Localizing the Production of Global Cities: A Comparison of New Town Developments Around Shanghai and Kolkata', *City & Community*, vol. 8, no. 4, pp. 433–65.

Chien, SS 2008, 'Local Responses to Globalization in China: A Territorial Restructuring Process Perspective', *Pacific Economic Review*, vol. 13, no. 4, pp. 492–517.

Chowdary, TH 1999, 'Telecom demonopolization - Why did India get it so wrong?', *Innform*, vol. 1, no. 3, pp. 218–24.

CIVIC 2007, *Spatial impacts of large infrastructure projects on the periphery of Bangalore*, Citizens Voluntary Initiative for the City, Bangalore.

Cook, S 2006, 'Structural Change, Growth and Poverty Reduction in Asia: Pathways to Inclusive Development', *Development Policy Review*, vol. 24, no. s1, pp. 51–80.

Cox, K (ed.) 1997, *Spaces of globalization : reasserting the power of the local*, Guilford Press, New York.

D'Costa, AP 2011, 'Geography, uneven development and distributive justice: the political economy of IT growth in India', *Cambridge Journal of Regions, Economy and Society*, vol. 4, no. 2, pp. 237–51.

Dasgupta, K 2007, 'City Divided? Planning and Urban Sprawl in the Eastern Fringes of Calcutta', in A Shaw (ed.) (ed.), *Indian Cities in Transition*, Orient Longman Private Ltd., Hyderabad, pp. 314–40.

Davies, JS 2003, 'Partnerships versus Regimes: Why Regime Theory Cannot Explain Urban Coalitions in the UK', *Journal of Urban Affairs*, vol. 25, no. 3, pp. 253–70.

Debroy, B & Bhandari, L 2009, *Gurgaon and Faridabad - An Exercise in Contrasts*, Freeman Spogli Institute for International Studies, Stanford, USA.

Deccan Herald 2011, *Devanahalli aerospace park & SEZ gathering steam*, Deccan Herald,, viewed 17 August 2012, <http://www.deccanherald.com/content/39488/devanahalli-aerospace-park-amp-sez.html>.

Deccan Herald 2012, *Two bills in limbo*, Deccan Herald Group,, viewed 28 August 2011, <http://www.deccanherald.com/content/274245/two-bills-limbo.html >.

Department of Town and Country Planning 2007, *Gurgaon - Manesar Master Plan 2021*, Government of Haryana, Chandigarh.

Dhungel, DN, Pun, SB & Thapa, AB 2009, 'Access to Sea: Kosi Canal Waterway', in DN Dhungel & SB Pun (eds), *The Nepal–India Water Relationship: Challenges*, Springer Netherlands, Dordrecht, pp. 197-220, DOI 10.1007/978-1-4020-8403-4_7, <http://dx.doi.org/10.1007/978-1-4020-8403-4_7>.

DiGaetano, A & Strom, E 2003, 'Comparative Urban Governance: An Integrated Approach', *Urban Affairs Review*, vol. 38, no. 3, pp. 356–95.

District Administration Jhajjar 2011, *SEZ Jhajjar*, District Administration Jhajjar,, viewed 30 November 2011, <http://jhajjar.nic.in/sezjjr.aspx>.

Dohrmann, JA 2008, 'Special Economic Zones in India - An Introduction', *ASIEN*, vol. 106, pp. 60–80.

Dossani, R & Kenny, M 2003, *Went for Cost, Stayed for Quality?: Moving the Back Office to India*, Centre on Democracy, Development and The Rule of Law, Freeman Spogli Institute for International Studies, Stanford, USA.

Drucker, P 1987, *The Frontiers of Management*, Heinemann, London.

Dupont, V 2007, 'Conflicting stakes and governance in the peripheries of large Indian metropolises - An introduction', *Cities*, vol. 24, no. 2, pp. 89–94.

Dupont, V 2011, 'The Dream of Delhi as a Global City', *International Journal of Urban and Regional Research*, vol. 35, no. 3, pp. 533–54.

Dupont, V & Sridharan, N 2006, *Peri-urban dynamics: Case Studies in Chennai, Hyderabad and Mumbai*, New Delhi.

Eriksen, TH 2007, *Globalisation - The Key Concepts*, Berg, Oxford.

Friedmann, J 2005, 'Planning Cultures in Transition', in B Sanyal (ed.), *Comparative planning cultures*, Routledge, New York.

Fuerstenberg, K 2010, *The West Bengal Panchayet Model in Peril? A Survey-based Appraisal of West Bengal Panchayets*, South Asian Institute, Heidelberg University, Heidelberg.

Gereffi, G, Wadhwa, V & Rissing, B 2008, 'Getting the Numbers Right: International Engineering Education in the United States, China, and India', *Journal of Engineering Education*, pp. 13–25.

Ghosh, A 2005, 'Public-Private or a Private Public? Promised Partnership of the Bangalore Agenda Task Force', *Economic and Political Weekly*, vol. 40, no. 47.

Ghosh, J 2010, *Poverty reduction in China and India: Policy implications of recent trends*, Department of Economic and Social Affairs, United Nations, New York.

Giddens, A 1999, *Runaway World: How Globalisation is Reshaping our Lives*, Profile, Londom.

Gissendanner, S 2004, 'Mayors, Governance Coalitions, and Strategic Capacity', *Urban Affairs Review*, vol. 40, no. 1, pp. 44–77.

Goldman, M 2011, 'Speculative Urbanism and the Making of the Next World City', *International Journal of Urban and Regional Research*, vol. 35, no. 3, pp. 555–81.

Goodwin, M & Painter, J 1996, 'Local governance, the crises of Fordism and the changing geographies of regulation', *Transactions of the Institute of British Geographers*, vol. 21, pp. 635–48.

Goswami, O 1989, 'Sahibs, Babus, and Banias: Changes in Industrial Control in Eastern India, 1918-50', *The Journal of Asian Studies*, vol. 48, no. 2, pp. 289–309.

Government of Haryana 2000, *Haryana IT Policy*, Government of Haryana, Chandigrah.

Government of India 2012, *List of Special Economic Zones notified under SEZ Act*, Ministry of Law, Justice and Company Affairs, Government of India,, viewed 12 December 2012, <http://sezindia.nic.in/writereaddata/pdf/Sector-wise%20distribution-SEZ.pdf>.

Government of Karnataka 2000, *The Millenium IT Policy*, Government of Karnataka, Bangalore.

Government of Karnataka 2011, *Investment Opportunities in IT and Biotechnology Sectors*, Department of IT, BT and S&T, viewed 10 February 2011, <http://www.bangaloreitbt.in/index.html>.

Government of West Bengal 2003, *West Bengal IT Policy* Government of West Bengal, Kolkata.

Government of West Bengal 2012, *West Bengal IT Policy* Government of West Bengal, Kolkata.

Graham, S & Marvin, S 2001, *Splintering Urbanism*, Routledge, New York.

Gray, PS, Williamson, JB, Karp, DA & Dalphin, JR 2007, *The Research Imagination*, Cambridge University Press, New York.

Guha-Thakurta, G 2012, *Porshi muluk-er bazar dhorte IBM er kendro Kolkata (in Bengali)*, Ananda Bazar Patrika,, viewed 9 September 2012, <http://www.anandabazar.com/9bus2.html>.

Guha, R 2007, *India After Gandhi*, Macmillan, New Delhi.

Guha, R 2012, *The State of My State*, The Telegraph, viewed 4 August 2012, <http://ramachandraguha.in/archives/the-state-of-my-state-the-telegraph.html>.

Guhathakurta, S & Parthasarathy, B 2007, 'The Role of the World Markets and International Networks in the Evolution of India's High-tech Clusters: Riding the Coat-tails or Bucking the Trend?', in A Shaw (ed.), *Indian Cities in Transition*, Orient Longman Private Ltd., Chennai.

Gupta, A 2008, 'International trends and private higher education in India', *International Journal of Educational Management*, vol. 22, no. 6, pp. 565–94.

Guruswamy, M, Sharma, K & Mohanty, JP 2005, 'Economic Growth and Development in West Bengal: Reality versus Perception', *Economic and Political Weekly*, vol. 40, no. 21, pp. 2151–7.

Hamnett, S & Forbes, D 2011, 'Risks, Resilience and Planning in Asian Cities', in S Hamnett & D Forbes (eds), *Planning Asian Cities*, Routledge, Abingdon, Oxfordshire, UK.

Harvey, D 1989, 'From Managerialism to Entrepreneurialism: The Transformation in Urban Governance in Late Capitalism', *Geografiska Annaler. Series B, Human Geography*, vol. 71, no. 1, pp. 3–17.

Harvey, D 2003, 'The right to the city', *International Journal of Urban and Regional Research*, vol. 27, no. 4, pp. 939–41.

Hay, C 2002, *Political Analysis*, Palgrave, Basingstoke, Hampshire, UK.

Held, D & McGrew, A 2007, *Globalization / Anti-Globalization*, 2nd edn, Polity, Cambridge.

Hust, E 2005, 'Problems of Urbanization and Urban Governance in India', in E Hust & M Mann (eds), *Urbanization and Governance in India*, Manohar Publishers Pvt. Ltd., New Delhi.

Hutton, TA 2003, 'Service industries, globalization, and urban restructuring within the Asia-Pacific: new development trajectories and planning responses', *Progress in Planning*, vol. 61, no. 1, pp. 1–74.

Jain, AK 2003, 'Actioning new partnerships for Indian cities', *Cities*, vol. 20, no. 5, pp. 353–9.

James, A & Vira, B 2012, 'Labour geographies of India's new service economy', *Journal of Economic Geography*, no. April, pp. 1–35.

Jenkins, R 2000, *Democratic Politics and Economic Reform*, Cambridge University Press, Cambridge.

Jessop, B, Brenner, N & Jones, M 2008, 'Theorizing sociospatial relations', *Environment and Planning D*, vol. 26, pp. 389–401.

Joardar, SD 2006, '*Development Mechanism in Spatial Integration*', paper presented to 42nd ISOCARP Conference, Istanbul.

Jodhka, SS & Dhar, M 2003, 'Cow, Caste and Communal Politics: Dalit Killings in Jhajjar', *Economic and Political Weekly*, vol. 38, no. 3, pp. 174–6.

Jones Lang LaSalle 2010, *State of the Nation - Office, Retail, Residential*, Jones Lang LaSalle,, Mumbai.

Jones Lang LaSalle 2012a, *Monthly Real Estate Monitor (November)*, Jones Lang LaSalle,, Mumbai.

Jones Lang LaSalle 2012b, *Reaping the Returns - Decoding Private Equity Real Estate Exits in India*, Jones Lang LaSalle,, Mumbai.

Joshi, S 2009, *IT ITES as an Engine of Growth: An Exploration into the Indian Experience*, Working Paper Series No. E/294/2009, Institute of Economic Growth, New Delhi.

Kadekodi, G, Kanbur, R & Rao, V 2007, 'Governance and the 'Karnataka Model of Development'', *Economic and Political Weekly*, vol. 42, no. 8, pp. 649–53.

Kantor, P, Savitch, HV & Haddock, SV 1997, 'The Political Economy of Urban Regimes', *Urban Affairs Review*, vol. 32, no. 3, pp. 348–77.

Kasturi, K 2008, 'Of Public Purpose and Private Profit', *Seminar*, no. 582.

Kasturi, K 2009, *SEZs: engine derailed?*, India Together, viewed 7 September 2011, <http://www.indiatogether.org/cgi-bin/tools/pfriend.cgi>.

Kavi-Kumar, KS & Viswanathan, B 2008, 'Vulnerability to Globalisation in India: Relative Rankings of States Using Fuzzy Models', in M Nissanke & E Thorbecke (eds), *Globalization and the Poor in Asia: Can Shared Growth be Sustained*, Palgrave Macmillan, New York.

Keivani, R & Mattingly, M 2007, 'The Interface of Globalization and Peripheral Land in the Cities of the South: Implications for Urban Governance and Local Economic Development', *International Journal of Urban and Regional Research*, vol. 31, no. 2, pp. 459–74.

Kelly, PF 2006, 'The Politics of Urban-Rural Relations: Land Use Conversion in Philipines', in C Tacoli (ed.), *The Earthscan Reader in Rural-Urban Linkages*, Earthscan, London.

Kennedy, L 2007, 'Regional industrial policies driving peri-urban dynamics in Hyderabad, India', *Cities*, vol. 24, no. 2, pp. 95–109.

Kennedy, L 2012, 'The politics of SEZs in Haryana: Beyond the Rural-Urban divide', in R Jenkins, L Kennedy & P Mukhopadyay (eds), *The Politics of India's Special Economic Zones*, Oxford University Press, New Delhi.

Kennedy, L & Zerah, MH 2008, 'The Shift to City-Centric Growth Strategies: Perspectives from Hyderabad and Mumbai', *Economic and Political Weekly*, pp. 110–7.

Khomiakova, T 2007, 'Information Technology Clusters in India', *Transition Studies Review*, vol. 14, no. 2, pp. 355–78.

KMDA 2007, *Comprehensive Mobility Plan*, Kolkata Metropolitan Development Authority, Kolkata.

Kumar, R 2009, *The Development of the Software Industry in Postreform India: Comparative Regional Experiences in Tamil Nadu, Andhra Pradesh and Kerala*, Cambria Press, New York.

Kundu, A 2011, *Trends and processes of urbanisation in India*, International Institute of Environment and Development and United Nations Population Fund, London.

Labbé, D 2011, 'Urban Destruction and Land Disputes in Periurban Hanoi During the Late-Socialist Period', *Pacific Affairs*, vol. 84, no. 3, pp. 435–54, 20.

Lama-Rewal, ST 2009, 'Neighborhood Associations and Local Democracy: A Focus on Delhi Municipal Elections 2007', *Economic and Political Weekly*, vol. 44, no. 26 and 27.

Lama-Rewal, ST 2009, 'The Resilient Bhadralok: A Profile of the West Bengal MLAs', in C Jaffrelot & S Kumar (eds), *Rise of the Plebians? The Changing Face of Indian Legislative Assemblies*, Routledge, New Delhi, <http://books.google.com.au/books?id=t DN0MinxMigC&lpg=PT246&ots=WxSmGgnY5m&dq=Karnataka%20politics%20deve lopment&lr&pg=PP1#v=onepage&q=Karnataka%20politics%20development&f=false>.

Leaf, M 2002, 'A Tale of Two Villages: Globalization and Peri-Urban Change in China and Vietnam', *Cities*, vol. 19, no. 1, pp. 23–31.

Leclerc, E & Bourgignon, C 2006, 'Defining the urban fringe through population mobility: the case of Madhapur and its Information Technology Park (HITEC City)', in V Dupont & N Sridharan (eds), *Occasional Paper No.17: Peri-urban dynamics: Case Studies in Chennai, Hyderabad and Mumbai*, New Delhi.

Leftwich, A 1995, 'Bringing Politics Back In: Towards a Model of the Developmental State', *Journal of Development Studies*, vol. 31, no. 3, pp. 400–27.

Leftwich, A 2010, 'Beyond Institutions: Rethinking the Role of Leaders, Elites and Coalitions in the Institutional Formation of Developmental States and Strategies', *Forum for Development Studies*, vol. 37, no. 1, pp. 93–111.

Liu, Y, He, S, Wu, F & Webster, C 2010, 'Urban villages under China's rapid urbanization: unregulated assets and transitional neighbourhoods', *Habitat International*, vol. 34, pp. 135–44.

Logan, J & Molotch, HL 1987, *Urban Fortunes: the political economy of place*.

Lubell, H 1974, *Calcutta - Its urban development and employment prospects*, International Labour Office, Geneva.

Luce, E 2006, *In spite of the gods: the strange rise of modern India*, Little Brown, London.

MacLeod, G & Goodwin, M 1999a, 'Reconstructing an urban and regional political economy: on the state, politics, scale, and explanation', *Political Geography*, vol. 18, no. 6, pp. 697–730.

Macleod, G & Goodwin, M 1999b, 'Space, scale and state strategy: rethinking urban and regional governance', *Progress in Human Geography*, vol. 23, no. 4, pp. 503–27.

Mahadevia, D & Parashar, A 2008, 'Dynamics of High Tech Urban Zones in Pune: Emerging Trends and Impacts', in C Ramchandriah, ACM van-Westen & S Prasad (eds), *High-Tech Urban Spaces: Asian and European Perspectives*, Manohar, New Delhi.

Maitra, S 2008, 'Dynamics of High Tech Urban Spaces:Lessons from IT Sector Expansion in the National Capital Region, India', in C Ramchandriah, ACM van-Westen & S Prasad (eds), *High-Tech Urban Spaces: Asian and European Perspectives*, Manohar, New Delhi.

Malik, A 2011, 'Didi's long march', *Tehelka Magazine*, vol. 8, no. 20, May 21.

Marshall, F, Waldman, L, MacGregor, H, Mehta, L & Randhawa, P 2009, *On the Edge of Sustainability: Perspectives on Peri-urban Dynamics*, STEPS Centre, Institute of Development Studies, Sussex, Brighton.

Mayers, J 2001, 'Economic reform and the urban/rural divide: Political realignment in West Bengal 1977-2000', *Journal of South Asian Studies*, vol. 24, no. 1, pp. 17–42.

McDuie-Ra, D 2012, 'Tribal Labour and Denationalised Urban Space: Economic Inclusion and Social Exclusion in Neo Liberal Delhi', paper presented to Asian Studies Association of Australia 19th Biennial Conference, Paramatta, NSW, 11–13 July.

Mckinsey Global Institute 2007, *The 'Bird of Gold': The Rise of India's Consumer Market*, Mckinsey Global Institute,, Delhi.

Mckinsey Global Institute 2010, *India's urban awakening: Building inclusive cities, sustaining economic growth*, Mckinsey Global Institute,, Delhi.

McLean, D 2001, 'Tension between state and capital in West Bengal', *South Asia: Journal of South Asian Studies*, vol. 24, no. 1, pp. 93–115.

Messner, W 2009, *Working with India*, Springer, Berlin.

Miller, S 2009, *A Capital Dilemma: is Delhi a 'World City'*, Bennet Coleman Group, viewed 15 February 2011, <http://articles.timesofindia.indiatimes.com/2009-02-15/all-that-matters/28022082_1_prb-world-city-population-reference-bureau>.

Ministry of Law and Justice 2005, *Special Economic Zones Act (2005)*, Government of India,, New Delhi.

Minnery, J 2007, 'Stars and their Supporting Cast: State, Market and Community as Actors in Urban Governance', *Urban Policy and Research*, vol. 25, no. 3, pp. 325–45.

Mohan, R & Dasgupta, S 2004, 'Urban Development in India: Policies for Accelerating Urban Growth', paper presented to Fifth Annual Conference on Indian Economic Policy Reform, Stanford, June 4–5, 2004.

Mukhopadhyay, P & Pradhan, KC 2009, *Location of SEZs and Policy Benefits: What Does the Data Say*, Centre for Policy Research, New Delhi.

Mundle, S, Chakraborty, P, Chowdhury, S & Sikdar, S 2012, 'The Quality of Governance - How Have Indian States Performed?', *Economic and Political Weekly*, vol. 47, no. 49, pp. 41–52.

Myint-U, T 2011, *Where China Meets India*, Farrar, Straus and Giroux, New York.

Nair, J 2000, 'Singapore Is Not Bangalore's Destiny', *Economic and Political Weekly*, vol. 35, no. 18, pp. 1512–4.

Nair, J 2005, *The Promise of the Metropolis: Bangalore's Twentieth Century*, Oxford University Press, New Delhi.

Nair, J 2012, *Mysore Modern - Rethinking the Region under Princely Rule*, Orient Blackswan, New Delhi.

Narain, V 2009, 'Growing city, shrinking hinterland: land acquistion, transition and conflict in peri-urban Gurgaon, India', *Environment and Urbanization*, vol. 21, no. 2, pp. 501–12.

Narain, V & Nischal, S 2007, 'The peri-urban interface in Shahpur Khurd and Karnera, India', *Environment and Urbanization*, vol. 19, no. 1, pp. 261–73.

Narayana, MR 2010, *ICT Sector, Globalization and Urban Economic Growth: Evidence from Bangalore (India)*, Helsinki.

NASSCOM 2011, *Strategic Review 2011*, NASSCOM,, New Delhi, <http://www.nasscom.in/upload/60452/Executive_summary.pdf>.

NASSCOM 2012, *Strategic Review 2012*, National Association of Software and Service Companies, viewed 4 September 2012, <http://www.nasscom.org/indian-itbpo-industry>.

NASSCOM 2013, *Indian IT-BPM Industry FY2013 Performance Review*, National Association of Software and Service Companies, viewed 24 January 2014, <http://www.nasscom.org/indian-itbpo-industry>.

NASSCOM & A.T.Kearney 2009, *Location Roadmap for IT-BPO Growth: Assessment of 50 Leading Cities*, National Association of Software and Service Companies, New Delhi.

Nielsen, KB 2010, 'Contesting India's Development? Industrialisation, Land Acquisition and Protest in West Bengal', *Forum for Development Studies*, vol. 37, no. 2, pp. 145–70.

O'Connor, D 2003, *Of Flying Geeks and O-rings: Locating Software and IT Services in India's Economic Development*, OECD Development Centre, Issy-les-Moulineaux, France.

Ohmae, K 1995, *The End of the Nation State*, The Free Press, New York.

Pal, A 2006, 'Scope for bottom-up planning in Kolkata: rhetoric vs reality', *Environment and Urbanization*, vol. 18, no. 2, pp. 501–21.

Parthasarathy, B 2004, 'India's Silicon Valley or Silicon Valley's India? Socially Embedding the Computer Software Industry in Bangalore', *International Journal of Urban and Regional Research*, vol. 28, no. 3, pp. 664–85.

Pemberton, S & Goodwin, M 2011, 'Exploring the Changing Governance of London - the politics of state rescaling, scale perodization, and local political strategy', paper presented to 3rd World Planning Schools Congress, Perth, WA, 4–8 July 2011.

Pemberton, S & Searle, G 2012, 'Exploring the Changing Governance of London - the politics of state rescaling, scale perodization, and local political strategy', paper presented to 26th Annual Congress of the Association of European Planning Schools, Ankara, 11–15 July.

Pierre, J 2005, 'Comparative Urban Governance', *Urban Affairs Review*, vol. 40, no. 4, pp. 446–62.

Planning Commission of India 2006, *Eleventh Five Year Plan (2007–2012)*, Government of India, New Delhi.

Planning Commission of India 2012, *Real Growth Rate of States GDP*, Government of India, New Delhi.

Prime, PB 2009, 'China and India Enter Global Markets: A Review of Comperative Economic Development and Future Prospects', *Eurasian Geography and Economics*, vol. 50, no. 6, pp. 621–42.

Punch, KF 2008, *Introduction to Social Research*, Second edn, Sage Publications, London.

Purfield, C 2006, 'Is Economic Growth Leaving Some States Behind?', in C Purfield & J Schiff (eds), *India goes global:its expanding role in the world economy*, International Monetory Fund, Washington D.C.

Raghuram, G & Sundaram, SS 2009, *Lessons from Leveraging Land: A Case for Bangalore Mysore Infrastructure Corridor*, Indian Institute of Management, Ahmedabad.

Ram, TLR & Kakani, RK 2009, 'Framework for Evaluation of Land Aquisition in India: Sustainable Development Perspective', in N Mohanty, R Sarkar & A Pandey (eds), *India Infrastructure Report 2009: Land - A Critical Resource for Infrastructure*, Oxford University Press, New Delhi.

Ramanathan, U 2011, 'Land Acquisition, Eminent Domain and the 2011 Bill', *Economic and Political Weekly*, vol. 46, no. 44–45, pp. 10–4.

Ramchandriah, C & Prasad, S 2008, 'The Makeover of Hyderabad: Is it the 'Model" IT City', in C Ramchandriah, ACM van-Westen & S Prasad (eds), *High-Tech Urban Spaces: Asian and European Perspectives*, Manohar, New Delhi.

Ramsay, M 1996, 'The Local Community: Maker of Culture and Wealth', *Journal of Urban Affairs*, vol. 18, no. 2, pp. 95–118.

Rao, MG & Singh, N 2005, *Political Economy of Federalism in India*, Oxford University Press, New Delhi.

Rawal, V 2008, 'Ownership Holdings of Land in Rural India: Putting the Record Straight', *Economic and Political Weekly*, vol. 46, no. 21, pp. 43–7.

Ray, S & Ray, I 2011, 'An Insight into the Vision of Charismatic Leadership: Evidence from Recent Administrative Change in West Bengal Province of India', *European Joournal of Business and Management*, vol. 3, no. 9.

Ray, SC 2011, *The Political Economy of Decline of Industry in West Bengal: Experiences of a Marxist State Within a Mixed Economy*, University of Connecticut, Storrs,CT.

Raychaudhuri, A & Basu, GK 2007, *The Decline and Recent Resurgence of the Manufacturing Sector of West Bengal: Implications for Pro-Poor Growth from an Institutional Point of View*, IPPG Programme University of Manchester, Manchester.

Reserve Bank of India 2012, *Handbook of Statistics on Indian Economy*, Reserve Bank of India,, viewed 13 August 2012, <http://www.rbi.org.in/scripts/AnnualPublications. aspx?head=Handbook%20of%20Statistics%20on%20Indian%20Economy>.

Rigg, J 2006, 'Evolving Rural-Urban Relations and Livelihoods in Southeast Asia', in C Tacoli (ed.), *The Earthscan Reader in Rural-Urban Linkages*, Earthscan, London.

Sainath, P 2005, *"Take That, Tom Friedman" Indian Elites' Neoliberal Idol Shattered Yet Again: Urban Masses Stubbornly Reject NYT's Hero*, counterpunch.org, viewed 25 April 2010 2010, <http://www.counterpunch.org/sainath10062005.html>.

Sassen, S 2001, *The Global City - New York, London, Tokyo*, Princeton University Press, Princeton.

Sassen, S 2012, *Cities in a Global Economy*, Pine Forge Press, Thousand Oaks, Calif.

Scoones, I 2003, *Making policy in the new economy: the case of biotechnology in Karnataka, India*, Institute of Development Studies, Brighton, Sussex.

Sen, R 2009, *The Evolution of Industrial Relations in West Bengal*, International Labour Organisation viewed 24-11-2011 Paper 79, <http://digitalcommons.ilr.cornell.edu/ intl/79>.

Sen, S 2011, 'For a Left Resurgence', *Economic and Political Weekly*, vol. 46, no. 24, pp. 14–6.

Shankar, R & Shah, A 2003, 'Bridging the Economic Divide Within Countries: A Scorecard on the Performance of Regional Policies in Reducing Regional Income Disparities', *World Development*, vol. 31, no. 8, pp. 1421–41.

Shastri, S 2009, 'Legislators in Karnataka: Well-entrenched Dominant Castes', in C Jaffrelot & S Kumar (eds), *Rise of the Plebians? The Changing Face of Indian Legislative Assemblies*, Routledge, New Delhi, <http://books.google.com.au/books?id=t DN0MinxMigC&lpg=PT246&ots=WxSmGgnY5m&dq=Karnataka%20politics%20deve lopment&lr&pg=PP1#v=onepage&q=Karnataka%20politics%20development&f=false>.

Shatkin, G 2004, 'Globalization and Local Leadership: Growth, Power and Politics in Thailand's Eastern Seaboard', *International Journal of Urban and Regional Research*, vol. 28, no. 1, pp. 11–26.

Shatkin, G 2007, 'Global cities of the South: Emerging perspectives on growth and inequality', *Cities*, vol. 24, no. 1, pp. 1–15.

Shatkin, G 2011, *Reading the Indian City: Assessing Recent Research on State, Space and Citizenship*, Gradutate School of Design, Harvard University, viewed 6 May 2012, <http://www.youtube.com/watch?v=cANNUTEJdsM>.

Shaw, A & Satish, MK 2007, 'Metropolitan restructuring in post-liberalized India: Separating the global and the local', *Cities*, vol. 24, no. 2, pp. 148–63.

Shen, J 2004, 'Urban Competitiveness and Urban Governance in the Globalizing World', *Asian Geographer*, vol. 23, no. 1–2, pp. 19–36.

Shen, J 2007, 'Scale, state and the city: Urban transformation in post-reform China', *Habitat International*, vol. 31, no. 3–4, pp. 303–16.

Shivaramakrishnan, KC 2011, *Re-visioning Indian Cities: The Urban Renewal Mission*, Sage, New Delhi.

Sinha, A 2005, *The Regional Roots of Developmental Politics - A Divided Leviathan*, Oxford University Press, New Delhi.

Srinivasan, TN & Krueger, A 2005, 'Information-Technology-Enabled Services and India's Growth Prospects (With Comments and Discussions)', *Brookings Trade Forum*, pp. 203–40.

Stone, CN 1993, 'Urban Regimes and the Capacity to Govern: A Political Economy Approach', *Journal of Urban Affairs*, vol. 15, no. 1, pp. 1–28.

Stone, CN 2004, 'It's More than the Economy after All: Continuing the Debate about Urban Regimes', *Journal of Urban Affairs*, vol. 26, no. 1, pp. 1–19.

STPI 2010, *Annual Report*, Software Technology Parks of India, New Delhi.

Sundaram, R 2009, *Pirate Modernity*, Routledge Studies in Asia's Transformation, Routledge.

Suri, SN 2011, 'Making Indian Cities Livable: Challanges of India's Urban Transformation', in C Gossop & S Nan (eds), *Livable Cities: Urbanising World*, International Society of City and Regional Planners, The Hague.

Swyngedouw, E 1997, 'Neither global nor local -"Glocalization" and the politics of scale', in K Cox (ed.), *Spaces of globalization : reasserting the power of the local*, Guilford Press, New York.

Tacoli, C (ed.) 2006, *The Earthscan Reader in Rural Urban Linkages*, Earthscan, London.

Tan, T-Y 2007, 'Port cities and hinterlands: A comparative study of Singapore and Calcutta', *Political Geography*, vol. 26, no. 7, pp. 851–65.

The Economist 2012a, *Comparing Indian states and territories with countries*, The Economist,, viewed 5 August 2012, <http://www.economist.com/content/indian-summary>.

The Economist 2012b, 'Special report: India - Aim higher', *The Economist,*, vol. 29 September no. 29 September 29 September <http://www.economist.com/node/21563414 http://www.economist.com/blogs/graphicdetail/2012/09/india-figures-interactive-guide>.

The Economist 2012c, *Special report: India - Aim higher*, The Economist, viewed 30 September 2012, <http://www.economist.com/node/21563414 http://www.economist.com/blogs/graphicdetail/2012/09/india-figures-interactive-guide>.

The Hindu 2005, *IT row: attacks becoming more personalised, say leaders*, The Hindu Group, viewed 29 August 2012, <http://www.hindu.com/2005/11/07/stories/2005110712390400.htm>.

The Hindu 2008, *BMIC is country's biggest fraud: Deve Gowda*, The Hindu Group, viewed 29 August 2012, <http://www.hindu.com/2008/12/21/stories/2008122152740400.htm >.

The Telegraph 2010, 'London Dreams', *The Telegraph,*.

The Telegraph 2011a, 'Blow to varsity politics - Govt. mulls sweeping changes in education acts', *The Telegraph,*.

The Telegraph 2011b, *CM warning on syndicates*, Ananda Bazar Patrika Group, viewed 4 December 2012, <http://www.telegraphindia.com/1111204/jsp/bengal/story_14836443.jsp>.

The Telegraph 2011c, 'Eye on Calcutta', *The Telegraph,*.

The Telegraph 2011d, *To IT: Just tell me, I will do it – Mamata offers industry 'whatever support is needed'*, Ananda Bazar Patrika Group, viewed 9 December 2012, <http://www.telegraphindia.com/1111209/jsp/frontpage/story_14859444.jsp>.

The Telegraph 2011e, 'Wheel deal with eye on London', *The Telegraph,*.

The Telegraph 2012a, *CM roots for non-SEZ sops*, Ananda Bazar Patrika Group, viewed 28 April 2012, <http://www.telegraphindia.com/1120428/jsp/calcutta/story_15426946.jsp>.

The Telegraph 2012b, *Govt/ land role but with 80% consent*, Ananda Bazar Patrika Group, viewed 9 August 2012, <http://www.telegraphindia.com/1120809/jsp/nation/story_15833821.jsp>.

The Telegraph 2012c, *Masters of the name game – Supply Syndicates in new Avatar*, Ananda Bazar Patrika Group, viewed 9 February 2012, <http://www.telegraphindia.com/1120209/jsp/frontpage/story_15112662.jsp>.

Thite, M & Russel, R 2007, 'India and Business Process Outsourcing', in J Burgess & J Connel (eds), *Globalisation and Work in Asia*, Chandos Oxford.

Times of India 2003, *Premji drives on the road ahead; will others follow?*, Bennet Coleman Group, viewed 24 August 2011, <http://articles.timesofindia.indiatimes.com/2003-08-17/bangalore/27212732_1_roads-sarjapur-highways>.

Times of India 2009, *Land acquisition fire smouldered at wellness hub for years*, Bennet and Coleman Group, viewed 21 December 2012, <http://articles.timesofindia.indiatimes.com/2009-08-24/kolkata/28200312_1_land-acquisition-vedic-village-rajarhat>.

UN Habitat 2011, *The Economic Role of Cities*, UN Habitat, Nairobi.

United Nations 2011, *World Urbanization Prorspects*, United Nations Department of Economic and Social Affairs, viewed 24 May 2013, <http://esa.un.org/unpd/wup/CD-ROM/Urban-Agglomerations.htm>.

Upadhya, C 2004, 'A New Transnational Capitalist Class? Capital Flows, Business Networks and Entreprenaures in Indian Software Industry', *Economic and Political Weekly*, vol. 39, no. 48, p. 5141.

Upadhya, C 2007, 'Employment, Exclusion and 'Merit' in the Indian IT Industry', *Economic and Political Weekly*, vol. 42, no. 20, pp. 1863–68.

Upadhya, C & Vasavi, AR 2006, *Work, Culture and Sociality in the Indian IT Industry*, National Institute of Advanced Studies, Bangalore.

Urban Age 2007, *Urban India - Understanding the Maximum City*, London School of Economics, London, <http://lsecities.net/ua/>.

Vang, J & Asheim, B 2006, 'Regions, Absorptive Capacity and Strategic Coupling with High-Tech TNCs: Lessons from India and China', *Science Technology and Society*, vol. 11, no. 1, pp. 39–66.

Wadhwani, K 2009, 'Opportunities and Challanges of Investing in Indian Real Estate', Master of Science in Real Estate Development thesis, Massachusetts Institute of Technology.

Webster, D 2002, 'On the Edge: Shaping the Future of Peri-urban East Asia', *CIAO Working Paper*, <http://www.ciaonet.org/wps/wed03/index.html>.

Webster, D 2011, 'An Overdue Agenda: Systematizing East Asian Peri-Urban Research', *Pacific Affairs*, vol. 84, no. 4, pp. 631–42.

World Bank 2012, *World Development Indicators*, World Bank, viewed 27 December 2012 2012, <http://data.worldbank.org/indicator/NY.GDP.MKTP.CD>.

Yadav, B 2000, 'Haryana's Rising 'Critical Insider(s)'', *Economic and Political Weekly*, vol. 35, no. 50, pp. 4383–5.

Yin, RK 2003, *Applications of case study research*, Thousand Oaks: Sage Publications, London.

Yin, RK 2009, *Case study research: design and methods*, Fourth edn, Applied Social Research Mehods Series, Sage Publications, London.

Index

www.ingramcontent.com/pod-product-compliance
Lightning Source LLC
Chambersburg PA
CBHW071847270326
41929CB00013B/2132